Timothy Darvill

PREHISTORIC BRITAIN

B. T. Batsford Ltd London

For Michael and Winnie Darvill,
to help explain some of the ancient monuments
they have seen on their holidays!

First published 1987
Reprinted 1988, 1990, 1992

Typeset by Keyspools Ltd., Golborne, Lancs.
and printed in Great Britain by
Courier International Ltd., East Kilbride
for the publishers
B. T. Batsford Ltd
4 Fitzhardinge Street, London W1H 0AH

British Library Cataloguing in Publication Data
Darvill, Timothy
  Prehistoric Britain.
  1. Man, Prehistoric—Great Britain
  2. Great Britain—Antiquities
  I. Title
  936.1'01   GN806

ISBN 0 7134 5180 7

Contents

List of Illustrations

Glossary

Acculturation   Transference of ideas, beliefs, traditions and sometimes artefacts by personal contact and interaction between societies. Assimilation through contact.

Artefact   A product of human workmanship. Including tools, weapons, ornaments, utensils, houses, buildings, monuments etc.

Assemblage   An associated set of artefacts.

Band   A simple, small, autonomous family-based group, the definition of which may be no more than the fact that its members feel closely enough related that they do not intermarry. There are no specialized or formalized institutions or groups which can be recognized as economic, political or religious, for the band itself is the organization that undertakes all roles. Leadership and the division of labour is usually by age or sex differentiations.

Chiefdom   A form of social organization characterized by the existence of a chief who exercises central authority at the head of a social hierarchy in which an individual's status is determined by birth and nearness by kinship to the chief. The chief occupies a central role socially, politically and economically. Characteristically, the chief operates some kind of redistribution system wherein food and/or goods from separate sectors of the chiefdom are brought together and then dispersed according to fixed social rules.

Ecological   Having to do with the relationship between man and his environment.

Excarnation   The exposure of human bodies to the elements to facilitate the decomposition of the flesh before the bones are gathered up for burial or disposal.

Exchange   Transfer of goods, services or information between individuals or groups of individuals. Such transfers may not necessarily involve payments or reciprocation with equivalence. The term is often used by prehistorians wishing to avoid the modern connotations of the word trade.

Ideology   The belief system, true or false, shared by members of a society or a collectivity of members within a society. The sharing is not a coincidence because subscribing to the beliefs is an obligation of membership.

Material culture   The sum total of artefacts made, used, or owned by a given society. Used to refer to physical possessions rather than the spiritual or ideological side of a culture.

Power   Generalized capacity to make decisions and make them binding on others.

Procurement strategy   Method or methods devised to acquire food, goods or information.

Settlement pattern   The distribution of archaeological sites within a particular geographical area.

Social change   A variation in the structuring or execution of activities within a society. Such variations do not necessarily represent a 'development' in the sense of change for the better.

Stratification   The differentiation of the population on either a prestige scale or kinship affinity.

Subsistence   Having to do with the provision of basic human requirements, principally food supplies.

Tool-kit   Collection of tools used for specific and/or general purposes.

Trade   The regular exchange of goods or information between societies or between groups within a society. Not to be confused with modern notions of trade which include overtones of profit and a formal buyer-seller relationship.

Tribe   An association of a large number of kinship segments or lineages tied together by political links and associated with a specific territory. Leadership may be contested and may be based on achievement rather than inheritance. There are no identifiable political, economic or religious sectors of society, but ranking and unequal status by birth, sex or achievement may be present. Each lineage or sector preserves a good deal of autonomy and may detach itself from the tribe as a whole at any time.

Preface

One of the most exciting aspects of archaeology as a subject is the way that new discoveries and new research continually extend and reshape our understanding of the past. Prehistoric archaeology is no exception to this, and in many respects leads the field within the discipline. Over the last 25 years the pace of discovery through excavation and research has increased dramatically through greater public awareness and interest in what is being damaged and destroyed by urban expansion, civil engineering works, and many of the other highly intensive activities that today's landscape is forced to host.

One result of this quickening tempo of discoveries has been a tendency for prehistoric studies to become highly specialized, focusing, for example, on environmental studies, prehistoric technology, settlement, or perhaps one particular period. At the same time, both the natural sciences and the social sciences have influenced the direction of archaeological research, and played a formative role in refining and extending archaeological theory. This is, of course, only natural in a developing and expanding discipline, but for the non-specialist the tangle of information, often cast in almost intractable language and frequently published in almost unobtainable publications, makes it easy to lose track of what is going on. It was during an attempt to bring together the results of some of this recent work into a coherent overview of prehistory for a series of lectures and day schools for Bristol University Department of Extra-Mural Studies that the idea for this book was born.

Naturally, everything that is new is not necessarily any more correct than earlier work, and a high degree of selectivity has had to be exercised while choosing source material and relating it to what is already known. By its very nature, research proceeds step by step off the back of earlier work, so that even studies which effectively lead down a *cul de sac* may make contributions to knowledge in the long term. However, the basis for selecting material for this book was its relevance to current understandings of the prehistoric past rather than what might be expected of a particular approach in future.

The layout adopted here is basically chronological, starting with the earlier periods and working progressively towards Roman times. Throughout, emphasis is given to six themes: subsistence, technology, ritual, trade, society and population. There is nothing particularly new in this approach, although one claim to novelty is the abandonment of the traditional, but often confusing, nomenclature for the successive periods of prehistory — palaeolithic, mesolithic, neolithic, Bronze Age and Iron Age. Instead, an absolute prehistoric calendar based on radiocarbon dates is adopted which largely overcomes the difficulties of period definition, differential regional development and the implied sharp breaks between periods which were inherent in the old system.

Radiocarbon chronologies have become an important part of prehistoric archaeology, sharpening up our appreciation of the age of things under investigation and providing many new insights into development and change within prehistoric societies in Britain. Radiocarbon dating is not, however, without its problems. Throughout this book raw radiocarbon dates are used for the period before AD I, and are cited as years BC; but, as will be explained in Chapter 1, radiocarbon dates do not correspond exactly with solar years, or calendar years, such as we use today when speaking of the date. For the more recent past the difference between radiocarbon years and calendar years is not great, but the gap widens at an uneven rate backwards into prehistory, so that, for example, a date of 2000 radiocarbon years BC actually means about 2400 calendar years BC. At present no single calibration curve matching radiocarbon years with calendar years has been universally accepted and so no attempt has been made to calibrate the dates used here. Moreover, it must be emphasized at the outset that radiocarbon dates are simply estimates of the actual age of the material tested. Accordingly, dates are quoted with a standard deviation (e.g. 2000 ± 70 BC) expressing the statistical concept that the actual date has a 68 per cent probability of lying within the limits specified either side of the mean value (in this case within the range 2070–1930 BC). Doubling the standard deviation raises the probability level to 95.5 per cent. For the period after AD 1 historically derived dates which approximate to calendar years are used, and cited as years AD.

Prehistoric archaeology has also come to rely on an increasingly extensive specialized vocabulary describing entities or concepts relevant to its field of interest. Some such jargon has been carried over from other disciplines, in other cases it has developed within prehistoric archaeology itself, often to avoid having to use words or phrases which include strong overtones of twentieth-century westernized practice which may be wholly inappropriate in a prehistoric context. No apology is made for perpetuating the use of some of these words, although a conscious effort has been made to minimize their use and to explain their meaning, where appropriate, in the text or in the glossary (*p. 10*).

All the line drawings in this book have been specially redrawn to a common set of conventions. Every effort has been made to ensure that they remain accurate and faithful to the originals, although some detail has occasionally been omitted for clarity. Because of the small scale of reproduction used here, those wishing to check points of detail, such as measurements or alignments are advised to refer back to the larger scale originals acknowledged in the figure captions. Figures 9, 12, 15, 18, 22, 28, 39, 48, 49, 55, 57, 67, 70, 71, 79, 92, 93, 94, 95B, 97, and 100 were kindly drawn by Jane Timby.

The preparation of this book would not have been possible without the help of many individuals and organizations. First and foremost, thanks must go to Graham Webster, the series editor, and Peter Kemmis Betty of Batsford for their help and constant encouragement in shaping a vague idea into the form of this book. Of the many people who answered queries, provided information and supplied photographs and illustrations, special thanks go to Don Benson, Bob Bewley, Richard Bradley, Bill Britnell, Dave Buckley, Tony Clark, John Coles, Barry Cunliffe, Andrew David, John Dent, Andrew Fleming, Mike Fulford, Clive Gamble, John Gowlett, Stephen Green, Colin Haselgrove, John Hedges, Roger Jacobi, Margaret Jones, George Lambrick, Roger Mercer, Harold Mytum, Georgina Plowright, Francis Pryor, Alan Saville, Mick Sharp, Charles Thomas, Stephen Upex, Blaise Vyner, Geoffrey Wainwright and George Williams. Thanks also to friends and colleagues Mick Aston, Bob Bewley, Richard Bradley, David Fraser, Clive Gamble, Richard Hingley, Roger Jacobi, Mark Maltby, John Smith and Graham Webster for their invaluable comments and criticisms of early drafts of part or all of the text, although the author naturally takes full responsibility for all remaining misinterpretations. Finally, special thanks go to Jane Timby for her intellectual and moral support and encouragement throughout the preparation of this book, and for her sterling work at the drawing-board.

1 The Prehistoric Past

Archaeology in the Present

Introduction

In this age of high technology, mass communication and the passion to record even the most mundane details of everyday life in as many different ways as possible, it is sometimes hard to imagine a time when there was no writing, no sophisticated technology, and communications largely depended on word of mouth. Yet such conditions prevailed for half a million years or so before the Roman Conquest of Britain in AD 43, and during that time some of the foundations for life and culture as we know it today were laid down.

The absence of written records does not mean that nothing is known of these early societies in Britain. Quite the contrary. Man interfered with the landscape during prehistory just as today, influencing its topography, building structures and monuments which were subsequently abandoned, and littering the countryside with discarded tools and piles of rubbish. In this way communities etched an enduring record of their actions on the landscape, and from what has survived over the millennia down to the present day something of these distant times can be reconstructed.

Almost every parish in Britain can boast the presence of prehistoric remains, and much can still be seen above ground level. On the rolling downs of southern England, for example, there are long barrows, tumuli, hillforts and boundary earthworks which are as much a part of the landscape today as the tiny villages, narrow lanes and sheep pastures. The rugged uplands of the north and west of Britain bristle with the remains of hut circles, camps, stone rings, standing stones and brochs; in a few areas, notably parts of Cornwall, modern field walls still follow boundaries established over 3000 years ago.

For every site visible above ground there are perhaps ten times more hidden from view. Even superficially less-promising looking landscapes are rich in prehistoric remains. Flat peaty areas, such as the Somerset Levels or the Cambridgeshire Fens, preserve timber trackways and marsh-side settlements in their acid waterlogged soils, while the heavily cultivated arable lands along the main river valleys of southern and eastern England preserve a variety of prehistoric remains just below the plough soil.

The wealth of evidence visible in the countryside is supplemented by an abundance of material stored and displayed in museums up and down the land, most of which has come to light over the past few centuries. Objects, or artefacts, of prehistoric date ranging from stone axes to iron swords, and from dug-out canoes to highly decorated cinerary urns, abound.

Each of these monuments and objects is part of Britain's prehistoric heritage and contributes to the complicated and intriguing story of its past, of long-vanished human societies and the way they changed through time. The story is one of good times and bad, of crisis, opportunity and endless change. More particularly it is a story of communities wresting a livelihood from the environment while retaining their identity among fellow groups, controlling their internal relationships and, above all, ensuring their continuity.

This book is an attempt to outline that story up until the Roman Conquest. It tries to look beyond the spectacular and the familiar to glimpse the people behind the evidence, at least as far as they can be seen from the archaeological evidence currently available. There are two basic aims: firstly to set the evidence which can be seen in the countryside and in our museums into its wider context as a record of prehistoric society, and secondly to look at how and why those societies changed over time. Naturally it is not possible to cover every region of Britain in the detail it deserves in a book of this length, and accordingly some generalization must be excused. But the shortcomings can be overcome by reference to the abundant literature relating to prehistoric Britain, and to this end a select bibliography follows the text.

Britain BC

Few people can fail to be interested in or inspired by the field monuments or the rich artefacts: the magnificence of Stonehenge in Wiltshire, or the splendour of the gold pectoral from Mold in Clwyd which is now displayed in the British Museum. But when looking at sites in the landscape or fine exhibits in museums it is easy to forget that these are the remains of living, breathing people. Alongside the imposing sites and fine objects must be set the prosaic bric-a-brac of everyday life and the commonplace features of the landscape such as settlements, fields and trackways. Moreover, to appreciate prehistoric sites and objects to the full it is necessary to know something of the environment in which they were set, the climate, and the animals and plants present at the time.

Although prehistoric people were physically not so different from ourselves they would have seen the world through very different eyes, and had quite different beliefs and values from those of today. Clearly it is impossible to read the minds of prehistoric people, but some insight into what they deemed important can be glimpsed from what they left behind and the way they treated and deposited different objects.

Often, the prehistoric past is perceived as a relatively undifferentiated period, but again the reality was very different. Over the half million years or so before the Roman Conquest there were a great many changes—changes in the ways of finding and producing food, changes in technology, changes in religious ritual, indeed changes in every aspect of life. Against such a background it would be quite wrong to elevate prehistory to the status of a 'Golden Age' when life was simple and close to nature. In fact, there is no reason to think that life in those distant times was not every bit as complex and, at times, as traumatic as today.

Other misconceptions about events in prehistory also abound in the popular imagination. Mention may be made of a few of the more far-fetched, such as the idea of early man hunting dinosaurs, of Druidical ceremonies at Stonehenge, of the presence of a dwarf-like undersized population, and of the existence of 'ley lines' linking sites together by linear force-fields apparently well known to prehistoric communities but totally forgotten today. Such ideas originated in the minds of the over-imaginative using inadequate evidence, and will, hopefully, be dispelled by what follows in later chapters. As a prelude to the detailed treatment of the evidence, however, it is perhaps helpful to look first at the development of interest in the subject, and then at the range of methods, theories and techniques commonly used today by prehistorians investigating the remote past.

The idea of prehistory

Today's knowledge of prehistory relies on evidence accumulated during several centuries of study and investigation. The existence of pre-Roman inhabitants in these islands, Ancient Britons as they were often called in the formative years of archaeological studies, was known before the sixteenth century because of references to them by classical writers such as Caesar and Tacitus. Although early antiquaries like John Leland (?1506–1552) and William Camden (1561–1623) between them recorded many prehistoric sites in their books, they had no conception of the relative antiquity of the remains they described. It was the Wiltshireman John Aubrey (1626–1697) who really first began to assign particular sites and monuments to the pre-Roman period. On the orders of Charles II, for example, he prepared a discourse on Stonehenge, and in the 1640s did much the same thing for the great circular henge monument at Avebury in north Wiltshire. Aubrey's greatest work, *Monumenta Britannica*, which contains a wealth of notes and drawings of prehistoric and later sites, languished as a manuscript in the Bodleian Library in Oxford until 1982 when it was published for the first time some 285 years after the author's death.

The work of Leland, Camden and Aubrey stimulated others, such as William Dugdale, Thomas Hobbington, Edward Lhwyd and Robert Plot, to record the monuments in their own neighbourhoods. All were constrained by the lack of a chronological framework within which to order the accumulating evidence, for the early history of man was immutably enshrined in the words of the Bible. In 1650 James Ussher, Archbishop of Armagh, calculated that on the basis of genealogies presented in the Bible the world began in 4004 BC. For several centuries this date was widely accepted as authentic, and perhaps explains why little progress was made in advancing knowledge of ancient times during the eighteenth century. The idea of prehistory had, however, been born, and interest in it continued. Shortly before 1718 the Society of Antiquaries of London was formed and in 1754 was granted a Royal Charter.

Digging, recording and the Three Age System

By the mid eighteenth century simply recording monuments was occasionally supplemented by a more ambitious method of investigation—digging. William Stukeley (1687–1765) was perhaps the most eminent antiquary and field archaeologist of the eighteenth century, investigating a number of barrows in Wessex, and undertaking the first detailed studies of Stonehenge and Avebury. Stukeley made a substantial contribution to knowledge, but the work of many antiquaries is more difficult to evaluate. The Rev. Bryan Fausett (1720–1776), for example, is known to have dug into hundreds of sites in south-east England, plundering no less than 106 barrows around Gilton, Kent, over a period of only three years. Very few records of this work exist, and the

evidence he excavated is therefore lost for all time. Others did much the same elsewhere.

The work of the eighteenth century set the scene for major changes in approach and understanding during the nineteenth century. Digging and recording (although not necessarily together!) continued through the work of men like Richard Colt Hoare, William Cunnington, General Pitt Rivers and others. Wessex was the centre for much of this practical work but the real advances came in conceptual changes which happened elsewhere.

It was the intellectual climate of the mid nineteenth century that really changed the face of prehistoric studies. Differences in the type of objects and sites investigated had been noted since the middle of the eighteenth century, but not codified or explained. The first breakthrough came in the early years of the nineteenth century in Denmark where Christian Jurgensen Thomsen, who was charged with sorting out the collections of the newly-established National Museum of Denmark, developed a three-fold classification based upon an age of stone, an age of bronze and an age of iron. These were seen as three technologically defined ages or stages in man's development, thus providing both a classification and a rudimentary chronology.

1 Nineteenth-century engraving of an inhumation burial discovered in 1855 at Roundway, Wiltshire. [*Reproduced from* Archaeologia *volume 43 (ii) for 1871, by permission of the Society of Antiquaries of London*]

The Three Age System, as it became known, was first published in English in 1848 by Thomsen's pupil John Jacob Worsaae, but its immediate effect here was slight. Thomas Bateman was an early advocate of the system, and it appears in his book *Vestiges of the Antiquities of Derbyshire* published in 1848. The British Museum adopted the scheme in 1866, but before this the Museum of the Society of Antiquaries of Scotland in Edinburgh (now the Royal Museum of Scotland) became the first museum in the English-speaking world to arrange its collections according to the Three Age System. Daniel Wilson was the instigator of these developments in Edinburgh, and in 1851 he published *The archaeology and prehistoric annals of Scotland*, the first book to use the work 'prehistory' in the sense of meaning the time before history.

The development of the Three Age System was only one of several events which profoundly changed the course of prehistoric studies in the nineteenth century. Advances in the field of geology by Charles Lyell and in the field of biology by Charles Darwin and others made their mark on prehistoric archaeology too. Together these works swept away traditional beliefs that man and animals were absent from the Earth when the rocks were formed and that man was a separate creation. The accumulated evidence of associations between early stone tools and the bones of extinct animals led to the proposition that prehistory was of considerable duration. Darwin, or course, suggested that man evolved from predecessors in the animal kingdom. Fundamental to the practical study of prehistory was the development of the law of stratigraphy which asserts that where deposits representing several phases of actions or events are superimposed, the layer at the bottom will be the oldest and the one at the top the most recent. This principle underpins all modern excavation and the interpretation of archaeological deposits.

The effects of these developments caused something of a revolution in prehistoric studies and ushered in an avalanche of new work, some of it supporting the new ideas, some against them. The second half of the nineteenth century was a great period of excavation and discovery, and standing earthworks such as barrows and hillforts came in for much attention. Among the most memorable archaeologists of the time were Canon Greenwell, John Thurnam, Thomas Bateman, Charles Roach Smith, Arthur Evans, and General Pitt Rivers. Public works such as railways, road schemes and the growth of towns brought to light much new evidence. Public

interest grew as well, and it was at this time that many county archaeological societies came into being. In 1865 John Lubbock (later Lord Avebury) published the first major synthesis of British prehistory, entitled *Prehistoric Times*. This book subsequently went through seven editions, the last published in 1913 just after his death.

Prehistory in the twentieth century

By 1900 prehistory was firmly established as a discipline, a branch of archaeology, and many of the techniques and premises which dominated prehistoric studies in the twentieth century had been developed. The Three Age System provided the chronological framework, while detailed study of artefacts and sites allowed individual pieces of evidence to be fitted onto the scheme. Assigning dates to periods or phases in prehistory remained difficult. The best hope was seen in closely ordering the evidence into a sequence and tying this up with established chronologies such as were available in the Classical world and Ancient Egypt.

The periodic syntheses of prehistory published through the first half of the twentieth century, notably those by Gordon Childe, Stuart Piggott and Grahame Clark, trace the development of interpretation. The two notions of invasion and migration were invoked to explain what were seen as major discontinuities in the story of prehistory: the first arrival of farming, the appearance of beaker pottery, the early use of iron, and so on. Gordon Childe developed the idea of recognizing distinct prehistoric 'cultures' through recurring patterns of material remains, and cultural units became the basis for many archaeological interpretations. O. G. S. Crawford, the first archaeological officer with the Ordnance Survey, took these ideas further by adding the spatial dimension to the culture model so that by plotting out the distribution of specific types of object, cultural areas could be defined. Sometimes cultures were credited with ethnic identity, even race, and ideas of ethnic replacement were battled about. In retrospect it is easy to see why these ideas developed when colonialism was a strong ideology in Britain, and Marxism (which greatly influenced Gordon Childe, for example) was expanding its intellectual and political influence.

Over the past three decades, prehistoric studies have undergone another revolution. The cause was not so much new techniques, although some, like radiocarbon dating, have certainly completely changed our chronological perspectives, but more fundamentally because the opportunities for archaeological work have been greater than ever before. The building boom in the 1960s and 70s brought to light a wealth of archaeological evidence on a scale previously unimagined. Greater public awareness brought increased funds for the discipline. Professional archaeologists became more numerous and the number of practising archaeologists, both amateur and professional, in field archaeology and in academic archaeology increased dramatically between 1960 and 1975. With these new resources much new and exciting work has been possible, principally in five spheres: recovery of the evidence, analysis, archaeological theory, dating and environmental studies. Together these provide a rather more solid basis upon which to reconstruct the prehistory of Britain.

2 Aerial view of cropmarks at Langford, Oxfordshire. The dark marks result from the plants drawing water and nutrients from sub-surface ditches and pits while the surrounding crop has ripened faster over undisturbed subsoil where root penetration is less. Enclosures, trackways and circular buildings can be seen.
[*Photo: author, Pilot: Ron Locke; copyright reserved*]

Recovery of the evidence

There is no direct link, such as historical documents, that allows us to step back into the prehistoric past to reconstruct pictures of early life in Britain. Everything we know about the prehistoric past must be derived from mute remains which, largely by chance, have survived the ravages of time through many thousands of years. What we have is an archaeology which exists in the present representing a residue of what once was. Moreover, that residue is not large and is biased towards those types of evidence which survive most easily.

In the popular imagination excavation is often thought to be the main, if not the only method used by prehistoric archaeologists to obtain information about the societies they are studying. But while it is true to say that excavation is certainly important it is by no means the only technique used. Indeed, because excavation is expensive to undertake and can only be entertained on a limited scale, many archaeologists argue that is should be used far less frequently than it is so that resources can be channelled in other directions. All the techniques used by prehistoric archaeologists have one thing in common—they are ultimately designed to coax information about the past out of the ground. Five such techniques may briefly be considered, although of course in practice slight modifications have to be made to the basic principles to take account of soil

17

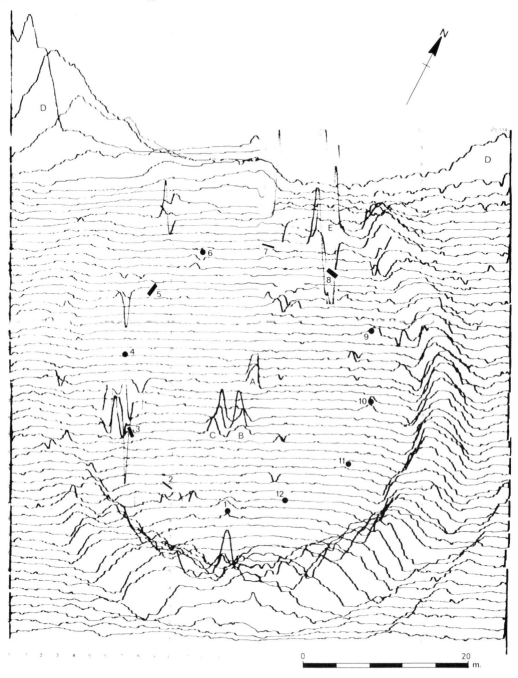

3 Magnetic survey plot of the Stones of Stennes, Orkney. The stones of the circle are numbers 1–12. The ditch shows clearly as an anomaly reaching 50 nanoteslas, with an entrance at the top. The anomaly at A proved upon excavation to be a stone-lined cist; those at B and C were ritual pits. E is an anomaly caused by buried iron, while natural anomalies can be seen at D, in this case caused by intrusions of igneous rock.

conditions, terrain and the type of site under investigation.

Fieldsurvey, the observation and recording of ancient features in the landscape through careful scrutiny of the ground surface, is the oldest and still the most commonly used technique in prehistoric archaeology. The information recorded is mostly spatial in the sense that it allows plots to be made of the landscape at different times. In some upland areas of Britain, for example Dartmoor, the Cheviots or the Scottish Highlands, recent surveys have brought to light a bewildering amount of detail tantamount to complete relict landscapes.

Aerial photography as an archaeological technique was pioneered in the early inter-war years. Careful use of low-angle sunlight and correct camera position can reveal even the slightest undulations in the ground surface and allow ancient features to be picked out. In the late summer differential crop growth over infilled ditches or pits can be clearly seen from high above and allows sites to be recognized and their plans drawn. A single flight can cover a wide area which makes this particular technique very cost effective, especially in areas difficult of access. Computer enhancement of photographs and computer plotting techniques allow accurate and rapid analysis of pictures. On the light gravel soils of the main river valleys, aerial photography is especially effective in detecting cropmarks. The Thames valley, the Avon valley in Warwickshire, the Trent valley and the Ouse valley have been well studied and literally thousands of sites recorded.

Techniques which look through the soil — geophysical surveys of various sorts — are also important and have been greatly improved by the electronics revolution and the availability of microprocessors and computers for image analysis. Most work by measuring minute changes in either soil resistance or magnetic intensity caused by the presence of underlying pits, gullies, hearths and so on.

Wherever the ground is disturbed there is the opportunity to search for prehistoric remains. Despite the great antiquity of prehistoric sites most have only a thin cover and so buried features are frequently disturbed, for example by ploughing. By carefully plotting the position of all the finds visible on the top of disturbed ground it is possible to work out the position and extent of buried sites. Such evidence can be used to build up pictures of activity patterns within a given area of landscape in much the same way as fieldsurvey does.

In comparison to the techniques mentioned so far

excavation can only take place on a small scale, perhaps a few thousand square metres. The size of excavations has tended to increase in recent years for two reasons. Firstly, it has become clear that in order to understand what when on at a site a significant portion of it must be examined, and secondly the scale of potential threats affecting known sites has increased. At Mucking on the Thames gravels near Gravesend, Essex, for example, approximately 15 hectares (37 acres) have been investigated in advance of gravel quarrying, while at Fengate near Peterborough, Cambridgeshire, sporadic trenches over an area of about 1000 by 500 metres (3280 by 1640 feet) in advance of industrial development provide a clear insight into land use on the edge of the Fens throughout prehistory. Several hillforts in southern England have been substantially excavated, among them Danebury, Hampshire, and Crickley Hill, Gloucestershire.

The quality of evidence from excavation is, or should be, high. By carefully removing one layer at a time within a deposit the sequence of deposition can be built up and the finds and structures carefully related to one another. Even a medium-sized site will have several thousand individual layers and in some cases thousands of finds, each representing a particular episode or event in its complex history and development. The law of stratigraphy established back in the nineteenth century remains the basis for determining which deposits are earlier and which are later.

Analysis

The evidence available from the various techniques just discussed is only of use if it is analysed to search for patterns and regularities that can tell us something about life in prehistory: the way tools were made, how houses were built, preferred orientations for the dead, and so on. Such searching for patterns falls into two categories: data handling and technical studies.

Data handling has been revolutionized by the widespread use of computer-based systems in archaeological research. These are ideal for storing, sorting and cross-referencing the sort of descriptive and statistical information produced by most excavations and surveys. Sophisticated computer programs are now available to assist in the recognition of posthole patterns which might indicate the position of buildings, and by comparing the different types of finds from individual layers examined by excavation it is possible to work out the sorts of activities undertaken in different parts of a site.

Technical studies are only limited by the technology available. Many focus on characterizing materials found on excavations. As early as 1923, for example, pieces of bluestone from Stonehenge were petrologically studied by H. H. Thomas and identified as spotted dolerite from the Prescelly Mountains of Dyfed. Since that time numerous techniques of physical and chemical analysis have been directed towards prehistoric materials, among them optical emission spectroscopy, neutron activation analysis and X-ray diffraction, all of which allow the chemical composition of materials to be determined and therefore compared one with another, and with materials of known source, to determine origins and associations.

The biological sciences have made a significant contribution too, and environmental studies represent one of the expanding branches of prehistoric archaeology. By collecting samples of soil from different layers within a site it is possible to extract microscopic remains of once-living organisms such as insects, pollen, pieces of charcoal and tiny seeds which all contribute to building up a picture of the environment within a part of a site or landscape, and the possible range of activities taking place in the vicinity.

Archaeological theory

Archaeology in general, and prehistory in particular, has always been a highly theoretical subject. This is inevitable since the very subject matter under enquiry is remote and cannot be directly interrogated, or even observed working. Early theoretical propositions such as the Three Age System, based as it was on progressive technological development, or the diffusionist notion of cultural change based on the effects of invasions and the dissemination of new ideas from the Mediterranean to Britain, have already been touched upon, and something of their inadequacy highlighted.

Coincident with the expansion field archaeology in the 1960s and early 1970s came the questioning of many of the assumptions and principles which provided the basis for archaeological interpretations until that time. An overt concern for theory developed. Good theory, it was hoped, could link the archaeologist working in the twentieth century with the societies under study in the distant past. Drawing on work in other disciplines, notably social

anthropology and the philosophy of science, a more holistic approach to prehistory developed which concerned itself not just with reconstructing static pictures of society at particular points in time but, more importantly, looked at the dynamics of prehistoric societies through time. Anthropology offered many ready-made theories appropriate to the study of primitive societies and some were pounced upon and applied to archaeological examples. Retrospectively, this shift in interest within prehistoric studies has become known as the development of the 'New Archaeology'.

Since the 1970s the theoretical basis of prehistoric archaeology has moved forward on several fronts. At the most fundamental level much attention has been given to the formation of the archaeological record and the way it is interpreted and analysed. What were flint tools used for? How were houses built? What do collections of animal bones mean? And what was the function of rock-cut pits? These were among the many questions asked, and by carrying out experiments and closely observing the behaviour of present-day and recently recorded extinct primitive societies it has been possible to establish a range of possibilities in response to such questions. On occasion, by comparing the results of observations and experiments with what can be seen in the archaeological record fairly specific answers can be found. Thus the wear patterns on tools provide insights into the ways they were used and the different materials on which they were used. At the other end of the scale, work at the Butser Hill Iron Age Research Farm in Hampshire has demonstrated the efficiency of rock-cut pits as grain storage silos and the robustness of round houses. Different types of animal bone assemblages representing, for example, primary carcass dismemberment, butchery and food preparation can be distinguished on the basis of the different proportions and types of bones present. When undertaken rigorously, experimentation and careful observation can lead to the identification of new things to look for in the archaeological record, tell-tale signs of particular activities or processes.

One school of archaeological theory which has had a particularly powerful influence on prehistoric studies, and which had its origins before the development of New Archaeology, is the ecological approach. Pioneered by Grahame Clark and Geoffrey Dimbleby, this school emphasized the environmental constraints on social development and focused on the relationships between prehistoric societies and the environment in which they lived.

Social and economic prehistory

Over the last 20 years much attention has been directed towards understanding the form, organization and complexity of prehistoric societies. Technological classifications such as 'neolithic' or 'bronze age' say nothing of the internal workings of the society which could differ widely among stone-using or bronze-using communities in different areas. Working again from progress made in the field of anthropology more socially meaningful classifications were adopted and applied to the evidence from prehistory. Elman Service suggested that the following three types of primitive society could be recognized on the basis of social organization: bands, tribes and chiefdoms. In contrast, Morton Fried put forward the suggestion that political structure might be more important, and accordingly suggested the identification of egalitarian societies, ranked societies and stratified societies. The problem for prehistorians was to translate these ideas into the sort of evidence which might be recovered archaeologically. Studies of the spatial arrangements of societies represented by their monuments and settlements, together with investigations into the relationships that existed between groups as represented by exchanged goods, provided the most successful lines of enquiry, but the search for types of society has now largely been abandoned in favour of studies connected with social dynamics.

Social dynamics and social change together provide the theme for much archaeological theory since the mid-1960s. At first, objective attempts to understand social change drew heavily on what is known in the social sciences as Systems Theory. Applied to British prehistory by David Clarke, Systems Theory was used in an attempt to examine complex entities as a series of separate components or sub-systems. The operation of each sub-system, and its relationships with other sub-systems, form the focus of interest. Change could either originate from within the system by fluctuations in the operation of one or more sub-system, or could be forced upon the system from outside its bounds. In looking at prehistoric societies, topics such as economics, subsistence, trade, population and ritual formed the basis for defining sub-systems. Specific analytical approaches to these themes were developed, often focusing on the spatial implications of patterns of activity within each because spatial relationships could, at least in theory, be recovered archaeologically.

Amongst the most successful lines of enquiry was the analysis of production and exchange. Anthropo-

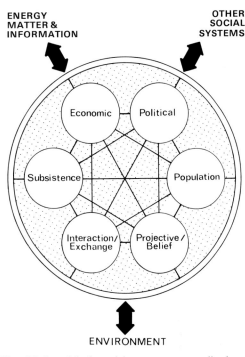

4 Simplified model of a social system conceptualized as a set of six subsystems each defined as groups of related everyday activities. Possible relationships between subsystems are shown, and the main interactions between the system and its environment are described. [*Source: author*]

logical studies demonstrated that among primitive societies trade does not take place in the same way as in modern western societies, but rather is dominated by varying degrees of obligation between exchange partners. Thus at the household level items may pass between individuals frequently and with no obligation to reciprocate, but on a wider scale exchanges between communities may only take place at specified times, in specified ways, with very clear rules of reciprocation which may be far from simply matching the value of goods going one way with some commodity going the other. Exchange practices between particular sections of societies, for example exchanges between group leaders, were also documented. From these observations it was suggested that different practices would be represented archaeologically by different patterns in the distribution of artefacts recorded away from their source—fall-off patterns as they are called. Through plotting fall-off curves, showing the frequency of objects found against distance from source, local production is able to be distinguished from regional production and

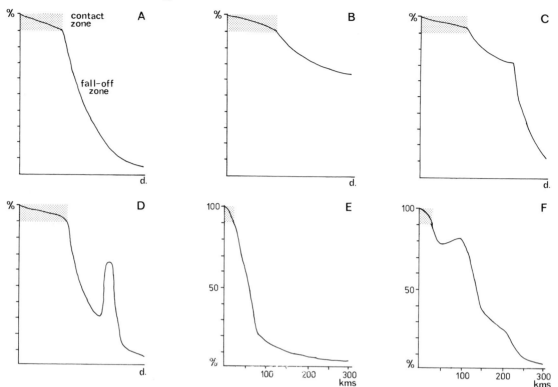

5 Distance decay curves modelling the decreasing frequency of goods (fall-off) with distance from source. Expected fall-off curves for: (A) down-the-line gift exchange; (B) prestige goods exchange; (C) freelance trading; (D) directional trading with trading outposts or redistribution centres. Recorded fall-off curves for (E) group VII stone axes made at Graig Lwyd, Gwynedd; (F) group XII stone battle-axes and axe-hammers made at Corndon Hill, Powys. (NB: d. = distance) [*(A)–(D) After Renfrew 1972, 466–470; (E) and (F): author*]

several different types of exchange systems identified.

Systems Theory is, by its nature, strongly functionalist in its outlook and promotes a rather mechanisitc view of the operation of society. Its principal attraction is the way it focuses attention on specific fields of activity and gives roughly equal weight to a wide range of different factors which may stimulate social change. Alternative and more flexible approaches to the study of prehistoric societies have, however, developed over the last ten years, largely out of a revival of interest in Marxist analysis. In this, emphasis is placed upon the way that individuals, groups, and societies as a whole develop specific systems of thought, belief and association of ideas, which they then articulate through the manufacture and use of objects, the construction of monuments and structures, and recurrent patterns of behaviour. The assumption is made that material culture, the objects and constructions of everyday life, are somehow meaningfully constituted in relation to a set of symbolic schemes. Whether this framework will ever provide a general theory for prehistoric studies remains to be seen.

The increased awareness of the theoretical basis of prehistoric studies over the last 20 years has undoubtedly promoted a more critical approach to the interpretation of archaeological evidence. At present there is no single unified set of theory relating to prehistory, although the discipline is now moving towards a more mature understanding of the complexity of prehistoric societies as they are represented in the archaeological record. There have, of course, been many casualties along the way, the most notable being the rejection of the old idea that waves of newcomers from the Continent were largely responsible for changes in Britain, and that all of the important changes seen in Britain ultimately derived from developments in the Mediterranean world. It is not doubted that movements of people took place on occasion, but it is generally agreed that many of the changes which can be seen in the archaeological record, for example the introduction of farming or the development of metalworking, result from far more complicated and deep-rooted social processes which cannot be explained away simply by the arrival of new people. The importance of both internal and external factors in social change, the role of politics and ideologies within given societies, and the ecological constraints imposed upon them must all be balanced out to provide what Colin Renfrew has called a 'social archaeology'.

Dating

The Three Age System, developed in the mid nineteenth century, provided the main chronological framework for prehistoric studies for over 100 year. The earliest of the ages, the Stone Age, was sub-divided into palaeolithic, mesolithic and neolithic (meaning literally old, middle and new Stone Age respectively), and, together with the Bronze Age and the Iron Age, gave five sucessive periods in prehistory. Artefacts and sites were assigned to specific periods according to their type, and many attempts were made to further sub-divide each period by developing complex typological sequences based on the development or degeneration of traits exhibited in the design of individual pieces or sites. This type of dating is called relative dating. The laws of stratigraphy provided the ultimate test for any proposed sequences, and many failed.

In the late 1940s a new technique became available, radiocarbon dating. Developed by the American physicist Willard Libby, radiocarbon dating provided, for the first time ever, a method which could determine the age of any animal or vegetable matter recovered from archaeological sites (e.g. charcoal or bone). The method itself was based on the principles of atomic physics and so the results were not open to the same criticisms as relative dating.

The principles of radiocarbon dating are basically fairly simple. All living matter contains a fixed ratio of the stable isotope carbon 12 (^{12}C) and the

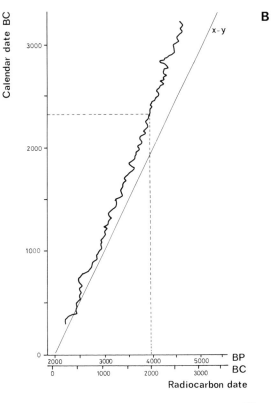

6 Radiocarbon dating. (A) Part of the radiocarbon accelerator at Oxford. (B) Calibration curve to convert radiocarbon dates to calendar dates based on tree-ring samples of known age. As an example a dotted line leads from a raw radiocarbon date of 2000 BC up to the curve and across to give the calibrated date of about 2400 BC.
[*(A) Reproduced by permission of John Gowlett, Oxford Radiocarbon Accelerator Unit, Oxford; (B) after Pearson et al.* 1983]

radioactive isotope carbon 14 (^{14}C). The ratio between these is maintained during the life of the organism by the absorption of ^{14}C from the atmosphere. However, from the time of death no new ^{14}C is taken in, and what is present begins to decay at a roughly fixed rate while the ^{12}C remains stable. Carbon 14 decays very slowly such that after about 5568 ± 30 years half of what was originally present has gone. By measuring the ratio of ^{12}C to ^{14}C in an ancient sample it is possible to say how much time has elapsed since the organism died. Carbon 14 is, of course, present in all living matter as very small quantities (one atom of ^{14}C to every million million atoms of ^{12}C) so the measuring equipment has to be very sensitive. Furthermore, because ^{14}C is naturally present in the atmosphere the equipment has to be able to filter out background 'noise'. Several different types of counter are now in use and some of the more sophisticated ones can measure very small concentrations of ^{14}C.

The first few dozen radiocarbon dates for British prehistory shook many of the established ideas on chronology by suggesting that many familiar types of monuments were in fact much older than was imagined. Still greater surprise came when it was found that because of fluctuations in the amount of ^{14}C present in the atmosphere in the past, radiocarbon years did not correspond with calendar years. In an effort to produce a calibration curve matching radiocarbon dates with calendar years, samples of wood from Bristlecone Pine trees were dated. The Bristlecone Pine grows in the White Mountains of California, and individual tress live to be up to 4000 years old. By counting back the annual growth rings in the trunk, pieces of wood of known age could be dated and the real age compared with the determined age. In this way a rather wiggly curve was produced, and there is still no universal agreement on its exact form. Accordingly, all the dates cited in this book are given in raw (uncalibrated) radiocarbon years BC.

Over 5000 radiocarbon dates are now available for British prehistory and allow an objective prehistoric calendar to be established. The proposition that all the ideas adopted in Britain originated in the great early civilizations of the Mediterranean (Egypt and Greece) can no longer be substantiated because in some cases the north European evidence is much earlier than supposed prototypes. Of course the traditional terms like neolithic and Bronze Age still provide a useful shorthand to refer to a period of time, much as we might refer to the Victorian Age or the Middle Ages, but their use is not perpetuated in this book out of preference for the more precise terminology of millennia and centuries BC.

The prehistoric environment

Although the basic topography and geology of Britain has remained substantially the same since the end of the last Ice Age, other facets of the natural environment—climate, sea level, vegetation cover and the natural animal species present—have been continually changing. The environment at different times is described in later chapters, but clearly the relationships between the various factors are immensely complex. Changing climate means changes in vegetation cover which in turn changes the range of animal species that can be supported, and so on. Man too has had a considerable impact. Over-exploitation of resources, even as far back as the second millennium BC, caused marked changes in the appearance of the landscape and in some areas led to soil erosion and loss of soil fertility. Although it may seem that natural landscapes still exist, for example the uplands of northern and western Britain, even these have been changed beyond recognition by man and nature during and since prehistoric times.

A number of techniques have been developed to document past changes to the environment using evidence drawn from natural deposits and man-made contexts. Vegetation history can be reconstructed from the analysis of pollen grains. Slowly developing peat bogs and lake sediments trap pollen from the atmosphere in each successive layer. Pollen is very resilient and can be attributed fairly accurately to the species of plant from which it came. Since all plants give off pollen at some time during the year a picture of the relative abundance of the different types of plants growing in the vicinity of the bog or lake can be built up. By examining successive layers of peat or lake sediment the changing spectra of the vegetation can been seen. By radiocarbon dating distinctive layers some appreciation of the age of successive pictures can be obtained.

In areas where pollen is not preserved (for example on alkali soils) snail shells can be analysed to provide glimpses of past landscapes. Snails have distinct habitat preferences—some only live in woods, some only in permanent grassland, some only on cultivated land. By documenting the species present in any given context the conditions prevailing when the context was formed can be determined.

Date (BC/AD)	Geological period		3 Age System	Archaeological period		Metalworking stage*		This book
1,000,000	Q U A T E R N A R Y	P L E I S T O C E N E	S T O N E A G E	P A L A E O L I T H I C	lower			Chapter 2
500,000					....			
100,000					middle			
30,000					....			
					upper			
10,000		H O L O C E N E OR F L A N D R I A N		M E S O L I T H I C	early			
6000					....			
					late			
3500				N E O L I T H I C	early			Chapter 3
2900					....			
					middle			
2500					....			
					late			
2000			B R O N Z E A G E		early	I II III IV V VI		Chapter 4
1500					.... middle	VII Arreton VIII Acton Park		
1000					.... late	IX Taunton X Penard XI Wallington/ Wilburton		Chapter 5
600						XII Ewart Park XIII Llyn Fawr		
			I R O N A G E		early			
300					....			Chapter 6
100					middle			
					....			
1 BC/AD					late			Chapter 7
AD 43			THE ROMAN PERIOD					

*After Burgess 1980.

Table 1 Prehistoric time-chart showing the correspondence between conventional terminology and the chapters in this book (not to scale).

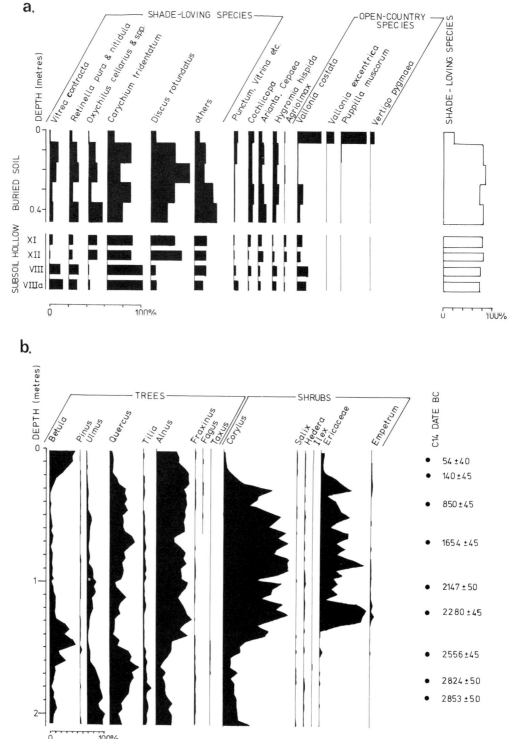

7 Snail assemblage and pollen frequency profiles. (a) Snail assemblages recovered from the buried soil and sub-surface hollows at Ascott-under-Wychwood, Oxfordshire. The top of the soil dates to the early third millennium BC. Changes in the frequency of shade loving species, indicating woodland conditions, and open country species, indicating grassland conditions, can be clearly seen. (b) Pollen profile from the Abbot's Way site, Somerset, showing frequency of tree and shrub pollen. [*(a) After Evans 1971 figure 5. (b) after Beckett and Hibbert 1979 figure 4*]

Thus snails from beneath the long barrow at South Street, Wiltshire (constructed about 2810 ± 130 BC) were predominantly open-country loving species and indicate that a dry grassland environment prevailed at the time the barrow was built. A similar assemblage was found in the topsoil underlying a barrow of about the same date at Ascott-under-Wychwood, Oxfordshire.

Animal bones preserved in archaeological deposits allow insights into the range of animal species present at different times, while studies of the structure of soils provide valuable information on past land-use and misuse. Changes in sea level are reflected in coastal deposits such as raised beaches and submerged forests.

Climate is the most difficult aspect of the environment to reconstruct yet it is so crucial. Plant and animal species whose distribution is precisely controlled by climate—indicator species—provide one source of information, but on a wider scale ancient weather patterns are now being studied through analysis of deep sea cores and sections through the polar ice caps which, it seems, preserve tell-tale signs of past conditions in their chemistry.

Understanding the prehistoric past

It will have become clear by now that the study of prehistory is not as straightforward as might at first appear. There is a constant feedback between developing appropriate theoretical perspectives, re-covering new evidence, formulating reconstructions of the past and then going back to review both the theory and the evidence. The contribution from other disciplines to our understanding of the prehistoric past is also considerable.

There are some things which will never be known. The thoughts of prehistoric people are beyond the reach of the archaeologist, so are the languages spoken, and in many cases so is much of the material culture which they used. Wood, leather, and organic fibres, for example, only survive in exceptional and rare circumstances, yet were probably the most widely used materials in many communities. These deficiencies must be borne in mind when considering what is known of prehistoric communities.

In the course of developing reconstructions of the past it is common practice to build a 'model' of whatever aspect is under consideration. Such a model is simply an attempt to portray the known pieces of the picture of the past and suggest relationships between them. They are really summaries of often complicated patterns and serve as a proposition to be tested against new evidence as it is found. Much is already known about the prehistoric past, but the following account can only be regarded as an interim statement, a series of models of the past. New evidence will come to light, new theory will be developed and more dates will allow greater refinement of the prehistoric calendar. Each of the following chapters will deal with a recognizable episode of prehistory dated by radiocarbon determinations.

2 Bands on the Run

Hunter-gatherer Societies to 3500 BC

Ice and man

For over 99 per cent of the time that human communities have lived in Britain, hunting and gathering were the mainstays of the subsistence economy. Naturally, such a lifestyle involves a high degree of mobility and the minimum of equipment and possessions, which in turn leaves behind very little trace in the archaeological record. No structures except basic shelters were erected by hunter-gatherers; they lived within the constraints of the environment rather than by modifying it.

Human groups arrived in northern Europe during the Pleistocene Ice Age. This was not a single event but a series of successively advancing and retreating ice caps. Traditionally four main episodes of glaciation are distinguished, although in Britain only three are represented by known physical residues; these are termed the Anglian, Wolstonian and Devensian glaciations. Before the Anglian, and between each subsequent glaciation, there were warm periods known as interglacials: the Cromerian, Hoxnian and Ipswichian. The period following the last (Devensian) glaciation is known as the Flandrian (or Holocene) period and is the warm phase in which we now live, seen by many as merely another interglacial episode. This general pattern is complicated by the fact that glacial phases were interrupted by short warm periods known as interstadials, and likewise interglacials were punctuated by cold spells, or stadials. The picture of fluctuating warmer and colder periods can be fairly accurately reconstructed back to the effective maximum range of radiocarbon dating, about 30,000 BC, but beyond this both the sequence of events and their absolute age are far less certain. Recent analysis of ice cores from the polar ice cap and deep sea ocean cores

suggests that since about 700,000 BC there may in fact have been anything up to eight periods of polar ice cap growth with intervening periods of shrinkage. For the time being, however, the accepted British terminology for glacial and interglacial episodes provides a sufficiently detailed framework within which to examine the archaeological evidence.

The amount of water in the oceans changed in harmony with fluctuations in the ice caps, and this in turn brought about changes in sea level. Thus at

8 Pleistocene climatic fluctuations based on oxygen isotope stages. [*After Wymer 1985 figure 107*]

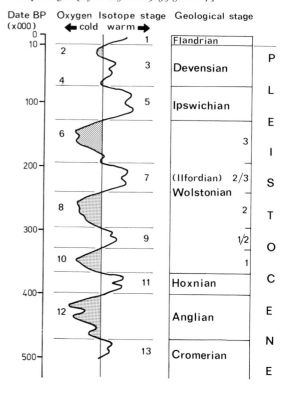

28

times of glacial advance, when much water was locked-up as ice, the mean sea level fell and Britain, as we now know it, was simply a peninsular extension of a European land-mass. Conversely, during warm periods, when the ice melted and water was released, Britain became an island. These factors, of course, affected the climate and vegetation, which in turn determined the animals and plants available as food sources for hunter-gatherers. During glacial advances those parts of Britain not covered by ice may have been arctic tundra, probably not unlike some areas within the arctic circle today. During warm periods woodland and forest regenerated and animals suited to such conditions spread from regions further south. Richard West has identified four phases in the development of soils and vegetation after glacial episodes: first a pre-temperate phase when boreal trees such as pine and birch establish themselves; secondly an early temperate phase when mixed oak forest develops; thirdly a late temperate zone when there is an expansion of late immigrant tree such as hornbeam at the expense of the mixed oak forest, and finally a post-temperate zone when boreal elements predominate again and the woodland becomes more open. Naturally these changes would not have been perceived by people living at the time for the progression was far too slow to be noticeable.

Exactly when human groups first made their way into what is now Britain is not clear, but it was probably during, if not before, an interstadial within the Anglian glacial episode, some time before about 450,000 BC. By world standards this is late in the spread of the human species; early hominids had been living in the equatorial zone since about four million years BC, and by about one million years BC a fairly advanced hominid species known as *Homo erectus* had spread widely across Africa, southern Europe and Asia. One of the great difficulties of working with evidence from Britain, however, is that each successive glacial episode disturbed whatever evidence had been left by man before, and carried tools and objects away from where they were dropped or abandoned. In effect glacial episodes wiped the landscape clean of earlier traces, and it is only by chance that evidence for these early periods of settlement survives *in situ*.

Traces of early man in Britain suggest periodic visits during the warmer periods within the Anglian glaciation and during the early Hoxnian interglacial. Among the remains so far known two distinct traditions can be recognized on the basis of tool-making technologies. These are known as the

Clactonian and Acheulian. John Wymer had postulated that on typological and stratigraphic grounds the Clactonian tradition is the earlier of the two, although there may be some overlap in their use.

The Clactonian

The Clactonian tradition is named after a rich collection of material from Clacton-on-Sea, Essex. The tools which characterize the tradition are mostly made of flint and comprise flake tools—that is implements made using flakes of flint struck from nodules called cores. Some tools are, by later standards, crude and hardly seem to warrant the term 'tool' at all. In addition to the flake tools some cores were worked to a rough edge as choppers or chopping tools.

Riverside sites seem to have been favoured by the users of the Clactonian technology, possibly because of the advantages such places provided as a focus for resources—animals coming for water, a rich variety of plants, and a range of aquatic species. At Clacton-on-Sea itself, excavations in gravel deposits at the golf course site revealed what had formerly been a river bank in early Hoxnian times. The site, which was probably simply a temporary camp, showed that deer, bison, horse, elephant and rhinoceros had either been hunted or successfully scavenged. Pollen indicated that the surrounding landscape was dominated by open woodland with some grassland nearby. Analysis of the wear patterns on the flint tools betrayed their use for butchering meat, hide-scraping, and wood working. A waterlogged deposit at Lion Point, Essex, preserved the end of a yew wood spear which had been shaped with flint tools and was probably a thrusting weapon rather than a throwing spear.

A rather similar type of site is known south of the Thames at Swanscombe, Kent. Here deposits known locally as the 'lower gravels' contain distinctive Clactonian type artefacts, probably from a campsite in the vicinity again situated beside a river. In contrast to Clacton, however, pollen suggests that here at Swanscombe reed swamps, fen habitats and light woodland surrounded the site, thus providing a slightly different potential range of resources. The animals available to the occupants of the Swanscombe area at this time included straight-tusked elephants, fallow deer, horse, wild ox, red deer and rhinoceros. Other Clactonian findspots include Little Thurrock, Essex, and Barnham St Gregory, Suffolk, which were again in waterside locations. No Clactonian tools have so far been recorded from occupation layers within caves.

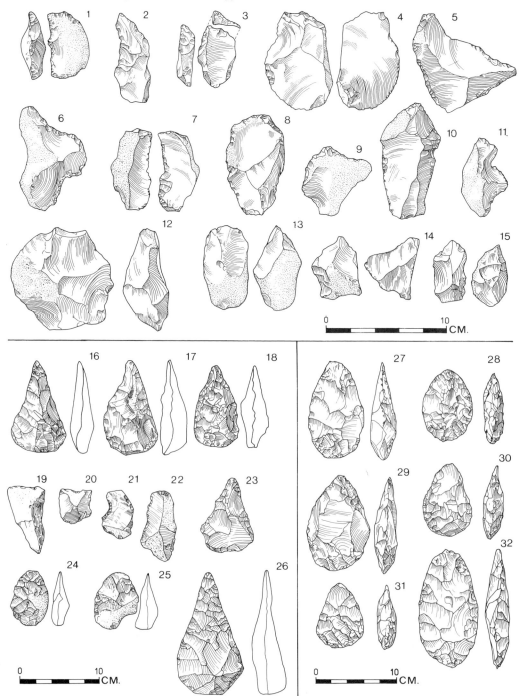

9 Clactonian and Acheulian tradition flint tools.
(a) Clactonian tools from Jaywick Sands, Clacton, Essex: 1–11 = worked flakes/flake tools; 12–15 = cores.
(b) Acheulian artefacts from the middle gravels at Swanscombe, Kent: 16–18 and 23–26 = hand-axes; 19–22 = flake tools. (c) Acheulian ovate hand-axes from the upper loam deposits at Swanscombe (nos. 27, 28, 31 and 32) and Pearson's Pit, Dartford, Kent (nos. 29 and 30). [*(a) After Oakley and Leakey 1937 figures 3, 4, and 5. (b) after Roe 1981 figure 3.6. (c) after Roe 1981 figure 3.7*]

The early Acheulian

Acheulian tradition technologies are characterized by rather different types of tool of which the most distinctive are bifaces or hand-axes. These are core tools made by flaking down a nodule of flint or some other fine-grained rock into the desired form. Early examples were made using a stone hammer and often appear to have a rather heavy butt and a thicker cross-section than some later examples. Hand-axes were multi-purpose tools used as knives or choppers in various domestic and hunting activities. Other tools include variants on the hand-axe theme—for example less pointed hand-axes known as cleavers— as well as scrapers and trimmed flakes.

Riverside and lakeside locations attracted groups using early Acheulian type tools, no doubt for the same reasons as the users of Clactonian industries favoured them, but caves were also exploited for habitation. Dating some of these early deposits and determining their cultural affinities can be most difficult. At Fordwich, Kent, for example, many tools have been recovered from gravels beside the river Stour, but whether they all derive from a single occupation area is not known. Other possible early Acheulian sites include Farnham, Surrey, and Warren Hill, Suffolk. Two cave sites may be mentioned. The first, at Westbury sub-Mendip, Somerset, is not a cave proper but a fissure connected to a cavern system in which occupation material has become trapped and thus survived the effects of later glaciations. The site was discovered in 1969 and analysis of the material is still in progress. Finds include flint flakes and bones of bear, jaguar, wolf, horse, rhinoceros, and other mammals. These deposits highlight another problem of dealing with evidence of this antiquity, namely that human groups were not the only users of caves, for animals frequently adopted one as a den and of course would sometimes have taken their prey there to eat. The point here is that not all bones recorded from cave excavations necessarily belong with any human occupation of the site.

The second cave to mention is Kent's Cavern, Devon, which was first excavated in 1825-9 and is truly a cave in the sense of an accessible cavern suitable for occupation. In the lowest levels investigated hand-axes were recovered along with the bones of sabre-toothed tiger and two species of vole which are thought to have become extinct before the end of the Anglian glaciation or early in the Hoxnian.

Whether human groups consistently hunted large mammals such as elephant and rhinoceros, or whether they simply took advantage of kills made by other animals is not clear. Likewise, uncertainty surrounds the identity of the makers of these pre-Hoxnian and early Hoxnian tool traditions. No human skeletal remains of this date have been recovered, so whether two quite different early hominid species were responsible for the identifiable tool-making traditions, or whether the variations can be explained by chronological development or functional requirements connected with the exploitation of different resources cannot at present be determined. However, on present evidence it is tempting to associate these early visitors to Britain with the northward expansion of *Homo erectus*.

The Hoxnian expansion and after

The middle of the Hoxnian interglacial marks the first major expansion of hunter-gatherer exploitation in Britain. John Evans has shown that the Hoxnian period was characterized by a mild oceanic climate with mixed deciduous woodland dominated by hazel, yew, alder, oak and elm, together with open grassland in the river valleys. Herds of large herbivorous mammals were plentiful and carnivores such as bear, wolf and lion roamed the land. For most of the period Britain was probably connected to the Continent, which may account for the fact that well over 3000 findspots of Hoxnian and Wolstonian period tools have been recorded and is suggestive of a relatively high population by Pleistocene standards, or at least frequent visitation by mobile groups exploiting the north European Plain.

During the early part of the Hoxnian period Clactonian industries similar to those of earlier periods were in use, but by the middle of the Hoxnian period Acheulian technologies alone flourished. River valleys and lakeside situations were still favoured for settlement, probably for much the same reasons as previously. The Thames valley in particular has yielded abundant traces of occupation of this period, although most of the evidence is contained within disturbed glacial drift deposits. Taking the distribution of known sites as a whole there seems to have been a preference for situations near the confluence of rivers, as for example in the middle Thames and further west where the Bristol Avon meets the Severn.

The site of Hoxne, Suffolk, which gives its name to the interglacial as a whole, has two distinct levels of Acheulian occupation. The site lay beside a lake at this time and the lower and earlier level is characterized by a tool assemblage made using fine quality black flint and dominated by refined cordate/ovate hand-axes. Products of the Hoxnian period and later were finished by flaking with a soft hammer which produced a much more regular finish than is found on early Acheulian tools. Bones from the site suggest that horse was the principal animal hunted or scavenged, with deer, bison, wild cattle and elephant present in lesser numbers. Analysis of the tools showed that butchery, woodworking and plant processing were practised at or near the camp. Stratified above this industry was a second artefact-rich level, rather different, although still of Acheulian character, with mainly pointed hand-axes and large numbers of scrapers found in discrete clusters suggestive of hide cleaning.

Another riverside site reoccupied at this time was Swanscombe. Above the early Clactonian industries in the 'lower gravels' is an Acheulian industry which is probably of middle–late Hoxnian date. Environmental evidence suggests relatively open conditions, and horse and wild oxen were the main animals found. The number of flint flakes worked up as tools at Swanscombe was less than at Hoxne, perhaps reflecting a slightly different range of activities at the two sites. From the Acheulian levels at Swanscombe

come three fragments from the skull of one of the inhabitants. It is difficult to say much from the pieces found because they all derive from the rear of the skull, but they seem to have belonged to a hominid somewhat more developed than *Homo erectus* but not yet fully comparable with modern man, *Homo sapiens sapiens*.

Other waterside sites with hand-axes of this period include Stoke Newington, London, Hitchin, Hertfordshire, and Foxhall Road, Ipswich, Suffolk. At Hoxne, Suffolk, and also Mark's Tey, Essex, there is some evidence for a period of deforestation and the deposition of charcoal in the vicinity of each site at about the same time as human groups arrived. Possible explanations of this must of course include natural disasters such as lightning strikes, but another suggestion is that human groups were deliberately interfering with nature by setting fire to the forest, perhaps to encourage the growth of new shoots and scrub which would attract herds of animals and so make sources of food more predictable. Whether this is so or not, the skill of these early hunter-gatherer groups in exploiting the environment in which they lived should not be underestimated. They undoubtedly had a deep knowledge of

A

B

10 Acheulian flintworking floor of the Wolstonian glacial period under excavation at Red Barns, Portsmouth, Hampshire. (A) General view of the excavation showing the depth of glacially deposited overburden sealing the floor, scale totals 2 metres. (B) Detail of part finished tool and flintworking debris on the working floor, scale totals 0.2 metres. [*Photos: Clive Gamble and Arthur Apsimon; copyright reserved*]

their surroundings and the behaviour of their prey. To judge from hunter-gatherer societies recorded in modern times, hunting strategies were probably complicated and well co-ordinated.

Waterside sites were not the only places occupied at this time. Acheulian type hand-axes have been found on high ground over 100 metres (330 feet) above sea level on the Chilterns, in north Hampshire, on the Wiltshire Downs, and possibly even on the Cotswolds. Coastal sites may also have been used to exploit marine resources, as perhaps at Boxgrove and Slindon, Sussex, occupied after a phase of high sea level. Another attraction of coastal sites in southern England would have been the supplies of fresh flint available from cliff falls.

In the uplands of North Wales a cave at Pont-newydd, Clwyd, was occupied in post-Hoxnian times about 225,000 BC. Settlement was apparently confined to the entrance area of the cave and tools included hand-axes and scrapers of late Acheulian type made from local rock. Stephen Green, the excavator of the site, suggests that the evidence recovered is compatible with the use of the cave for transitory settlement, probably as part of a hunting strategy, in which local raw materials were used for the production of *ad hoc* tool-kits. Human bones

were also found at the site, including teeth which are comparable with examples belonging to early *Homo sapiens neanderthalensis* (Neanderthal Man).

From the late Hoxnian or early Wolstonian period a new mode of flintworking became fashionable, the so-called 'Levallois technique'. The aim was to remove flakes of a predetermined size and shape, and

B

11 Pontnewydd Cave, Clwyd. (A) Excavations inside the cave in progress. (B) Hominid bones—adult molar and a fragment of a juvenile mandible. [*Photos: by permission of the National Museum of Wales; copyright reserved*]

A

this was accomplished by first preparing a block of flint as a core by surface flaking one face to produce what is often rather aptly called a 'tortoise core'. Once this was done flakes could be detached along the axis of the core, each flake retaining a distinctive pattern of converging surface flake-beds on its back or dorsal face. Tools made using this technique are known from Pontnewydd and other sites of similar date.

Mousterian industries

Dating finds to the Wolstonian glacial period is not easy since tool types remained similar to those in use during the Hoxnian. Cave sites do not seem to have been favoured, perhaps because many were blocked by ice or out-wash material, but an open campsite in the lower Thames valley at Baker's Hole, Northfleet, Kent, demonstrates the presence of groups in Britain at this time as it seems to have been occupied in a very cold period during the Wolstonian. By the end of the period or the beginning of the Ipswichian the Levallois technique had become widely used, and the composition of most tool-kits had changed. Some new assemblages are generally described as belonging to the Mousterian tradition in which flake tools predominated, although hand-axes continued to be made as all-purpose tools.

Mousterian industries are common in France and indeed across wide areas of Europe where they are generally associated with Neanderthal communities. Other than the possible early Neanderthal bones from Pontnewydd, no remains of this species have been found in Britain so far, although some Neanderthal teeth were found in 1910 at La Cotte de Saint-Brelade, Jersey, in the Channel Islands. It is impossible to say whether communities using Mousterian style tool-kits made their way into Britain in pursuit of animal herds or whether the traditions were adopted by existing communities. During much of the Ipswichian period Britain was probably an island, cut off from the Continent and so occupation may have been confined to the beginning and ends of the interglacial.

During the early phases of the last glacial period, the Devensian, Mousterian industries include various scrapers and forms comparable to those used in the Acheulian traditions and these gave rise to what are known as 'Mousterian of Acheulian' tradition assemblages. Among the distinctive tools added at this time were *bout coupé* style hand-axes which differ from earlier hand-axes in having a more U-shaped form.

Caves were again widely used for occupation in the early Devensian, although overall open sites far outnumbered cave sites because of the geographically restricted distribution of caves. Mammoth hunting was widespread at this time, and the development of the Levallois flaking technique may have been linked with the increasing exploitation of this species during the late Wolstonian. At Ealing in north London a pointed Levallois flake was discovered lying among the bones of what appears to have been a complete mammoth skeleton. Overall, the number of sites dating to the early Devensian is large, but spread over the enormous time period involved suggests that the density population was low, perhaps less than five groups spread across the whole country at any one time, and there might indeed have been times when Britain was unoccupied for long periods. The size of any group is hard to estimate. Hunter-gatherer societies are often very fluid, with fissioning or partitioning of the community at times when resources are scarce followed by fusion or the coming together of groups into maximum units or bands when circumstances permit, possibly on a yearly cycle. Local bands cannot have fallen below about 25 members since this is the minimum number of persons required to maintain a reproductive population. At all times, group size and dispersion must have been governed by the resources available and what could be exploited.

No evidence of structures or dwellings of this early date are known on open sites, but they would probably have been simple wooden or hide-covered shelters. Group territories defined in terms of the cycle of movements undertaken may have covered very large areas, and communities staying in southern Britain from time to time may have been just as familiar with large areas of the Rhine valley as with the Thames valley. Whether communities penetrated the uplands of northern Britain is not known. No artefacts or sites have so far been recorded from these areas, but this could simply be a product of uneven preservation rather than a real preference for the hunting grounds of southern and eastern England as an extension of the north European Plain.

The first modern man

By about 40,000 BC anatomically modern man, *Homo sapiens sapiens*, was present in Europe, and undoubtedly appeared in Britain during the middle stages of the Devensian. Whether Neanderthal Man was replaced by modern man, or whether the Neanderthals somehow evolved into modern man, or whether modern man developed along some other evolutionary path, perhaps from *Homo erectus*, is not known. Uncertainty also surrounds the nature of settlement during the middle Devensian which was characterized by a fluctuating climate before the onset of a full glacial advance from about 26,000 BC.

Flintworking technologies in the middle Devensian period underwent further changes, and the range of items in the average took-kit increased greatly. Hand-axes, which had been in use for the previous 200,000 years or more in Europe, were finally replaced by a range of tools adapted to specific tasks. Roger Jacobi has argued that these changes broadly follow patterns of development evidenced on the Continent. Particularly distinctive was the adoption of a blade-based technology in place of the earlier reliance on flakes. Blades are long narrow flakes generally defined as being at least twice as long as they are wide and in the middle Devensian they were detached from elongated cores using a soft hammer or punch. The most distinctive new tool form to appear at this time was the 'leaf-shaped' point. These are large, usually 10–15 centimetres (4–6 inches) long, and shaped by carefully executed surface chipping of both sides of the blade (bifacial working). Assigning a function to these pieces is not easy, but their most likely role was as spear-tips. Among the remainder of the tool-kit blades, forming knives and scrapers were common, but various other points were also usually present.

Only about 15 or 20 sites can be confidently assigned to the middle Devensian, and of these most are cave sites in Devon, the Mendips of Somerset, Wales and the southern Pennines round Creswell Crags, Derbyshire. Open sites do exist, as at Barnwood in the Severn valley, Gloucestershire, but they are rare. Perhaps this is not unexpected at a time of deteriorating climate and the destruction of sites by natural processes.

Kent's Cavern, Devon, was one of the cave sites occupied in the early Devensian, probably about 26,770 ± 450 BC according to a radiocarbon date from bones loosely associated with flint tools from the site. Many leaf-shaped points were found in the Great Chamber, together with animal teeth, which might, as John Campbell has suggested, indicate an area in which tasks connected with the dismemberment and butchering of carcasses brought back by hunting parties were carried out. The presence of hyena bones suggests that man was not the only inhabitant of the cave, and for this reason it is difficult to be certain which of the great many animal bones of horse, woolly rhinoceros, deer, bison and great Irish elk fed humans and which were brought to the cave by hyena.

Comparable with Kent's Cavern is the site of Badger's Hole, on the Mendips, Somerset. This site was probably a base camp, but round about are other caves of the same period with markedly less artefactual material. This may suggest that they were used as temporary shelters by hunting parties working their way across the Mendip uplands and is perhaps the first evidence for a functional difference between sites. Analysis of pollen from the Hyena Den Cave, also on the Mendips, indicates a fairly open environment at this time with a high proportion of grasses and herbs and a few willow and juniper bushes interspersed between occasional pine, oak and lime trees. One of the great problems with this early period of prehistory, however, is assessing the contemporaneity of adjacent findspots and matching evidence recorded at one site with that from others.

Burials of middle Devensian date are extremely rare, according to present evidence, but one, the so-called 'Red Lady of Paviland', discovered in Goat's Cave, Paviland, Glamorgan in 1823 by William Buckland, has attracted much attention. In fact the burial is that of an adult male who had been sprinkled with red ochre after being placed in a shallow grave within the cave. The body seems to have been deliberately placed in association with the skull of a mammoth, and accompanying the interment were a number of mammoth ivory rods, two ivory bracelets and some perforated shells. The date of this burial, which represents the oldest known formal burial in Britain, has become a matter of some debate. A radiocarbon date of 16,510 ± 340 BC was determined on a very small sample of bone from the skeleton, but this would mean the burial had been made at the very height of the Devensian glacial advance when the edge of the ice cap was probably no more than a few kilometres away from Paviland. Recently Roger Jacobi has argued that the radiocarbon date could be too young and that the burial belongs with the middle Devensian occupation of the cave, which is dated to about 25,000 BC. This would be supported by the typological affinities of the ivory rods and the bracelet, and the ochreous staining on flint tools of middle Devensian types.

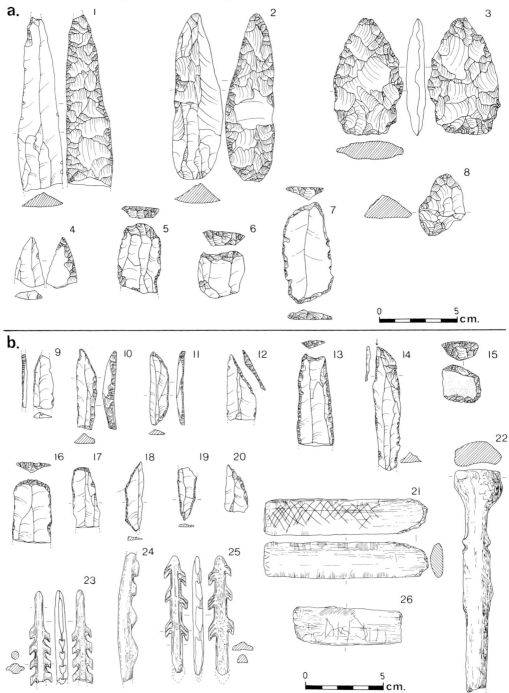

12 Selection of equipment and objects from late Pleistocene hunter-gatherer sites. (a) Early Devensian date flint tools from Kent's Cavern, Devon: 1–4 = leaf-shaped points; 5–8 = scrapers. (b) Late Devensian and early Holocene date (Creswellian) tools, weapons and decorated bone: 9–14, 16, 19 and 20 from Anston Cave, South Yorkshire; 15, 17 and 21 from Gough's Cave, Somerset; 18 from Langwith Cave, Derbyshire; 22 from Paviland Cave, Glamorgan; 23 and 24 from Kent's Cavern, Devon; 25 from Avelines Hole, Somerset; 26 from Robin Hood's Cave, Derbyshire. [*After Megaw and Simpson 1979 figures 2.4, 2.10 and 2.11*]

Late Devensian discontinuity

After about 25,000 BC the effects of the Devensian glacial advance were being felt throughout Britain. Northern areas were covered by ice and by about 18,000 BC the ice cap had penetrated as far south as the Bristol Channel and across England and Wales along a line drawn roughly between Swansea and The Wash. South of this line periglacial conditions prevailed.

During this time of maximum glacial advance there are virtually no traces of settlement in Britain, or indeed in northern France which was connected by land to southern England throughout the Devensian period. The length of this discontinuity in settlement is a matter for debate. Roger Jacobi has suggested that occupation is absent from Britain between about 25,000 and 10,000 BC, but others would prefer a break of shorter duration. Until more radiocarbon dates are available it is only possible to speculate, but the longer chronology of abandonment seems to fit currently available data rather better. However, the possibility of occasional forays northwards from the densely settled parts of France, for example round the Dordogne, cannot be ruled out, and if the radiocarbon date for the Paviland burial is taken at face value then its deposition may have taken place on just such an expedition by communities far from home.

The resettlement of Britain

The ice caps of the last main episode of glaciation began to retreat about 15,000 BC, and by 12,000 BC all of southern Britain was again available for settlement. Large numbers of elk, horse, reindeer, red deer and many other small animals moved back into northern France and Britain from their southern retreats to join the large mammals more accustomed to living in a periglacial environment. Man moved northward again following the animals.

The retreat of the last glaciation was not a single smooth process. Several readvances can be identified and after a period of climatic amelioration known as the Windermere interstadial, between about 11,000 and 10,000 BC, one such readvance, known as the Loch Lomond stadial, heralded a brief cold spell known to Continental climatologists as the younger Dryas. It was against this background of complex climatic fluctuations that the repopulation of Britain took place, although the details are only now just beginning to be sorted out. In terms of British prehistory this phase of resettlement is particularly significant because it probably marks the beginning of an unbroken period of occupation and continuous social development which is still in progress.

Technologically the communities repopulating Britain in the late Devensian had advanced little in the 14,000 years or so since the retreat southwards of the middle Devensian groups. Blade-based industries still predominated, but backed blades of various types appear for the first time. The leaf-shaped points had been replaced by shouldered and tanged points, and steeply retouched awls, burins and end scrapers had become common. These industries, which are usually termed 'Creswellian', were supplemented by greater use of bone and antler in toolmaking. Barbed uniserial or biserial points, probably used as harpoons, were an important innovation, and bone was also used for awls and needles.

Settlement and economy

Initial resettlement appears to have favoured the same parts of Britain used before the Devensian ice maximum. Caves in the south west, the Mendips, Wales and the southern Pennines were again occupied at this time. There is also a notable extension of settlement into the uplands with use of Victoria Cave, North Yorkshire and Kirkhead Cave,

13 The Victoria Cave near Settle, North Yorkshire. [*Photo: author; copyright reserved*]

Cumbria. In lowland areas open settlements are known, indicating a wide scatter of occupation. Sea levels were still low at this time and southern Britain was part of a huge basin extending across part of what is now the North Sea into Denmark, the Netherlands, Belgium and northern France, and across the English Channel into western France. Occupation was probably widespread in these areas, but is now under the sea. Artefacts characteristic of the period occasionally come to light in fishing nets.

Large mammals such as mammoth, bison, woolly rhinoceros and lion became extinct in Britain by the time of the late glacial resettlement and so the attention of the hunters shifted to the smaller mammals, especially horse, red deer, wild cattle and elk. This marked an important change in hunting strategy and set the course for the development of technology and society for the next few millennia.

A vivid example of late Devensian hunters at work is provided by the skeleton of an elk found in lacustrine muds at High Furlong, near Blackpool, Lancashire. Examination of the bones, and the artefacts found with them, allows the last weeks of the life of this creature to be reconstructed. It seems that during one winter, some time about 10,000 BC, the beast was attacked, possibly with hard-tipped projectiles and a chopper of some kind; wounds were inflicted on the limbs and rib cage. The animal escaped alive but three weeks or more later was attacked again, this time with spears tipped with uniserial bone points. One tip lodged in the left hind foot, another in its flank. Again the animal escaped, badly wounded, but seems to have died shortly after while crossing a marshy lake.

Among the most notable occupied caves of this period is Kent's Cavern, Devon, which seems to have continued its earlier role as the base for a hunting community. In the uppermost 'black band' in the entrance chamber the usual assemblage of backed blades and a uniserial bone point were found. Horse was the major prey of these hunters, along with giant Irish elk and perhaps cave bear. On the Mendips in Somerset, Gough's (New) Cave has produced one of the richest collections of material of this date, including all the usual tool forms together with two examples of a rather unusual type of tool known as a *bâton de commandement*. These are simply perforated bones which were probably for straightening spearshafts. Remains of horse and red deer indicate the main species hunted in the area. Further north a number of caves were occupied at this time along Creswell Crags, Derbyshire. Evidence from excavations in the mouth of Robin Hood's Cave

provides some insights into the organization of the occupation area, with a hearth under the opening, and a meat processing area at the rear. Nearby, at Mother Grundy's Parlour, pollen studies emphasize the changing environment during the late glacial occupations as the landscape became covered in woodland dominated by pine and birch.

In the lowlands important settlements have been excavated at Sproughton, Norfolk, and Hengistbury Head, Dorset. The latter now overlooks Christchurch harbour but in late glacial times, about 10,000 BC, lay on a ridge overlooking a wide, probably wooded, valley containing the confluence of two rivers. The tools and flintworking waste recovered from this site show that it was essentially a hunting and meat processing camp, perhaps carefully chosen on a route regularly used by migrating animals.

Art and death

The earliest known art in Britain comes from late glacial sites, and although confined to a few pieces of incised bone, the inspiration behind the designs clearly stems from the same traditions as are exemplified by the famous cave paintings in southern France and Spain which mostly date from the Devensian period. Among the pieces from Britain are the decorated horse mandible from Kendrick's Cave on the Great Orme, Gwynedd, radiocarbon dated to 8050 ± 120 BC; a rib bone bearing the engraving of a horse from Robin Hood's Cave, Derbyshire; an ivory point which carries a fish design from Pin Hole Cave, Derbyshire, and from the same site a reindeer rib on which is portrayed a masked figure. A number of bones from sites as far apart as Gough's Cave, Somerset, and Great Ormes Head, Gwynedd, have groups of cut-marks along one of more edges as if the bones had been used as a tally of some kind. Various possible uses have been suggested, among them the idea that the bones were primitive calculators or some kind of calendrical record.

No formal burials of late glacial date are known in detail, but isolated human bones have been found at a number of cave sites, among them Aveline's Hole and Sun Hole on the Mendips in Somerset.

The wildwood and the rising sea

By 8000 BC the development of post-glacial woodland was well advanced. Soils were beginning to

0   1000
KM.

14 Provisional reconstruction of the north European mainland about 7000 BC, with some of the main contemporary sites known in Britain. [*After Clark 1972 and Jacobi 1973 figure 4*]

mature, and pine and birch dominated the tree cover in most areas. The flora within these woods depended largely on soil type, for these were not managed woods but what Oliver Rackham has termed 'wildwoods'—self-regenerative woodland which is highly variable in density and cover. Animals such as wild ox, red deer, roe deer and wild pig, which were all suited to woodland, could be found in lowland areas. Some of the higher upland peaks may have remained open.

In response to these changes, hunting strategies and the equipment for procuring food also changed. Uniserial bone points continued to be made, but greater reliance was placed upon composite tools made from small blade-based pieces known as microliths set in wooden shafts. The microliths provided sharp tips or barbs for hunting weapons. Spears remained in use, but bows-and-arrows had become widespread by this time, and were no doubt a useful innovation in the forest where the noise of closing in on an animal to use a spear might give

alarm and cause it to escape. Another new tool type was the flaked axe or adze, again useful in woodland for general carpentry and the construction of temporary shelters. All of these technological developments followed more general pan-European patterns of change, for at 8000 BC Britain was still very much a part of the Continental mainland.

The majority of known occupation sites for the period 8000 to 6000 BC are open sites. A few caves were still used, but they account for rather less than one per cent of all known occupation sites. Riverside situations were again favoured, presumably because of their diversity of plant and animal resources, and perhaps because of the natural thinning of the woodland around such places. A few coastally situated sites are also known, but the biggest change is the spread of sites high into the hills, in some cases well above the 305 metre (1000 ft) contour.

Excavated sites in lowland areas include Thatcham, Berkshire, and Broxbourne, Hertfordshire, but Star Carr, North Yorkshire, is perhaps the best known early Flandrian site, and deservedly so because of the fine preservation offered to the remains of the settlement by the waterlogged conditions which have prevailed in the area since late glacial times. The site was excavated in 1949–51 by

39

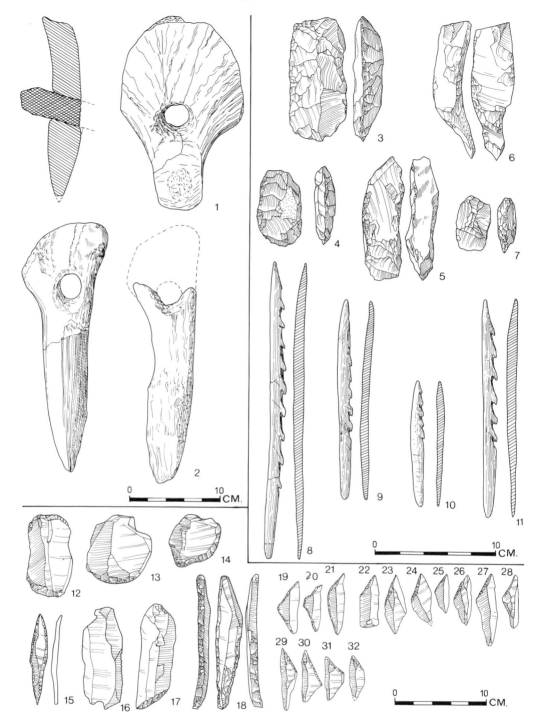

15 Selection of tools and weapons from the eighth-millennium BC campsite at Star Carr, North Yorkshire. 1–2 = elk antler mattocks/picks; 3–7 = flint axes/adzes; 8–11 = barbed antler points; 12–14 = scrapers; 15–18 = awls/points; 16–17 = trimmed flakes; 19–32 = microliths. [*After Clark 1954 figures 35, 38, 39, 40, 43, 64 and 69*]

Grahame Clark and was found to comprise a birchwood platform, on the edge of a lagoon, dating to about 7500 BC. Hunting was represented by the bones of a variety of animals including red deer, wild pig, wild cattle, elk, fox, wolf and pine marten. Birds were also represented, among them crane, white stork, grebe, lapwing and duck. Weapons found at the site included nearly 200 barbed antler points and over 240 microliths. Preservation was so good that one microlith retained traces of resin which had been used to affix it into a shaft. Equipment for processing animal skins—scrapers, flint knives and bone smoothers—were present, and the debris from the manufacture of barbed points from red deer antler was widespread. Flintworking also took place on the site. Among the tools abandoned on the platform were flaked flint axes, adzes, and bone mattocks and picks, which were possibly for grubbing up roots and tubers.

The inhabitants of Star Carr wore beads of shale and amber, probably made from raw materials collected from the nearby coast. Fragments of iron pyrites were also found, and had undoubtedly been used as strike-a-lights for fire-making. Most surprising were the 21 stag frontlets replete with antlers which displayed signs of modification and in some cases had perforations around the edge of the bone. What the purpose of these was is not clear; they could have been attached to some form of head-dress, and the most widely accepted explanation is that they were part of a disguise used during hunting, or ritual, or both.

Another important find at Star Carr was a wooden paddle-shaped object. If it was a paddle then it implies that boats were used nearby, but alternatively the object may have been a digging tool of some kind. In common with other groups of this period, the inhabitants of Star Carr kept a dog (a domesticated wolf), possibly for use in hunting as much as for companionship.

Exploitation of the uplands may have been intensive at this time. The Pennines, the North York Moors, the Mendips, and most other upland areas have yielded a large number of flint scatters containing microliths, typically located to command good visibility of the surrounding landscape and in many cases probably just above the prevailing tree-line. More sheltered spots within the main valleys penetrating the uplands were also used. Most are known only through surface scatters of flintwork, but at Deepcar, North Yorkshire, excavations on a site in a valley beside an upland stream revealed an extensive flint scatter suggestive of a settlement, together with slight traces of a small structure, possibly a shelter or a windbreak around at least three hearths.

Assessing which sites were actually situated on the coast at this time is not easy because of later changes in sea level, but coastal resources were certainly exploited, as shown by materials used at Star Carr. In south-west Wales, the site of Nab Head, Dyfed,

16 Excavations at Pointed Stone Site 2, North Yorkshire, an upland encampment dated to about 7000 BC. [*Photo: Roger Jacobi; copyright reserved*]

was probably occupied in the early Flandrian, and similar sites undoubtedly lie off the present shore elsewhere.

Territories, movements and population

How these various sites in different parts of the landscape related to one another is not known with certainty. Most are small and could hardly support a community all the year round. On the basis of the evidence from Star Carr some sort of seasonal exploitation of resources has been suggested and it is generally thought that communities each exploited a range of resources in different parts of the landscape through the year. Archaeologically the most difficult problem is determining when during the year a particular site was occupied. On the basis of the types of antler found at Star Carr, Grahame Clark suggested that this particular site was occupied in midwinter and springtime and that in summer the inhabitants moved away to higher ground or to the coast, but elsewhere the evidence is less clear cut.

Site	Microliths and microburins	Other tools
1. Upland		
Warcock Hill South, Yorkshire	70%	30%
Pointed Stone Site 2, Yorkshire	80%	20%
Pointed Stone Site 3, Yorkshire	85%	15%
Money Howe Site 1, Yorkshire	88%	12%
2. Lowland		
Star Carr, Yorkshire	25%	75%
Brigham, Yorkshire	43%	57%
Willoughton, Lincolnshire	41%	59%

[*Data from Jacobi 1978 figures 8 and 9 and page 315*]

Table 2 Incidence of microliths and microburins as a percentage of finished tools on upland and lowland sites in northern England.

Analysis of the flint tools at upland and lowland sites by Roger Jacobi has revealed that in the upland assemblages most of the finished tools are microliths, mainly from weapons used in hunting, while most of the waste pieces are microburins which are a by-product of making microliths. In contrast, at Star Carr and other lowland sites microliths and micro-

17 Simplified models of seasonal movements by hunter-gatherer groups in sixth–eighth millennia BC. [*Source: author*]

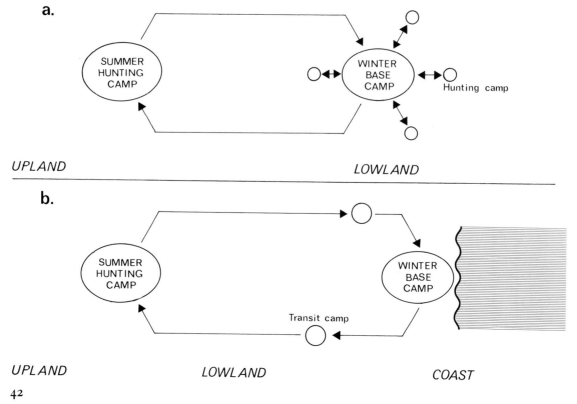

42

burins represent less than 45 per cent of finished tools. Instead the majority of tools were for meat processing and manufacturing activities. Moreover, analysis of the animal bones from Star Carr shows that only certain portions of slaughtered animals were brought to the site; less useful parts such as the pelvis and spine are missing and were presumably discarded at the kill site. The picture which begins to emerge is thus a complicated one involving a number of seasonally specific occupation sites for each group and long-distance movements between them. The annual range of these communities could have been considerable, perhaps as much as 80 kilometres (50 miles). Fissioning and fusion, the formal dispersal and subsequent reuniting of the group, probably played an important role in the distribution of population at different times of the year, and variations in the general pattern may be expected for groups living near the coast or some other particularly prolific source of food.

The size of individual groups at this time is hard to estimate. Working on the basis of evidence from Star Carr, a community of 25 people was suggested by Grahame Clark for this site, but in an analysis of other sites of the same period Paul Mellars suggests that Star Carr, with an area of perhaps 185 square metres (221 square yards), is larger than the average site. The general impression given by the evidence is that, although the range of resources used changed during the early Flandrian period, the basic pattern of social organization remained much as before with small bands as the basic social unit. Population levels for the country as a whole can only be guessed at. Don Brothwell postulated anything between 3000 and 20,000 people on the basis of hunter-gatherer population densities among recent groups, but this is probably an underestimate since the resources available in the developing post-glacial forest were very abundant by comparison with those available within the environments where hunter-gatherer groups have flourished in recent centuries.

Few burials of the period are known, which precludes study of the population itself. The best known and most complete burial so far recovered was found in Gough's (New) Cave, Cheddar, Somerset, in 1903. It was an unaccompanied inhumation of a young adult male (called 'Cheddar Man') and has been radiocarbon dated to 7130 ± 150 BC. Other cave burials also date to this period, as for example at Aveline's Hole, also on Mendip, where human bones have been dated to 7164 ± 110 BC and one deposit has been interpreted as the remains of a double inhumation accompanied by perforated animal teeth, animal bones and fossils. Some of the many undated cave burials elsewhere may well prove to be of this period.

As the glaciers receded northwards through the late glacial and early Flandrian, melt-water was released into the sea causing its level to rise. To some extent this was compensated for by the rising of the land as the weight of the ice was removed, but during the ninth and eighth millenia BC rising sea levels were beginning to have a real effect by reducing the land area of northern Europe available for settlement. It was at about this time that the spread of settlement into Scotland and the far north of England took place. Most settlements known here are coastal, exploiting marine resources, such as fish and shellfish, as well as whatever terrestrial resources were available. Among the earliest sites in Scotland are Morton, Fifeshire, and Glenbatrick Waterhole on the Island of Jura, Strathclyde. Occupation at both sites extended over a considerable area for many centuries.

Insular development and expansion

By 6000 BC Britain had become an island cut off from the mainland of Europe except by boat. In the following millennia technological and social developments continued, but they were essentially insular, with little or no Continental influence. The environment changed too. Woodland became more closed, with oak, alder, elm and lime taking over as the dominant species. Only the highest ground in the uplands remained free of woodland.

Tool technology continued to change, but, as Roger Jacobi has pointed out, isolation from the Continent led to a curtailment in the range and diversity of some aspects of material culture. The bone points of earlier periods were slowly abandoned while the shape and style of microliths changed to encompass a wide range of geometric forms, in some cases of minute size. These new forms probably indicate the introduction of new types of missiles, but what these might have been is not known. Flintworking itself continued in the blade tradition; very narrow blades struck from small cores were favoured. In areas where flint is scarce or absent especially frugal use was made of cores and waste flakes alike.

The increased density of population prompted by rising sea levels may also have been supplemented by rising population numbers from about 6000 BC or so onwards. Whereas earlier groups favoured light,

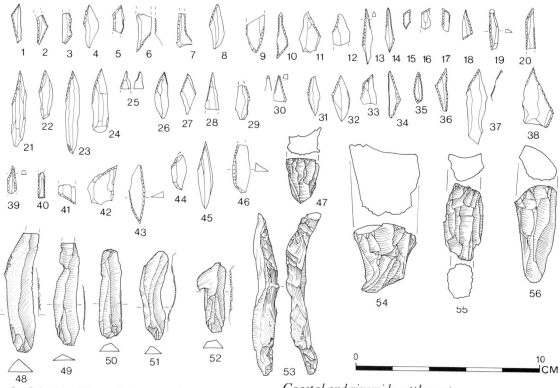

18 Selection of flint tools from an early sixth-millennium BC occupation deposit at Cherhill, Wiltshire. 1–46 = geometric and micro-triangular microliths; 48–52 = retouched and utilized blades; 53 = crested blade; 47 and 54–56 = cores. [*After Evans and Smith 1983 figures 17, 18 and 19*]

well-drained soils, almost all soil types were used to a greater or lesser extent from about 6000 BC onwards. Sites were often situated near the junction of different soils, and river valleys formed the focus of settlement in many areas. The reason for this was presumably easy access to a greater range of resources. Settlement in Scotland and the north expanded at this time; among the dated sites mention may be made of Barsalloch, Dumfries and Galloway, where charcoal from a hearth yielded a date of 4050 ± 110 BC.

The range of food resources available changed little after Britain's isolation from the Continent, although the elk may have been a casualty of over-exploitation by hunting groups since it disappears from the archaeological record about 7000 BC. It is, however, noticeable that the range of resources exploited at individual sites increases. This is especially visible at coastal sites which also increase in number greatly after about 6500 BC.

Coastal and riverside settlement

Settlements on or near the littoral are often characterized by substantial shellfish middens. Only about a dozen such sites have been proven to date to the seventh to fifth millennia BC, but many more can reasonably be included on the basis of their similarity of position, and stray finds of early prehistoric flintwork. At Westward Ho!, Devon, a large kitchen midden, loosely dated to 4635 ± 130 BC and comprising mostly oyster, mussel, limpet and winkle, lies well down the present beach and is sometimes exposed at low tide. But it was not only marine resources which were used by the occupants of this site, for red deer and wild pig bones were also present, suggesting the use of the local dry land environment too. This pattern is repeated at other sites round the coast, as for example at Culver Well on the Isle of Portland, Dorset, and in South Wales at Nanna's Cave, Caldey Island, Dyfed. Further north, in western Scotland, coastal communities were particularly numerous, and the Oronsay middens contain particularly good evidence of sea-shore exploitation in the form of crab, limpet, periwinkle, dog whelk, oyster and lobster as well as shallow water fishing, maybe with nets or spears, which yielded wrasse, saithe and ling. Radiocarbon dates from these middens, place them in the fourth

19 Hunter-gatherer coastal site at Nab Head, Dyfed. Excavations in progress on the headland. [*Photo: Andrew David; copyright reserved*]

millennium BC. Studies of the fish and shellfish remains suggest occupation for fairly long periods each year, notably the spring and early winter. At Morton on Tay, Fifeshire, occupation between 6000 and 4000 BC spread over a wide area. Excavations by John Coles revealed various structures and hearths as well as evidence for flintworking. Settlement may have been on a small scale each year but the range of resources exploited was wide. Sea-shore food was consumed in large quantities, but fishing supplied cod, salmon and sturgeon, and sea birds were also exploited. Dry land resources included grasses and at some periods red deer. At Lussa Wood on Jura, Strathclyde, a hearth or cooking place in the form of three conjoined circular settings of large stones was found in a midden and dated to about 6013 ± 200 BC.

Interest in sites with a wide range of resources is also reflected in the location of lowland sites inland. Some, such as Farnham, Surrey, reached a considerable size with many occupation foci within a wide spread of occupation, not all necessarily of the same date. Smaller sites continued to be used as well, for example at Broom Hill, near Romsey, Hampshire, dated between 6600 and 6400 BC. Riverside situations would have allowed the use of boats to exploit still wider environments. Assessing the range of resources exploited at these sites is difficult. The full range of ungulates is present wherever bones survive, and hazelnuts are a common find at most sites. Other plant foods must also have been used.

The uplands

In the uplands the size of site became smaller than in earlier times, but there is a certain amount of evidence to suggest that in some areas at least the range and predictability of resources was improved by some manipulation of the environment. In some organic deposits dating to the period 6000 to 3500 BC, evidence of woodland fires have been found in the form of bands of charcoal which are accompanied by traces of forest clearances represented in pollen profiles. Paul Mellars and others have argued that regenerated woodland would be particularly attractive to ungulates and that, although the overall number of animals might not increase, the abundant nutritious browse would help concentrate animals so that they could be more easily exploited. Some manipulation of resources may have taken place in lowland areas too. During the excavation of tombs of third-millennium BC date, for example at Hazleton, Gloucestershire, and Gwernvale, Powys, much earlier forest clearances with traces of fifth-millennium BC activities have been revealed.

Settling down and regional traditions

The main implication of the evidence for changes in the use of resources and in settlement patterns after 6500 BC is an overall reduction in group mobility. Some seasonal movement undoubtedly continued, and Roger Jacobi has developed a plausible model of coastal and upland exploitation in the south-west peninsula at this time which involves only a few summer months away from the main residence area

45

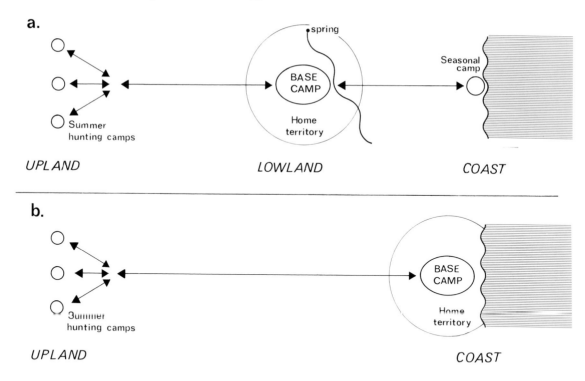

20 Simplified model of seasonal movements by hunter-gatherer groups in fourth and fifth millennia BC. [*Source: author*]

on the coast. Similar strategies were perhaps practised elsewhere, but in some places seasonal movement may have been abandoned altogether. Parts of central southern England, for example the Kennet Valley, were really quite heavily populated by 4000 or so BC. Despite the large number and wide distribution of occupation sites of this period almost nothing is known of burial practices. An exception might be a skull from the River Yare at Strumpshaw, Norfolk, possibly a hint that more remains to be discovered.

At this time also there is slight evidence for regional traditions in tool-making. The reasons for this are not fully understood, but a detailed analysis of microlith typology by Roger Jacobi has led to the definition of four or five large regional groupings or social areas in England; Welsh and Scottish material has not yet been analysed in the same detail. Whatever the nature of these groupings some interaction between communities within each must have taken place if only to promote the adoption of common tool types. Interaction probably went rather deeper than this, however, and the beginnings

of inter-group exchange systems may be glimpsed. Fine flint and other stone types for tool-making are not widely available and as mobility declined so ways of obtaining supplies of raw materials must have become established by groups living remote from resources. It is known that Portland chert from Dorset somehow made its way inland to communities as far north as the Cotswolds, while sandstone perforated maceheads may have been another commodity which travelled considerable distances. Verna Care has also shown that flaked axes and adzes were produced at a fairly limited number of locations in the flint-rich chalklands of Wessex and from there were widely disseminated to communities living off the chalk, either through some sort of exchange between communities or by being transported around the countryside by groups using the chalkland within the cycle of movements.

Exactly how these exchanges worked, or what the social areas meant, is far from clear, but the establishment of these institutions within hunter-gatherer societies in southern England, the presence of coastal and maritime-based economies, and a reduction in group mobility set the scene for one of the most important sociological changes visible in the prehistory of Britain.

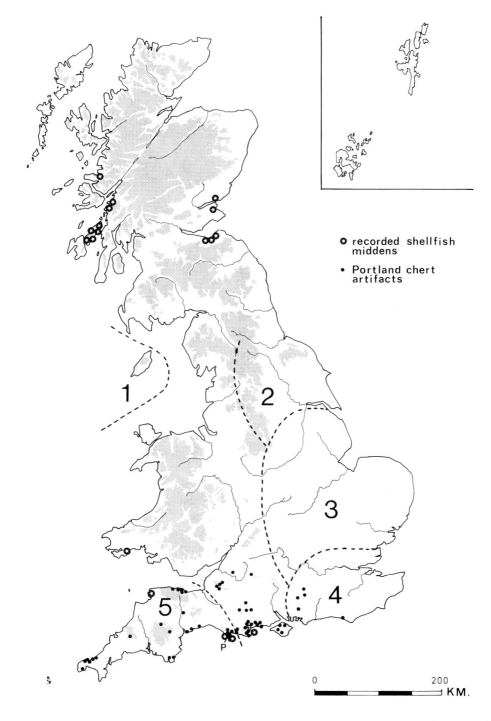

21 Distribution of recorded fourth- to sixth-millennium BC shell middens, Portland Chert artefacts (source marked P), and territories based on identifiable flint tool styles. [*Based on Jacobi 1979 figures 16 and 20; Palmer 1970 Appendix A*]. *Land over 240 metres OD (800 feet) stippled*

47

3 Harvest for the Year

Early Agriculturalists 3500–2500 BC

New beginnings

The hunter-gatherer societies described in the last chapter were remarkably successful; their survival over several millennia is testament to their skills in adapting to the changing environment. But during the later fourth millennium BC new types of artefacts, including sickles, querns, polished stone axes and pottery containers, appear for the first time in the archaeological record, replacing the microliths, points, digging sticks and spears of earlier times. New types of site appear, including permanent settlements and large ceremonial monuments. Civil engineering projects and communal works became a part of everyday life, and time and energy were invested in dividing and utilizing landscape resources on an unprecedented scale. The evidence currently available suggests considerable technological and sociological change too.

At the core of all these changes was a shift in the emphasis of subsistence activities, away from dependence on hunting and gathering to satisfy immediate needs, towards reliance on a single harvest for the year through manipulation of the biological reproduction of selected plant and animal species. Bound up with these changes was a shift in ideology. Hunting and gathering depended heavily on the skills and experience of individuals, while agriculture and animal husbandry depended on communal effort. This was the era of the first farmers in Britain, and, as such, possibly marks one of the most significant social transformations ever to have taken place, since, once established, the agricultural economy has supported society as a whole through more than five millennia down to the present day.

Continental origins?

Like many changes in Britain during prehistory, events on the Continent of Europe played a formative role during the development of farming in this country. By about 4000 BC the rich fertile loess lands of the major north European river valleys, such as the Rhine, the Meuse and the Weser, supported numerous farming communities who relied on the cultivation of wheat and barley, and the rearing of cattle. Most of these communities lived in small villages, such as at Köln-Lindenthal in Germany, which is typical of many and had an average of 21 houses over the seven successive phases of settlement represented on the site. All the houses were long rectangular structures and many served the combined role of providing a residence for a family unit, a byre for animals and a barn. But by the middle of the fourth millennium BC farming groups had begun to spread off the loess and into areas with less fertile soils. It was at this time that farming was first practised in Britain, and thereafter the development of farming societies on either side of the English Channel ran broadly parallel.

Traditionally the adoption of farming in Britain has been explained as the result of colonization by adventurous Continental farming groups, but this view does not fully square with the evidence. It is easy to see differences between hunter-gatherers and farmers in their material remains, since the equipment needed by each is specialized and very different. Might these differences mask a fundamental continuity of population who simply changed their subsistence base? The coastal communities along the southern and eastern seaboard of Britain must have been aware of the development of farming on the Continent. Indeed, in other parts of northern Europe, for example Denmark and Scandinavia, such groups quickly adopted the practices of the farmers further south simply by copying them. This process is known as acculturation and may have played an equally important part in the development of farming in Britain.

Support for the acculturation hypothesis may be found in the development of society during the preceding millennia. Group mobility among hunter-gatherers was greatly reduced in the sixth and fifth millennia BC. Seasonal movements took place, but in general fairly stable coastal and inland communities operated within relatively small territories. In some areas settlement had become dense. Attention was focused on a fairly restricted range of animal and plant resources, and there is the suggestion that in areas like the southern Pennines, where tree cover was less than elsewhere, sustained and controlled management of red deer herds took place. Interaction between groups through the exchange of tools, and even the emergence of identifiable regional traditions, are suspected. Attention to the whole community supporting itself rather than relying on a few individuals within it may also have been coming to the fore. Against this background, changing the resources exploited would be a small step, especially if obvious benefits could be seen among neighbouring groups. Localized factors such as food scarcities may have pushed some groups over the threshold from hunting and gathering to farming.

Whatever the relative contributions of direct migration and acculturation might have been for the establishment of farming in general, at least some of the first farmers in Britain were colonists. They must have carried with them to Britain the seed corn and animals necessary to provision a small farm, since neither domesticated cereals nor sheep are native to Britain. Even cattle and pigs, which were indigenous, were clearly brought here, because the early domestic examples are much smaller than the native strains. Other things, such as pottery, tools and farm equipment, or the skills to make them, were similarly introduced. Boats must have been used, possibly open skin-covered boats, but none has so far been found. Close study of the forms and types of objects associated with early farming sites in Britain shows that Brittany and the Lower Rhine valley provided the main sources of inspiration for colonists.

The first farmers and the landscape

At the time that farming was first practised in Britain much of the landscape was wooded. The post-glacial forest was past its prime but still determined the natural flora and fauna present countrywide. Pollen analysis shows that in southern England the woodlands were dominated by alder, oak, elm and hazel, while in western and northern areas birch and pine were more common than elsewhere. The very north of Scotland and the Western Isles may have already become treeless by the mid fourth millennium BC. The range of animal species present differed little from preceding millennia, although red deer populations may have declined. The climate was slightly more Continental than today, with longer growing seasons, freedom from drought, higher limits for cultivation and a reduced need to stall domestic animals over the winter. The soils were rich but regionally highly variable.

General conditions were therefore highly favourable for early farmers, but at a local level soil fertility and prevailing vegetation must have been major factors in the choice of settlement sites, bearing in mind the need for suitable agricultural land close at hand. The light soils of the coastal fringes and the major river valleys appear to have attracted early farming settlements. Where present, clearings made by hunter-gatherer groups may also have provided ideal land for early agriculturalists to take over.

Archaeological evidence for the first few centuries of farming in Britain is very sparse. Nothing comparable to villages such as Köln-Lindenthal is known, and indeed should not be expected. Early farming groups, whether they were indigenous societies experimenting with agriculture or colonists carving out new territory, were essentially pioneers.

At Shippea Hill, Cambridgeshire, a group established itself in a typical position on a small sandy ridge overlooking a stream. Rubbish, including pottery, broken flint tools and animal bones from the settlement spilled off the ridge into a nearby marshy area. The deposit explored by excavation was sandwiched between layers of peat yielding radiocarbon dates of 3515 ± 120 BC from below the debris and 3345 ± 120 BC from above. The pottery used at the site was well made, suggesting a knowledge of the production techniques, and the assemblage was dominated by open bowls with carinated sides and round bottoms. This type of pottery is known as Grimston-Lyles Hill ware after two sites where large quantities have been recovered. It is assumed that cereals were cultivated and animals reared by these

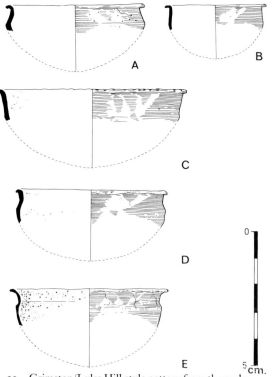

22 Grimston/Lyles Hill style pottery from the early levels at Broome Heath, Norfolk. [*After Wainwright 1972 figures 15, 16 and 17*]

pioneer farmers, but firm evidence is poor. At Broome Heath, Norfolk, occupation may have begun on a small scale as early as 3474 ± 117 BC, according to a radiocarbon date from layers sealed beneath a later earthwork, but the acidic soil failed to preserve any animal bones which would have provided evidence for the economy of the site.

The purely archaeological evidence is supplemented by the evidence from pollen spectra derived from lake sediments and peat bogs which suggest small-scale disturbances to the woodland cover. Analysis of peat from near Shippea Hill revealed that the woodland here was disturbed at a level contemporary with the appearance of the early pottery, and, most importantly, this disturbance was coincident with the appearance of several types of pollen indicative of the introduction of plant and animal husbandry. Other sites show similar evidence. At Crose Mere, Shropshire, for example, initial clearance of the woodland began about 3346 ± 150 BC. Taking the archaeological and palynological evidence together a pattern of small-scale farming settlement scattered widely over southern and midland England can be glimpsed. No houses or burials

have yet been found from this early period, and accordingly it is impossible to say anything about the social organization of these groups.

Farming spread rapidly across Britain during the pioneer phase. Settlements associated with evidence for early farming in the north and in Scotland are almost as early as those in southern England and the Midlands. At Thirlings, Northumberland, occupation traces including Grimston-Lyles Hill pottery and flint tools derived from pits have been dated to 3280 ± 150 BC. Further north still at Fochabers, Grampian, excavation of the Boghead Mound revealed pits and hollows dating to about 3081 ± 100 BC sealed beneath the mound. Again, Grimston-Lyles Hill style pottery was present. One attraction of these northern areas may have been the relatively open conditions compared with southern England.

Few if any of these early farming groups would have been alone in the landscape. In the far north and west, coastal communities supported by rich coastal fringe resources continued seemingly unaffected by farming groups until much later. On the island of Jura off the west coast of Scotland coastal hunter-gatherers continued to flourish down to the mid third millennium BC or later. Even in southern and midland England traditional hunter-gatherers probably existed alongside pioneer farmers. At Wawcott in the Kennet Valley, Berkshire, for example, a hearth associated with a typical hunter-gatherer encampment was dated to 3310 ± 130 BC. How these groups reacted with one another, or whether indeed they should be seen as separate at all, must await further analysis.

Established farming societies

Pioneer farming groups can be recognized for a period of perhaps three centuries, five or six generations. By 3000 BC farming life had changed appreciably and the distribution of farming groups expanded to include all but the uplands of the west and north, and even here communities established themselves on the low-lying peripheries and made use of whatever upland resources they could.

Pollen records from around the country support the archaeological evidence for expansion, and to judge from the number of sites now known the population must have increased. Settlements more the size of small villages came into being, and massive stone-built monuments began to be constructed in some areas. Social institutions, which can only be guessed at for the earliest farming societies, manifest themselves more clearly as communities faced up to new social pressures brought on by the changing values placed upon traditional resources. Two things come to dominate economic and social relations—the availability of land and the control and reproduction of labour. In the sections which follow, the importance of these two factors will become evident.

What became of the hunter-gatherers? Such groups all but vanish from the archaeological record by about 3000 BC except in a few coastal and northern areas. One theory holds that they simply faded out because their hunting grounds and their economy were disrupted by early farming groups. More likely, however, is that over time they adapted to farming. The rapid spread of farming in the centuries either side of 3000 BC could not have been achieved simply by migration or even a population explosion among the pioneer groups; the spread was rapid and is not accompanied by any new influx of ideas from the Continent. A combination of acculturation, limited migration, and population increase fits the evidence much better, and, as already indicated, the change from hunting and gathering to farming was probably a small step for many groups and the culmination of long-term processes of social change stretching back several millennia.

Farming and food

For the early farmers land became a critical resource for food production. The principal subsistence base of early farming communities was a combination of cultivated cereals—wheat and barley—and herded animals—cattle, sheep and pigs. These resources continued to be used as farming communities became more established. Naturally the contributions from each source varied from region to region according to the potential of the local environment, but assessing this is extremely difficult because only the waste debris from food production—bones and carbonized seeds—and processing equipment such as querns and knives are represented in the archaeological record.

Animal husbandry

The herding of animals was practised throughout Britain. On sites in southern England cattle bones invariably account for the majority of the domesticated animal remains found, with lesser numbers of sheep and pig bones. Cattle also predominated in the

English Midlands and the west, but pig usually takes second place over sheep here, possibly reflecting a less cleared landscape in which both cattle and pig browsed the woodland. In northern England and Scotland bone is often badly preserved or totally absent where it has been dissolved by the more acidic soils. However, at Northton on the Island of Harris, sheep equalled cattle in importance, and pig was absent. The rather less wooded landscape of the far north may be responsible for this pattern as sheep depend upon open grassland for grazing.

| | Species | | |
Site	Cattle	Pig	Sheep
Windmill Hill, Wiltshire*	60%	16%	24%
Robin Hood's Ball, Wiltshire*	76%	8%	16%
Knap Hill, Wiltshire*	88%	5%	7%
Hemp Knoll, Wiltshire	47%	6%	47%
Abingdon, Oxfordshire*	80%	0%	20%
Offham Camp, Sussex*	52%	17%	31%
Bury Hill, Sussex*	60%	26%	14%
Peak Camp, Gloucestershire*	52%	28%	20%
Gwernvale, Powys	67%	19%	14%
Northton, Harris	*c.*50%	00%	*c.*50%

*Enclosure sites. Remainder open settlement/occupation sites.

Table 3 Frequency of domesticated animal remains from early third-millennium BC sites.

Careful scrutiny of excavated bones reveals the marks left by carcass dismemberment and butchery. At Windmill Hill, Wiltshire, cut-marks made by flint knives were noted on some of the cattle skulls, indicating that the animals had been skinned, presumably to retain the hide for use as a raw material in making clothes or other items. All the domesticated animals were undoubtedly eaten as food, but determining what the frequency of animal bones means for diet is more difficult. After all, the meat yield from one cow is much greater than from a pig. Detailed studies by Tony Legge of the age and sex structure of the cattle population represented by the animal remains from Hambledon Hill, Dorset, and some other enclosure sites of early third-millennium BC date in southern England, revealed a high percentage of aged females. This implies a dairy herd rather than one maintained simply for meat production.

Crops and cultivation

The agricultural side of farming is represented by seed and grain impressions on pottery, carbonized seed and plant remains, traces of cultivation plots and equipment such as querns and sickles which were used during crop processing. Seed impressions and carbonized plant remains give direct evidence for the species of plant utilized. On the chalklands of southern England emmer wheat (*Triticum dicoccum*), with lesser quantities of einkorn wheat (*Triticum monococcum*), was the staple crop, but barley (probably *Hordeum vulgare*) was also grown. Wheat was especially well-suited to the soil and climate of southern England, and to judge from the evidence from Windmill Hill, Wiltshire, the size of the grain

compares well with wheat produced under modern conditions, whilst the barley grains were much smaller in comparison with modern samples. Robin Dennell has suggested that in the third millennium BC, as now, different soils and terrain favoured cultivation of a different range of crops—wheat being dominant on the heavier soils in western areas whereas there was a greater contribution from barley on the lighter downland soils of southern England. Emmer wheat was the main crop grown near Gwernvale, Powys, around 3000 BC, and at Aston on Trent, Derbyshire, a pit dated to about 2750 ± 150 BC contained a large quantity of carbonized grain, again mostly emmer wheat.

In the north cereals were also a major part of the farming regime. At Balbridie, Grampian, carbonized cereals have been found on an early third-millennium BC site variously interpreted as a settlement or burial monument. Slightly later in date is a deposit of over 300 seeds from inside the chambered tomb at Isbister, Orkney. In this sample barley predominated, with only one grain of wheat posi-

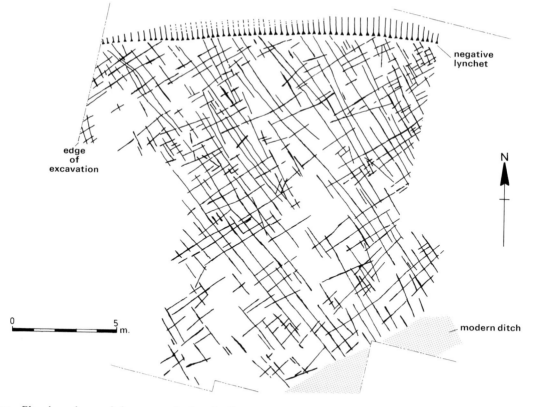

23 Plough marks revealed as grooves in the subsoil beneath the long barrow at South Street, Wiltshire. [*After Fowler 1971 figure 10*]

tively identified. Ann Lynch, who carried out this analysis, also recorded seeds from weeds commonly found in cultivation plots, including chickweed, curled dock and corn spurrey, which must have been harvested and processed alongside the cereals.

Examination of an early third-millennium BC old ground surface preserved beneath a burial mound at South Street near Avebury, Wiltshire, revealed traces of ploughing—criss-cross grooves scored into the subsoil surface. Peter Fowler believes that these grooves represent the practice of cross-ploughing with a simple ard, probably pulled by one or more oxen. No such ards have yet been found in Britain, but examples are known from the Continent. After a period of cultivation at South Street the ground was left open as pasture until the construction of the barrow several centuries later. In the north, excavations at Kilham, Humberside, by Terry Manby revealed evidence of cultivation prior to the construction of a burial monument about 2880 ± 125 BC. Throughout Britain, settlement sites commonly yield quernstones for grinding grain and flint sickles with characteristic silica gloss along the cutting edge resulting from harvesting cereals.

The impact of early farmers on the landscape was impressive. Pollen studies make it clear that in all but a few upland areas substantial inroads into the woodland or forest were made. Almost every pollen sequence so far studied in Britain shows declining tree pollen levels in the centuries around 3000 BC. Elm is often cited as one of the most distinctive indicators of these clearance episodes, but analysis by Margaret Girling of the insect remains preserved in peat on Hampstead Heath, London, has revealed the presence of beetles of the type responsible for transmitting Dutch Elm Disease as far back as the early third millennium BC, suggesting that in some cases at least a natural disaster may have been as important in changing the appearance of the forest as early farmers. Thus a decline in all tree species rather than just elm must be sought as evidence for interference.

Many farmers would, of course, have exploited naturally clear glades in the woodland, or areas cleared by cattle grazing, or perhaps areas cleared by hunter-gatherer groups in earlier millennia. Clearing woodland by hand must have been a laborious procedure which was also expensive in terms of labour requirements. Exactly how it was done is not known, but the most likely methods would have involved ring-barking trees to kill them, burning the dead wood, and then clearing what was left with polished stone or flint axes. Broken axes must have

littered the landscape in the third millennium BC because many thousands have come to light over the last few centuries. Once cleared, plots were used for cultivation and then later for pasture. Grazing animals effectively prevented regrowth of the forest and so the area of cleared land expanded in accumulative fashion. By the mid-third millennium BC large areas of the chalklands, the limestone ridges, the coastal plains and many of the river valleys were punctuated by substantial clearings. Further north, scrub and moorland had become common in the uplands, mostly it seems through processes of natural succession.

In western Britain it was not only trees which had to be cleared during the preparation of cultivation plots. Stones must have been a widespread problem and at Carn Brea, Cornwall, excavations revealed that stone clearance had indeed taken place on small plots along south-facing slopes adjacent to a large settlement dating to the early third millennium BC. These plots were presumably for cultivation. Possible clearance and cultivation features are also known on Bodmin Moor and in North Wales on Anglesey.

How land was owned and divided, whether it was communally or individually held, is not at present clear. It is, however, certain that once taken into use it remained so for long periods. Fences have been reported beneath a number of later burial monuments, as for example at Beckhampton Road, Long Barrow, Wiltshire. Indeed it is possible that many barrows were sited on boundaries to avoid causing disruption to farmland.

Hunting and gathering

Food was not derived entirely from farming. Wild fruits and nuts were gathered from the woods. Seeds of blackberries, sloes, crab apples, haws and hazel nuts have been recorded from settlement sites. A particularly vivid insight into the misfortunes of someone collecting nuts in the Somerset Levels came to light during the excavation of the Sweet Track. A pottery vessel, originally full of hazelnuts, was found smashed where it had been dropped beside the track which led across the wooded marshland of the Levels. The contents lay scattered round about, seemingly not recovered after the incident.

Animals were probably also hunted to supplement the food supply. Bones of red deer, horse, wild boar, wild cat, badger, beaver, hare, brown bear, wolf and many other smaller animals have been recorded from sites around the country and may have served to vary the diet a bit. In some cases these animals might of course have been unwelcome visitors to the homestead, or hunted for their pelts.

On the coast, marine resources continued to play an important role as a source of food. Dating these coastal sites is often very difficult, but where the ancient coastline is relatively well preserved, as in western Britain, a number of sites can be identified. At Coygan Camp, Dyfed, on the coast of south-west Wales, shellfish were loosely associated with occupation dating to about 3050 ± 95 BC, and at Knap of Howar, Papa Westray, Orkney, a shellfish midden surrounded and underlay a settlement dating to between 2815 ± 70 BC and 2395 ± 75 BC. Fish were probably more commonly used than the archaeological evidence would suggest since fish bones are very difficult to recover during excavation.

Technology and crafts

Farming required skills and equipment not familiar to hunter-gatherer societies. As the relationship between man and his environment became more complicated so did the technology to help control it. Being fairly permanently settled in order to tend crops and animals, the size and weight of tools and equipment were less important than for societies continually on the move. But there were disadvantages of being fixed in one place—for one thing the range of raw materials for making tools and equipment was less great. Thus it is notable that in areas where raw materials were scarce frugal use was made of every available piece. For example, Stephen Green has shown that flint leaf-shaped arrowheads tend to be much smaller in western and northern Britain than in areas where flint is plentiful. Likewise the amount of flintworking waste as a fraction of total assemblages tends to be less in non-flint rich areas.

Flint- and stoneworking

Flint, as the principal material used for making edged tools, continued to be worked through the third millennium and later in much the same way as it had been in earlier times. Pressure flaking and fine retouching characterize many assemblages. Leaf-shaped arrowheads, scrapers, knives, axes, adzes, points/awls and sickles were among the main types of tool made from flint. Over large parts of southern and eastern England flint suitable for making smaller

tools could be found on the surface, but larger nodules for making axes and finer implements could only be obtained by digging into a chalk hillside or by digging mines down to the prized nodules of natural flint which occur in bands within the upper chalk. The remains of some of these mines can still be seen, as for example at Cissbury, Sussex. Mining probably started in Sussex well before 3000 BC, according to a radiocarbon date of 3390 ± 150 BC from Church Hill, Findon. Indeed the availability of fine flint on the Sussex Downs may have been an important factor in promoting cross-Channel relationships in the fourth millennium BC.

The techniques of mining in the early third millennium followed methods established in northern France a millennium earlier. Shafts up to 15 metres (50 feet) deep were dug down to the level of the best flint, the floorstone, sometimes cutting through and ignoring less good layers. Once the flint was reached, radial galleries were dug to follow the bands and thereby maximize the return for the effort of digging the shaft. This must have involved many individuals and a considerable amount of time. Specialist mining communities may have been involved, but more likely whole communities undertook the work for a short stint as and when the demands of farming permitted. Once a mine had been exhausted a new one was sunk nearby, the spoil being used to backfill the previous shaft. All this work was done using antler picks, ox *scapulae* shovels, antler rakes and whatever wooden tools and baskets were available. These were, in fact, the main tools for all earth moving tasks from ditch digging to levelling off terraces for cultivation.

In the north and west of Britain fine metamorphic and igneous rocks, which behave in much the same way as flint when struck, were obtained from surface outcrops and used to make a wide range of tools. Smaller items such as scrapers and knives were used locally, but many of these rock sources are more well known for the fine polished stone axes which were transported all over Britain. At the stone sources themselves the quarrying and primary shaping (roughing out) of useful blocks created extensive spreads of working flakes and scree. These can still be seen at Penmaenmawr, Gwynedd, North Wales and Great Langdale in the Lake District. Over 30 different rock sources have now been pinpointed across Britain from Cornwall to Shetland. Many more undoubtedly remain to be discovered. The Great Langdale sources in the Lake District were certainly being exploited by the early third millennium BC, and a radiocarbon date from Killin,

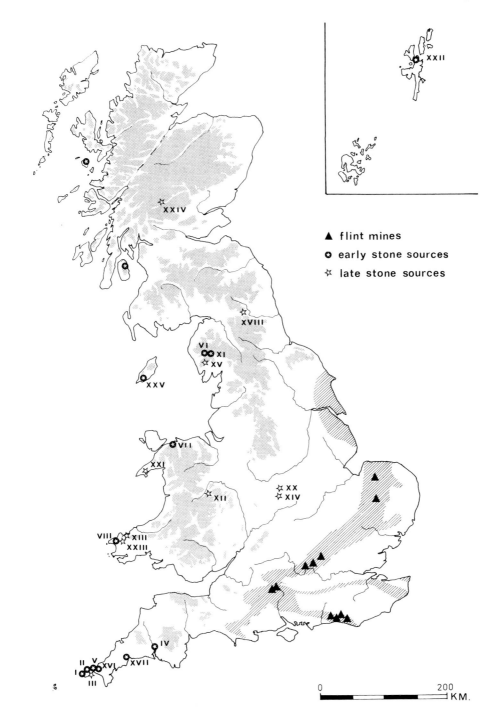

24 Sources of stone and flint used in tool-making during the early second and third millennia BC. Roman numerals indicate sources classified by the Council for British Archaeology Implement Petrology Committees.

Early sources are those in use during the first half of the third millennium BC; late sources are those which came into use after about 2500 BC. [*Source: author*]

Tayside, suggests that the calc-silicate hornfels available there were being worked from shortly after 2510 ± 90 BC, if not earlier.

Final working of both flint and stone tools was usually undertaken at settlement sites. Polishers of different shapes and sizes are found widely across Britain, often formed from sandstone blocks which have good abrasive properties. One of the largest examples lies among a scatter of sarsen boulders within the Overton Down Nature Reserve near Avebury, Wiltshire. Making a fine polished flint or stone axe could take several days, but arrowheads and scrapers could be manufactured in a matter of minutes.

Pottery making and other crafts

Many other manufacturing activities took place at or near the settlement. Pottery was made in a range of fabrics and forms according to the ultimate function of the vessel—cooking pots needed to have good refractive properties while porous storage jars were useful for keeping liquids cool. Vessels were fired in clamp kilns or bonfires, in which even fine-quality wares could be produced. Petrological studies of the clays used suggests that normally local sources available within a few kilometres of the settlement were exploited. In the course of time the typical carinated forms of the Grimston-Lyles Hill tradition were replaced by new forms with more marked regional variations in style and decoration.

Other skills evident at many sites include boneworking and stonecarving. Woodworking must have been among the most widely practised crafts, but the products are now almost entirely lost to us through decay. Many flint tools had handles or shafts. Houses, fences and other structures were also made of wood. Rare glimpses of the range of wooden objects produced at this time come from the peat deposits of the Somerset Levels. Bowls, pins, figurines, boat paddles, long bows, arrowshafts and a mallet are among the items recovered so far, but even this collection probably only represents a fraction of the range of objects made from wood during the third millennium BC, and no doubt further finds will be made in due course. Most important, however, is the evidence that woodworking skills included the ability to split trunks to make planks and to cut various mortice and tenon joints. No doubt these skills were applied during heavy-duty carpentry such as house building.

Woodland management is also demonstrated by the evidence from the Somerset Levels. Oliver Rackham has shown that coppicing and pollarding were practised in Somerset before 2430 ± 70 BC on the basis of wood recovered from trackways which includes not only coppiced poles but also the characteristic butt sections where a pole joined its stool. Coppiced poles have also been recovered from the waterlogged ditches of the Etton causewayed enclosure, Cambridgeshire, hinting that the practice was very widespread.

The use of other organic materials such as furs for clothing, reeds for baskets and matting, and leather for containers, clothes and other uses can only be guessed at. String and matting of early–mid third-millennium BC date have been found at the Etton causewayed enclosure, Cambridgeshire, where the deposits really highlight the wealth of evidence which is missing from sites where preservation conditions are less good.

A natural propensity for practical skills probably meant that some individuals were specialists or at least experts in one or more craft. Identifying particular skills with individuals is not easy. A rare example recently came to light during the excavation of an early third-millennium BC tomb at Hazleton, Gloucestershire. An adult male was found buried with a quartzite hammerstone in his left hand and a partly-used flint core in his right hand—a left-handed flintworker equipped in death as he was in life?

The technological abilities of early farming communities must not be underestimated. They had a rich empirical technology. Massive quantities of earth and stone were moved to make fields and build monuments and settlements, vast areas of woodland were cleared, and stones weighing up to 40 metric tonnes were moved during the construction of tombs.

Farmstead settlements

Farming activities throughout Britain in the early third millennium revolved around many small single farmsteads. The archaeological evidence for these units is generally poor, often comprising only a few pits, postholes from the house or some other building, and a scatter of houshold debris. These settlements were presumably surrounded by fields and grazing areas, but excavation has so far failed to reveal the full plan of such a site.

Farmstead settlements were characteristically sited in sheltered spots, often on well-drained soils, on low hills or in river valleys. A typical example

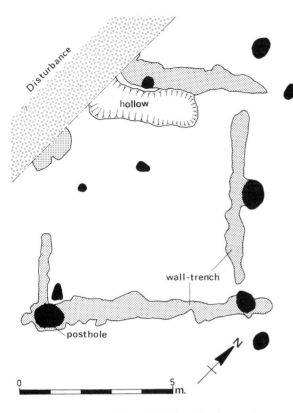

hollow

wall-trench

posthole

0   5
m.

25 Ground plan of the mid third-millennium BC house found at Padholme Road, Fengate, Cambridgeshire. [*After Pryor 1974 figure 4*]

came to light at Fengate, Peterborough, Cambridgeshire, during the construction of an industrial estate in 1971. The focus of the settlement was a small house dating to the middle of the third millennium BC. Rectangular in plan, about 7.5 by 6.0 metres (25 by 20 feet), this house was built of timber, with large posts supporting planked walls set in bedding trenches. There was probably only one room. Pottery, serrated flint blades, scrapers, a sickle blade and flintworking waste were found in the vicinity, together with part of a polished stone axe, a limestone pounder and a fine shale bead.

On the coastal plain of North Wales at Llandegai, Gwynedd, a rather larger house dating to the early third millennium BC was excavated in 1967. Here the arrangement of postholes defined an area about 15 by 8 metres (49 by 26 feet), and it seems likely that this structure had more than one room. On the hilltop of Clegyr Boia near St David's, Dyfed, two rectangular structures were recorded in association with a midden containing 50 or more broken pots, flint tools and animal bones. Over 100 similar sites are now known across the country, although most

are poorly documented and incompletely investigated. Many more undoubtedly remain to be found, and it is quite likely that some of the scatters of worked flints known from all areas of Britain represent the last vestiges of just such settlements.

The available house dimensions suggest that single family groups of perhaps six to twelve individuals occupied these small settlements. Their wooden construction makes interpretation of the internal features most difficult, but a rare glimpse of the organization of these houses is given by the stone-built examples dating to the mid third millennium BC at Knap of Howar, Papa Westray, Orkney. Here, two rectangular houses, each about 10 by 5 metres (33 by 16 feet) had been built on a midden of food refuse. Both had a single entrance in one of the short sides and a passage linked them together. Each had a central square-shaped stone hearth, and stone partitions subdivided the living space within each house into three areas. These may tentatively be identified as a sleeping area, a cooking and working area, and an open communal area.

Temporary settlements

The demands of subsistence activities have left their mark as temporary settlements related to the exploitation of particular resources. Coastal sites have already been mentioned, but by contrast in the uplands of Britain traces of hunting camps and herders' refuges are present. Caves were used wherever available. for example on the Mendips, North Wales, the Pennines and in Scotland. The small amounts of pottery and flintwork found at these sites suggest short-term occupation perhaps for summer grazing on the high ground. At Moel-y-Gaer, Clwyd, the remains of a wooden windbreak surrounded by flint waste from repairing broken arrowheads and weapons dating to about 2994 ± 40 BC suggests a temporary hunting stand. Small flint scatters in other upland areas may betray similar sites.

Enclosures and villages

In some parts of Britain, notably in the south-west, southern England and the Midlands, single farmsteads existed alongside large ditched enclosures. These enclosures are variously called causewayed camps, interrupted ditch systems or causewayed enclosures, because the ditches of many (but not all)

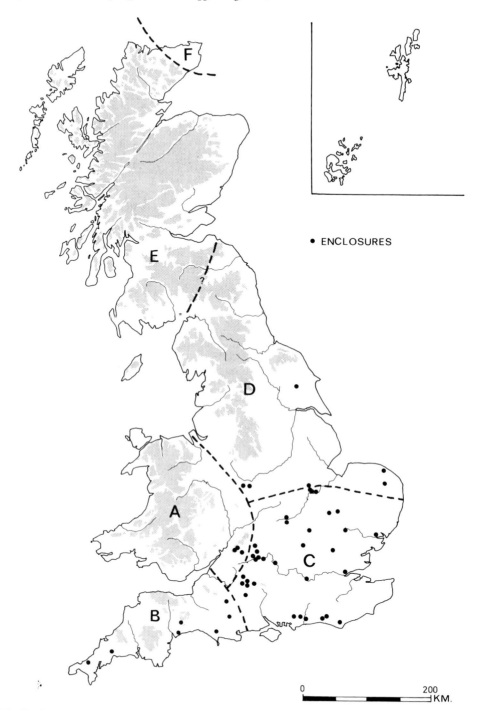

ENCLOSURES

26 Distribution of early-mid third-millennium BC enclosures and the spread of the main contemporary families of pottery. (A) = western styles; (B) = south-western styles (including Hembury wares); (C) = southern decorated wares (including Windmill Hill wares, Abingdon wares, Whitehawk wares; (D) = eastern styles; (E) = north-western styles (including Beacherra wares); (F) = north-eastern styles (including Unstan ware on Orkney). [*Source: author*]

are discontinuous, having been dug as a series of elongated pits separated by narrow causeways. The spoil from the ditches was used to build a rampart on the inside of the ditch, usually continuous except for the main entranceways. Largely thanks to aerial photography the number of these sites known has doubled since about 1970 so that now over 50 examples can be cited, although not all of them have been confirmed by excavation. They occur in a variety of positions including hill-top and promontory situations, on hill-slopes and even on valley floors. Their size, and the scale of the boundary ditches, varies greatly. Much debate has surrounded their interpretation and they have variously been seen as settlements, cattle enclosures, ritual centres and periodic meeting places. Underlying these difficulties of interpretation is the fact that the sheer antiquity of the structures has meant that many of those examined in southern England have been seriously damaged by ploughing since prehistoric times. In the West Country, on the harder rocks of the Cotswolds and the south-west peninsula, preservation is better, while in the east of England low-lying examples have occasionally been preserved by overburdens of alluvium. From excavations in these areas a more coherent picture is beginning to emerge which suggests that the enclosures performed a variety of functions, and that through time their role changed. Many can now be interpreted as settlements, which is indeed the function of comparable sites on the Continent.

One of the earliest enclosures known is at Hembury, Devon. Radiocarbon dates of 3330 ± 150 BC and 3150 ± 150 BC from the fill of the boundary ditch suggest it was established shortly before 3000 BC. Small-scale excavations revealed huts and storage pits within the enclosed area. Staying in the south west, Carn Brea, Cornwall, was also built prior to about 3000 BC. Here, a massive stone wall up to 2 metres ($6\frac{1}{2}$ feet) high enclosed an area of over 7000 square metres (8370 square yards). Approximately 30,000 man-hours would have been needed to build this wall—a colossal undertaking. Free-standing and lean-to structures, probably houses, were built against the inside face of the curtain wall. Taking into account the number and size of house platforms within the enclosure, Roger Mercer, the excavator, suggests that perhaps 150 to 200 people may have lived at the site at any one time.

Preliminary results from a long-term programme of research and excavation on Crickley Hill, Gloucestershire, suggest a similar type of site here on the Cotswold escarpment. The sequence of building and

change so far revealed is long and complicated. First, the enclosure was marked by a double line of interrupted ditches offering a boundary but not a defensive feature. The ditches were recut several times on the same alignment. Later, a single, much deeper, ditch with just two entranceways replaced the earlier arrangements and changed the site into nothing less than a fortified village. Within the enclosure there is evidence for the careful organization of activities, with houses arranged beside streets and areas set aside for flintworking, ritual and other activities.

Crickley Hill illustrates two other features typical of these enclosures. Firstly, situated on the Cotswold escarpment it sits astride the junction of two markedly different environments—the Severn Vale to the west and the Cotswold uplands to the east. Grahame Barker and Derrick Webley have identified similar contrasts in the land surrounding other enclosures and interpret this pattern as an attempt by the builders to be well placed for the exploitation of the widest possible range of land types. A second feature of Crickley Hill is that it has a neighbouring camp at The Peak near Birdlip, only 1 kilometre ($\frac{1}{2}$ mile) to the south. Pairs of enclosures and even clusters of several sites together have been recorded elsewhere, notably in the upper Thames valley, around Avebury, Wiltshire, and at Hambledon Hill, Dorset.

Carn Brea and Crickley Hill are small in comparison to some enclosures. At Windmill Hill in north Wiltshire the outer of three roughly concentric rings of ditches encloses about 9.6 hectares (24 acres). At Maiden Castle, Dorset, the causewayed enclosure underlying the later hillforts covers about 7 hectares (17 acres), and the main enclosure on Hambledon Hill, also in Dorset, covers about the same area. The average size of all known sites is about 2.5 hectares (6 acres). At some sites, where several rings of ditches are known, extension and expansion of the occupied site may be suspected.

The interior of most enclosures contains a variety of features including houses, pits, and, on occasions, burials. Severe erosion of many sites prevents full appraisal of the arrangements inside; in contrast, the ditches usually prove rich in artefacts. Broken pottery, animal bones, flintwork, broken axes and tools, and worn-out querns all lie discarded in deposits, suggesting that the ditches were used as middens. Soil was occasionally thrown over these deposits, probably to stifle the smell which must inevitably have been associated with such dumps. This practice, coupled with the problems caused by

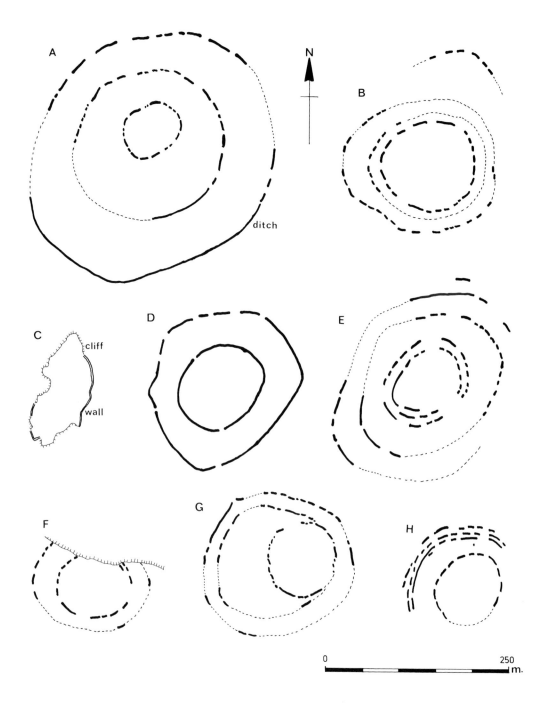

27   Plans of causewayed camps and enclosures. (A) Windmill Hill, Wiltshire; (B) The Trundle, Sussex; (C) Carn Brea, Cornwall; (D) Robin Hood's Ball, Wiltshire; (E) Whitehawk Camp, Sussex; (F) Coombe Hill, Sussex; (G) Briar Hill, Northamptonshire; (H) Orsett Camp, Essex. [*(A), (B), (D), (E), (F) after Mercer 1980 figure 4; (C) after Mercer 1981 figure 3; (G) after Bamford 1985 end figure; (H) after Hedges and Buckley 1978 figure 3*]

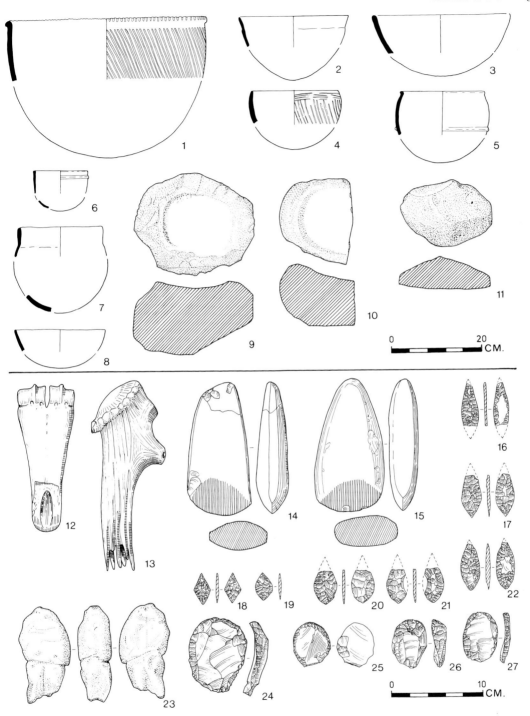

28 Selection of artefacts from the early-mid third-millennium BC enclosure on Windmill Hill, Wiltshire. 1–8 = pottery vessels; 9–11 = querns and grinders; 12 = bone chisel; 13 = antler comb; 14–15 = polished stone axes; 16–22 = flint leaf-shaped arrowheads; 23 = carved chalk figure; 24–27 = scrapers. [*After Smith 1965 figures 19, 24, 40, 45, 51, 52 and 53*]

A

B

29   Enclosure ditches under excavation. (A) Human skull on the floor of the main enclosure ditch at Hambledon Hill, Dorset. Scale totals 2 metres. (B) Semi-waterlogged deposits in the ditch at Etton, Cambridgeshire. [*(A) Photo: Roger Mercer; copyright reserved. (B) Photo: Francis Pryor (Fenland Archaeological Trust); copyright reserved*]

the occasional collapse of the internal ramparts, necessitated periodic redigging of the ditches.

The evidence for redigging of the ditches has been used to support the idea that many if not all enclosures were subject to periodic occupation, perhaps at festivals of some kind when the population from scattered farmsteads would gather together at a central point. The regular spacing of enclosures on the chalklands in Sussex and Wiltshire adds further weight to this idea. It is tempting to suggest that such activities were responsible for the origins of many enclosures, but that over time they became the sites of more permanent, and possibly fortified, settlements. Certainly the evidence from

Crickley Hill, Gloucestershire, would support this, but more excavations to establish the extent of regional variations will be required before firm patterns can be identified.

In addition to rubbish deposits most enclosure ditches also contain deliberately placed deposits. At several sites human skulls, often without their mandibles, and even whole bodies, were laid in the bottom of the ditches. Whether to act as guardians of the site, or simply out of convenience, is not known. At the waterlogged site of Etton, Cambridgeshire, where organic materials were preserved, two pots had been placed on a reed mat in a manner suggestive of an offering of some kind. At a few sites, among them the main enclosure at Hambledon Hill, Dorset, the ritual components of the ditch fills and the paucity of other evidence for domestic activities points to exclusive use of the enclosure for ritual purposes.

Clearly enclosures provided the scene for a variety of activities and generalization is very difficult. The close connection between what might be described as ritual and domestic activities should, however, come as no surprise since in the minds of many primitive peoples the two are inextricably linked.

Death and burial

Nowhere is ritual more strongly evident in the lives of these early farming groups than in their treatment of the dead and their arrangements for burial. Amongst the earliest evidence for burial rites are small monumental tombs, often stone-built in western parts of the country but elsewhere constructed from wood and turf. There is considerable regional variation in the types and styles of these monuments, no doubt reflecting regional traditions and perhaps the origins of the societies who used them. Four main types can, however, be recognized.

On the Cotswolds, and in areas surrounding the lower Severn valley, round stone cairns with a central cist—rotunda graves as they are called—were common. The example at Notgrove, Gloucestershire, is perhaps the best known and upon excavation was found to contain the bones of an adult male probably aged between 50 and 60 at death. The second type of monument, known as portal dolmen, are found in west Wales, the south-west peninsula, and to a lesser extent overlapping

B

30 Early third-millennium BC burial monuments. (A) Street House, Loftus, Cleveland showing the U-shaped façade trench, the burial deposits immediately behind and the square kerbed mortuary enclosure beyond. Scales each total 2 metres. (B) Portal dolmen at Carreg Coitan, Newport, Dyfed. Scale totals 2 metres. [*(A) Photo: Cleveland County Archaeology Section; copyright reserved. (B) Photo: author; copyright reserved*]

A

with the distribution of rotunda graves on the Cotswolds. Portal dolmen comprise four or more large upright slabs supporting a single capstone. The front of the tomb is defined by three of the uprights set in an H-shaped formation. These structures were probably never covered by a mound although many were surrounded by a low platform. Because of this they were open to the elements and as a result little is known about the burial rites involved. However, cremation was certainly practised at Dyffryn Ardudwy, Gwynedd.

In western and northern Scotland, and parts of northern and western Wales, a third type of monument can be recognized and these are usually called simple passage graves. They characteristically comprise a small rectangular or polygonal chamber approached by a short passage, the whole set within a circular mound or cairn. Sometimes the passage cannot be differentiated from the chamber, as at Mid Gleniron I, Dumfries and Galloway, where two such simple passage graves lay about 15 metres (49 feet) apart and both contained rectangular chambers/ passages built from large slabs of local stone.

The final class of burial monument comprises a variety of structures based on the theme of a square or rectangular mortuary area fronted by a façade of some description. Such monuments are found in eastern and south-western Scotland, north-eastern, central, and southern England, and are built in either wood or stone. At Dalladies, Grampian, a mortuary house dated to before 3240 ± 105 BC was excavated in 1970. It comprised three upright posts set in a line with a rectangular stone bank forming the edge of the structure and a pair of posts forming the entrance. A rather similar monument was found at Wayland's Smithy in Oxfordshire. Here, excavations by Richard Atkinson revealed a stone pavement, flanked by a low rubble bank, and bounded at either end by a large D-shaped post. It was approached through a funnel-shaped façade arrangement comprising six posts in two divergent lines. On the stone platform were the remains of 14 individuals. A single radiocarbon date places the construction and use of this monument to before 2820 ± 130 BC. A variation of this same general theme can be seen at Street House, Loftus, Cleveland, where a timber façade was set in front of a rectangular mortuary structure containing cremated human remains and a kerbed mortuary enclosure, all of which dated to about 2740 ± 30 BC. In south-western Scotland stone façades and rectangular cists replicate the wooden arrangements found elsewhere, as, for example, at Cairnholy, and Lockhill, both in Dumfries and Galloway. Apart from the regional diversity of these tombs they are noteworthy because they required relatively little effort to construct and were probably built as family vaults.

Long barrows and long cairns

In many parts of Britain burial monuments underwent significant changes during the centuries around 2800 BC when it became fashionable to construct larger tombs with a rectangular or trapezoidal mound covering one or more burial areas. The largest specimens, like West Kennet, Wiltshire, or Na Tri Shean, Highland, measure 80 to 100 metres (262 to 328 feet) long, and while smaller examples are common, all represent a considerable increase in the amount of energy expended on their construction. Bill Startin has estimated that a medium- to large-sized tomb may represent anything between 7000 and 16,000 man-hours construction time, depending upong the hardness of the local bedrock and the distance materials had to be moved. Whether this meant the work of many individuals for a short time, or a few individuals for a long time, or indeed several episodes of construction, is not known. Whichever was the case, the work is the equivalent of ten people working an eight-hour day, seven days a week for between three and seven months.

At some sites a long mound was added to earlier arrangements representing a second phase or re-modelling of the tomb. Thus at Dyffryn Ardudwy the portal dolmen was encapsulated within a rectangular mound and a new chamber was erected in the eastern-most narrow side; at Notgrove the rotunda grave was covered by a well-built trapezoidal mound, again with new chambers at the higher and wider eastern end; at Mid Gleniron I the two simple passage graves were smothered by a rectangular cairn, and at Dalladies the mortuary structure was covered by a large trapezoidal mound over 60 metres (197 feet) long and constructed on a different axis to the mortuary structure. A similar sequence of events took place at Wayland's Smithy where again a trapezoidal mound with new chambers in the eastern end completely covered the earlier tomb some time shortly after 2820 ± 130 BC.

Elsewhere, both the internal structures and the long mound itself appear to have been planned as one unitary structure, coherent in its design and constructed as a single operation. These represent new foundations in the period when the fashion for long mounds was at its height.

31 Large chambered tombs. (A) West Kennet, Wiltshire with the façade and chamber at the left hand end of the mound. The mound is about 100 metres long. (B) Camster Long, Watten, Highland, looking at the forecourt and stage at the front of the cairn with the entrance to the north-east chamber visible in the side of the cairn. [*Photos: Mick Sharp; copyright reserved*]

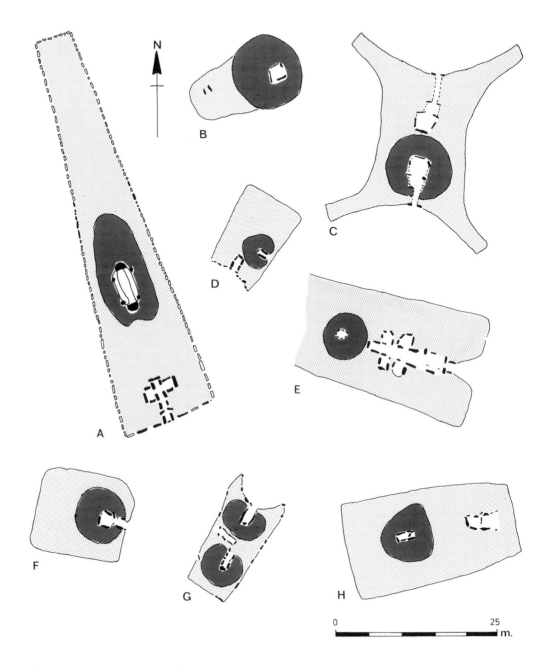

32 Multiperiod chambered tombs. First stage monuments are shown in dark toning, later additions and extensions in light toning. (A) Wayland's Smithy, Oxfordshire; (B) Pen-y-Wyrlod I, Powys; (C) Tulloch of Assery, Highland; (D) Mid Gleniron II, Dumfries and Galloway; (E) Notgrove, Gloucestershire; (F) Balvraid, Highland; (G) Mid Gleniron I, Dumfries and Galloway; (H) Dyffryn Ardudwy, Gwynedd. [*After Corcoran 1972 figures 1–3*]

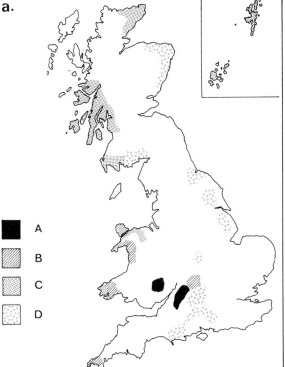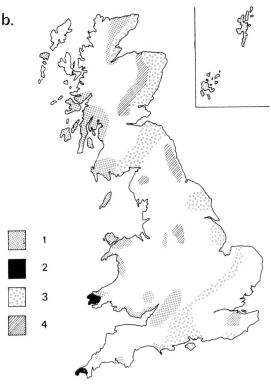

33 Distribution of late fourth- and early third-millennium BC tomb types. (a) Early types (mostly late fourth- to early third-millennium BC) A = rotunda graves; B = portal dolmen; C = simple passage graves; D = mortuary structures. (b) Later types (mostly early to mid third-millennium BC) 1 = chambered long cairns; 2 = portal dolmen; 3 = earthen long cairns; 4 = round cairns. [*Source: author*]

In all, several thousand tombs of this period are still extant around the country, especially where they have not been disturbed by recent farming. Their widespread distribution reflects the expansion of farming settlement between about 3200 and 2500 BC. The size and scale of each monument may in some general way reflect the surplus energy available within individual communities and, as such, can be related to the local economy and the prosperity of its builders. The smaller sites tend to concentrate around poor land in the west, where small groups with little surplus energy or time for monument building might be expected. Paul Ashbee has argued that on the Isles of Scilly a marine-based economy probably supported the construction of tombs at this time.

The changes in tomb design point strongly towards the imposition of a new ritual imperative,

but while the long mound represents a unifying theme, regional variations in form can still be found. In the Cotswolds, South Wales, North Wales, the north-east of England and western and northern Scotland large stones (literally *mega-lithic*) were used to build chambers which in turn were set within stone cairns. The material to build the cairns was either quarried from adjacent pits or collected from surface outcrops. Almost every known example is different in one way or another—the shape of the chambers, the positions of the chambers, the size of the forecourt and so on—although broad regional groupings can be discerned, often drawing on styles common in the earlier tomb forms. Thus a Cotswold-Severn group, a North Wales group, a Clyde group and so on can be defined. Other than the shape of the mounds or cairns, these tombs are linked by having some sort of forecourt arrangement at the wider and putatively higher end of the mound, and the fact that the stone chambers could be re-entered time and time again to insert additional interments.

In the east of England, in Wessex and in parts of eastern Scotland, superficially similar tombs to those of the west can be found, but these have wooden structures forming the focus of the monument. Forecourts were constructed at some, while in others

67

flat façades are found. It is unclear whether the wooden structures within these long barrows were accessible once the barrow mound had been erected, but at a few completely excavated sites it seems that the barrow was not built until relatively late in the life of the tomb, and that for a long period the wooden constructions provided the focus of attention. At Nutbane, Hampshire, the wooden structures underwent at least three rebuilds before the mound was finally piled over them.

Because of similarities in cairn shape and chamber arrangements between the British tombs and those found on the Continent, in Ireland and even in Spain and the Mediterranean, it was once thought that the idea of building such monuments spread from the Mediterranean northwards. Radiocarbon dates have, however, proved this suggestion incorrect, and demonstrated quite clearly that the tombs in northern Europe pre-date those of the Mediterranean by as much as a thousand years. Thus the tombs of northern Europe represent the earliest known style of traditional architecture in Europe.

Burial deposits

In both the long megalithic tombs of western Britain and the earthen long barrows of eastern and southern Britain multiple inhumation burial was the general rule. In both types of tomb the burial areas represent only a fraction, often less than five per cent, of the total tomb area. Up to 50 burials are represented in most tombs, and they apparently accumulated over long periods of time, perhaps up to 500 years. In some cases individual bodies may have been exposed to the elements while the flesh decomposed—excarnation as it is called—before the bones were placed in the tomb. In order to accommodate more bodies in the tiny chambers, and in order to satisfy required rituals, skeletons were frequently moved about, dismembered, and bones piled up in what at first sight looks like an unordered jumble. Michael Shanks and Christopher Tilley have, however, shown that in at least some monuments great care was taken when sorting the bones, and that the patterns of deposition represent an assertion of the collective basis upon which early farming groups operated and the denial of the individual and the differences between individuals in death.

There are, of course, exceptions. Two sites near Avebury, South Street barrow, and Beckhampton Road barrow were found to contain no burials at all when excavated, and indeed no provision in the way of chambers had been made to take bodies. A third site in the same area, the Horslip barrow, may also belong to this class of burial-less tombs, but ploughing had so reduced the mound prior to excavation that it is impossible to be certain. In Humberside and North Yorkshire instead of inhumation burial, cremation predominated, not single cremation but massed cremation—the incineration of disarticulated human bodies which had accumulated over a period of time in what is essentially a trench dug into the ground surface along the axis of the mound under the higher and wider end. At East Heslerton, North Yorkshire, the heat from the firing of the crematorium was sufficient to fuse the chalk rubble of the surrounding cairn.

Grave goods and ritual

Generally speaking, grave goods are sparse in long barrows and megalithic tombs. Those occasional items which are present amount to little more than personal objects—beads, pendants, necklaces and the occasional pottery cup or bowl. It is often hard to identify which individuals were associated with which objects because of the disarticulated nature of the burial deposits. Only about one in seven or perhaps one in ten of the interments could have been furnished with grave goods, unless of course objects were removed subsequent to the burials being made. There is no suggestion of provisioning the dead for an afterlife, rather the tombs give the impression of being storehouses for the bones of the deceased. Arrowheads are often found among the burials, and although some might be grave goods, a number were the cause of death for those in the tomb; at Ascott-under-Wychwood, Oxfordshire, a leaf-shaped arrowhead was fully embedded in a woman's spine, while at West Kennet, Wiltshire, a similar arrowhead was found in the area representing the thoracic cavity of an elderly male.

Upon excavation the forecourts of many tombs are found to contain fire pits, hearths and potholes. Human bones are frequently found scattered about in these areas. Bones were also seemingly removed from the tomb and its vicinity altogether during these rituals, or perhaps they never arrived at the tomb in the first place. At Ty Isaf in the Black Mountains of Powys, for example, the three chambers contained the remains of a total of 33 individuals, but three *humeri* were the only complete long bones, and while the remains of seven skulls were found, 22 mandibles were present.

A

B

34 Hazleton chambered tomb, Gloucestershire. (A) General view of the cairn after removal of the topsoil and overburden, looking east with the rubble-filled forecourt in the foreground. Quarry pits can be seen on either side of the cairn. The two chambers, which cannot be seen at this stage in the excavation, lie immediately beyond the unexcavated cross-balk. Scales each total 2 metres. (B) View into the north chamber showing the disarticulated burial deposit with skulls apparently preferentially placed around the chamber walls. Scale totals 0.3 metres. [*Photos: Alan Saville; copyright reserved*]

Round barrows

In north-eastern England and eastern Scotland large round tombs were built alongside the long tombs during the first half of the third millennium BC. Generally, the burial rites at these monuments were similar to those in the long mound tomb. For example, at Pitnacree, Tayside, built about 2860 ± 90 BC, a rectangular enclosure associated with the cremated remains of several individuals came to light during excavations, while at Seamer Moor, North Yorkshire, bodies were burnt *in situ* on a stone platform.

Tombs and population

Although most tombs contain multiple burials, sometimes up to 50 individuals, the total number of persons represented in them cannot account for the whole population at this time. Richard Atkinson has calculated that for eastern and southern England — the only area where enough excavations have taken place, and enough bone survives to arrive at an average number of burials per barrow — the burials found represent the dead from a total population which could not have exceeded between 40 and 75 persons, excluding infants, at any one time during the first half of the third millennium BC in the whole area. Such a low population would not even be enough actually to build the barrows themselves, and it must therefore be assumed that only a fraction of the population was interred within a barrow. Exactly what qualifications determined who was placed in a barrow remain unknown.

Other burials

Burials have also been recorded in a variety of other contexts. At Pangbourne, Berkshire, a female accompanied by a complete pottery vessel was buried in a pit, and a somewhat similar grave has been recorded at Handley Hill, Dorset, where it appears that a post was set up to act as a marker for the grave. Cist and pit graves without covering mounds have also come to light from time to time, as for example during the excavations at Fengate, Cambridgeshire, where four bodies were found in an oval pit, and at Sumburgh Airport, Shetland, a cist dated to 2445 ± 55 BC contained the remains of 18 individuals. The shafts of flint mines are often found to contain the remains of one or more individuals upon excavation. The boundary ditches of most enclosures contain human bones too. At Windmill Hill, Wiltshire, the complete skeleton of a child lay on the bottom of the outer ditch, and if the areas excavated are at all representative of the ditches as a whole, then a dead population of about 100 individuals may be represented by complete or disarticulated skeletons round the periphery of the site. Similar evidence was recorded at the main enclosure on Hambledon Hill, Dorset, and the practice of depositing burials and bones in enclosure ditches may help to explain some of the missing pieces from tombs.

Population and society

The human bones recovered from burial deposits allow insights into the structure of the population. Detailed anatomical studies of the bones from West Kennet, Wiltshire, by L. H. Wells provide a representative sample of the population a this time. In stature both males and females were marginally shorter than today. Adult males ranged from 1574 to 1803 millimetres (62 to 71 inches) in height while females ranged from 1498 to 1651 millimetres (59 to 65 inches). Their build was similar to the range present today. Diseases were common. Arthritis, especially in the back, was the plague of the community; hardly a single individual over 25 years of age failed to display some signs of the disease, and hands and feet were often badly affected. Spina bifida was noted in some individuals. The three most complete male skeletons all showed healed fractures of the upper limbs. Tooth loss before death was common, and a number of abscesses were noted. Similar evidence has been recorded by Judson Chesterman from the analysis of bones from Ascott-under-Wychwood, Oxfordshire, and Isbister, Orkney. Infant mortality in early farming societies was high, and the average age of death may have been as low as 30, although some individuals may have lived well past 50. Infant burials are more common in enclosure ditches than in tombs, but nowhere are they numerous enough to account for all infant deaths.

Estimating actual population numbers among early farming groups is notoriously difficult and there were certainly marked reginal variations in the distribution of population. Don Brothwell considers that an overall population of about 20,000 for the British Isles would be appropriate on the basis of analogies with recent primitive agricultural groups. This is probably much too low, and given the very extensive evidence for settlement a figure in the region of 200,000 may be more realistic.

From the distribution of tombs and the size of settlements it would seem that Britain was populated by small-scale groups, perhaps extended family units widely spread across the countryside, with some larger communities occupying enclosures. Andrew Fleming has suggested that the structure of the tombs themselves, the cellular subdivision of burial area, for instance, and the arrangement of the chambers, may somehow reflect the organization of the groups who built them. Although in most parts of Britain the average number of interments is roughly the same, the number of separate burial deposits or chamber areas varies greatly from region to region. Thus in many parts of Wales and western Britain single chambers hint at small single unit groups, while in southern England and much of the north multiple chambers point to close-knit family units bonded into groups by kinship.

Such small-scale autonomous groups have been

characterized by anthropologists as segmentary societies—repetitions of equivalent groups which are essentially self-supporting. There is very little evidence for ranking among early farming societies beyond the fact that as only a fraction of the population were interred in formal tombs some kind of selection criteria must have operated. Ian Hodder has argued that access to the tombs was related to the control of inheritance as a way of regulating claims to valued resources, particularly land as the main requirement for the production of food, and women as the reproducers of the human population.

Exchange and interaction

Despite their apparent political autonomy, early farming communities were not isolated. Rivers probably continued to provide lines of communications and elsewhere a network of trackways linked one group with the next, and all groups together. In most places such tracks would simply be worn paths very much like those criss-crossing the countryside today, but in the wet terrain of the Somerset Levels rather more substantial arrangements needed to be made and wooden tracks were built, sometimes stretching several kilometres. The most spectacular of the many tracks so far investigated is the Sweet Track, recorded for over 2 kilometres ($1\frac{1}{4}$ miles) between the Polden Hills and Westhay Island. Numerous radiocarbon dates indicate that it was built about 3200 BC and it comprised oak planks, each about 3 metres (10 feet) long and 60 centimetres (24 inches) wide, set end-to-end and held in place by pegs of hazel and alder. There were, of course, no wheeled vehicles at this time, and a pedestrian could easily walk along the narrow planks.

In addition to the known trackways, contacts between groups are evident from the many artefacts found on third-millennium BC sites which were made from materials only available many kilometres away. In general, such items can be divided into two groups: everyday items and prestige items. Heading the list of everyday items must be flint. Nodules up to 30 centimetres (12 inches) across were carried, presumably by people or pack animals, from the chalklands of southern and eastern England to areas of western and northern Britain. There they were broken down into cores which in turn provided the starting point for tool manufacture. Through prehistoric times many thousands of tonnes of flint must have been moved in this way.

It was not only raw materials which were moved.

35 The Sweet Track, Somerset. Part of the wooden trackway constructed about 3200 BC across the marshy ground between the Polden Hills and Westhay in the Somerset Levels. Pieces of the plank walkway and the bracing timbers which supported and stabilized the track can be seen. [*Photo: Somerset Levels Project; copyright reserved*]

Finely made flint axes, usually flaked into shape and then polished, were transported over much the same areas as flint nodules. In the west of England, Wales, northern England and Scotland, where fine igneous and metamorphic rocks were used to make tools, these too were transported great distances. Axes of Cornish origin are fairly common in Essex, for example, and Arran pitchstone axes are widely spread around Scotland. Axes from as far afield as Brittany, Northern Ireland and Scandinavia have come to light at various times in Britain, emphasizing the continuing links between British farming groups and their counterparts in Europe and around the western seaways.

Quernstones can only be made from certain types of rock. Good sandstones and conglomerates were sought out by those living near suitable sources, and the products exchanged with other communities round about who lacked such resources. Pottery too was sometimes moved considerable distances. Some of the pottery used at Windmill Hill, Wiltshire, was made from Jurassic clays available about 30 kilometres (19 miles) or so from the site. Petrological studies by David Peacock led to the identification of pottery made from gabbroic clays found only on the Lizard in Cornwall. This pottery was transported to most settlements and enclosures in south-western England, even as far afield as Dorset and Wiltshire.

It is possible that some communities recognized the significance of some of these exchanged objects and accorded them special attention. It is notable that some of the fine gabbroic pottery and finer axes are concentrated on the enclosure sites rather than the smaller settlements. Paramount among the objects singled out for special treatment must be jadeite axes. Although called axes, few could have functioned as such because most are very thin and would shatter or splinter on impact. Over 100

36 Distribution of stone axes in England and Wales. The contoured maps show the frequency of axes from particular sources (indicated) as a percentage of all stone axes known to date. Flint axes were not included in the analysis. [*After Cummins 1979 figures 4–8*]

examples are known from Britain, widely distributed from Cornwall to Orkney, but jadeite is not a rock which outcrops in Britain, and chemical studies have traced the sources to the Alps of southern France and Italy over 1200 kilometres (745 miles) away. A clue to the significance attached to these items may be glimpsed from the fact that one was found buried immediately beside the Sweet Track, Somerset, possibly as a ritual deposit or a foundation deposit of some kind to ensure appropriate spiritual protection for the track itself or those using it. Other prestige objects exchanged include shale beads, pendants, and other similar personal items, and these sometimes found their way into burial deposits.

The mechanisms whereby goods came to be moved about the countryside and exchanged between communities during the third millennium BC were undoubtedly complicated. Grahame Clark has suggested that some form of gift exchange was the main agent of trade, and some support for this derives from patterns in the fall-off frequency of goods measured against their distance away from their source when found. In gift exchange one community passes goods to the next without necessarily expecting immediate repayment. Indeed repayment, or reciprocity, may be delayed for months,

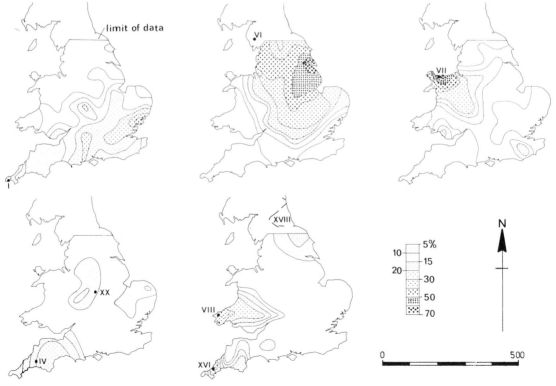

even years, and may take on an entirely different form from that of the original gift—food, for example, may be returned for pots. The important thing about gift exchange, and the thing that makes it so attractive to primitive societies, is that it makes groups obligated to one another. This in turn promotes alliances between groups and in effect creates a primitive insurance system whereby help can legitimately be expected from obligated groups during a time of crisis. Rare objects would be accorded the highest status and would be most sought after. The longer goods were in circulation the wider their distribution and the further they would move.

People, land and war

From the evidence currently available it is possible to glimpse something of the life-styles and social organization of the early farming groups. Taking the spatial distribution of the different styles of pottery, the distributions of dominant axe types, the clustering of enclosures and the designs of the tombs it is possible to discern perhaps seven or eight regional groupings within which interaction may have been more intensive, and common traditions bonded the population. In the south west, the coastal fringes and the periphery of the uplands were the focus of early farmer settlements, while in southern England the chalklands of Wessex, the downs of Sussex, the Thames valley and the Cotswold Hills were among the most intensively settled parts of Britain. Upland Wales, the Pennines and the Lake District may have served as summer grazing and source areas for fine stone, but most of the settlement was confined to the coastal fringes and upland peripheries. East Anglia was probably more intensively settled than current evidence suggests. Lincolnshire, Humberside and North Yorkshire were important foci of population and in some respects had developed a distinctive culture at this time. In the north of England and Scotland settlement was mostly confined to the main river valleys and along the coastal fringes, dense on fertile areas, but generally rather sparse at this time elsewhere.

Common to most areas was the construction of monumental tombs. Since they cost dearly in terms of man power input it is pertinent to enquire why they were built at all, and here the beliefs of the early farming groups are important. The communal monumental tombs undoubtedly had great symbolic meaning to their makers—a source of pride to the builders and perhaps envy to their neighbours. Colin Renfrew has suggested that, as monuments, the tombs may have acted as territorial markers for farming groups. By engraving their identity on a piece of land with a communal tomb, farming groups symbolized or legitimized their rights to the land. By creating a repository for the bones of their ancestors generation after generation could trace a direct link with the past and therefore with the ownership of specific areas of land. Such an arrangement may be interpreted as an ancestor cult in which the dead were though to play an important role in the lives of the living. Ian Hodder has, however, taken the symbolism expressed by the tombs further than simply the functional exigencies of territorial symbols. He suggests that all aspects of burial and other rituals can be linked to the society's concern with legitimatizing control of resources through an ideology of communal work and collective participation in all aspects of life. By coming together to build tombs and enclosures groups emphasized this belief and at the same time reduced the possibility of competing claims for the inheritance of resources by individuals.

Whatever the role of ritual and ideology in controlling and balancing resources, early farming societies were not as peaceful as might be imagined. Warfare was probably endemic, especially in areas where population density was high. Arrowheads are the most commonly found and widespread artefacts belonging to early farming groups and literally hundreds of thousands have been found over the last few centuries the length and breadth of the country. People were at least sometimes targets. The presence in tombs of individuals killed by arrowshots has already been mentioned and defended villages such as Carn Brea, Cornwall, and Crickley Hill, Gloucestershire, were little short of being strongholds relative to other contemporary settlements. At Peterborough, Cambridgeshire, four bodies were found in a pit grave. They comprised a male aged 25 to 30, a female of about the same age and two children, one aged 3 to 4, the other 8 to 12. A leaf-shaped arrowhead found between the eighth, and ninth rib of the adult male may have been responsible for his death, and it is tantalizing to speculate that here in this grave is a family group.

The development of warfare in early farming society is nowhere more clearly demonstrated than in the area around Hambledon Hill, Dorset. Preliminary studies of material recovered from a major programme of excavation directed by Roger Mercer allows a segment of the early third-millennium BC

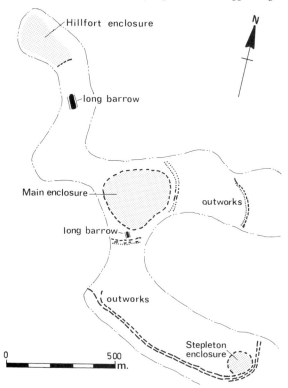

N

37 Simplified plan of early–middle third-millennium BC landscape at Hambledon Hill, Dorset; later features omitted for clarity. The chain line contour at about 130 metres above sea level indicates the extent of the hill-top. [*After Mercer 1985, 79*]

landscape to be reconstructed. At the beginning of the third millennium three enclosures probably existed, one on the main hill-top, one on the Stepleton spur to the south and one on another spur to the north. The main enclosure may have been a ritual site, possibly used for the excarnation, or exposure, of bodies while the flesh decomposed before they were buried in nearby tombs. Two long barrows lay outside this enclosure, one to the north west and one to the south. The Stepleton enclosure on the south-eastern spur was probably a settlement. Later, the boundary of the Stepleton enclosure was refurbished and strengthened and cross dykes were constructed across various spurs on the hill, giving additional protection to the main enclosure, the Stepleton enclosure, and the ground between. The area bounded was over 1.25 kilometres (1 mile) long. Sample excavations between the Stepleton enclosure and the main enclosure have revealed the presence of flint quarries, and grazing or cultivation may also have taken place here. Thus in its final phase most of the hill-top activity lay within a very large defended enclosure.

The potential threats to society's well-being, from rampant population growth, internal strife and under-production of food, were very real. A balance was maintained, possibly through ritual, ideological pressures and exchange, for a period of over 500 years, from the pioneer farming groups before 3000 BC to about 2500 BC. In the middle of the third millennium BC, however, a major episode of change took place in some areas of Britain, and entrenchment and consolidation in others.

4 Sunrises and Other New Beginnings

The First Chiefdoms 2500–1500 BC

Crisis and change

The relative stability of early farming groups during the first half of the third millennium BC came to an end about 2500 BC. Changes in the form and siting of settlements and monuments, and also in the types of pottery, flintwork and material culture allow several new regional traditions to be identified, some with separate and divergent patterns of development. In a few parts of Britain, notably southern England, these changes were seemingly preceded by tension between groups and, on occasions, open warfare. The mid third millennium has sometimes been described as a 'standstill' in the development of agricultural societies, but in many areas it was nothing less than a time of crisis.

Radiocarbon dating has radically altered perceptions of society in the late third and early second millennia BC. Many long-held theories of the rate and spread of change have been challenged, and regional diversity has been emphasized. Pottery types changed regularly over the period and provide a useful chronological framework. Field monuments, and in particular burial monuments, provide the majority of evidence for the centuries following 2500 BC. Two trends can be recognized which shaped the structure of society over the following millennium. Firstly, the decline of monumental tombs and the cult of the ancestors, and secondly, the substitution of community-centred ideologies with more overt ranking. Among the new beliefs which emerged as part of these changes came greater concern for celestial movements, particularly the rising and the setting of the sun and moon, and this is reflected in the form and layout of some monuments.

The environment changed very little. The climate remained warmer and drier than today, although by 2000 BC it was slightly cooler than it had been a millennium earlier. Peat bogs show signs of desiccation early in the second millennium BC, and with extensive tracts of woodlands cleared, wind erosion of soils became a real problem. At Broome Heath, Norfolk, wind-blown sand, probably derived from adjacent cultivated areas, was found beneath an earthwork built shortly after 2217 ± 78 BC. Beech and ash increased their contribution to the woodland flora. The coastline generally lay further out than today, although by about 1500 BC sea levels relative to the land were rising and marine transgressions characterized the mid second millennium BC. The wild fauna remained largely unchanged from earlier times, although aurochs became extinct during the second millennium. Brown bears may have been common to judge from the number of sites yielding their remains, and among the new species recorded at this time is the red squirrel.

Social discontinuity in the south

In southern England, the south-west peninsula, south-eastern Wales, the Midlands and East Anglia the social crisis of the mid third millennium BC can be seen in three changes: the blocking of monumental tombs, the abandonment of camps and enclosures, and the regeneration of woodland or the establishment of scrub-grassland in previously cleared areas.

Discontinuity in the use of chambered tombs and long barrows was widespread. In south-east Wales the chambers in the long cairn at Gwernvale, Powys, were sealed with rubble packed into the passages.

38   Blocking deposits in and around the entrance to the north chamber at the Gwernvale chambered tomb, Powys. Scale totals 1 metre. [*Photo: Bill Britnell for Clwyd Powys Archaeological Trust; copyright reserved*]

Radiocarbon dates of 2640 ± 75 and 2440 ± 70 BC were obtained for this event. Elsewhere in the Cotswold-Severn area tombs at Nympsfield and Notgrove, both in Gloucestershire, and Ty Isaf, Powys, were also apparently deliberately blocked at about the same time while many others simply fell out of use and became ruinous. In Wiltshire, the Lugbury and Lanhill tombs were blocked about 2500 BC, the huge West Kennet tomb a little later. Rectangular or trapezoidal earthen long barrows ceased to be built after the middle of the third millennium; Wor Barrow, Dorset, was probably among the last to be constructed about 2490 ± 70 BC. The same pattern can be found in Sussex and East Anglia. Analysis by Nick Thorpe of the burials from these late sites suggests that before the long barrow tradition ended, communal burial had given way to the deposition of single articulated inhumations under such mounds.

The trend toward the establishment of defended enclosures, and the development of warfare during the early third millennium BC, was described in the last chapter. Evidence from a number of enclosures shows that their defences were not built in vain. The final hours of occupation at Crickley Hill, Gloucestershire, witnessed a victorious attack on the settlement, which was then sacked and burnt. Hundreds of leaf-shaped arrowheads littering the ramparts and gateways were found during recent excavation. At Hambledon Hill, Dorset, a similar scenario can be glimpsed. Several bodies, at least one killed by an arrowshot, were found sprawled in the ditch with the remains of a collapsed portion of rampart crushing them. At Carn Brea, Cornwall, arrowheads were extremely numerous and therefore clearly an important component of the tool-kit kept inside the camp. There is no evidence that any of the enclosures in southern England continued to serve their original functions after the middle of the third millennium BC, and the ditches at most sites had substantially filled up with silt and rubbish by about 2400 BC.

Pollen records show that many areas previously cleared by early farming groups returned to woodland around the mid third millennium. At Hockham

Mere, Norfolk, regeneration was well underway by 2600 BC, and in the Somerset Levels woodland had closed in by 2400 BC. Around Dartmoor regeneration is evidenced too. On the chalklands of southern England pasture was widespread, and in a recent review of evidence from around Avebury in north Wiltshire, Bob Smith concluded that clearances became infested with weeds and invasions of bracken and scrub by about 2500 BC. The causes of these changes are difficult to pinpoint. Alasdair Whittle has suggested that population growth during the early third millennium created pressure on the agricultural system to the extent that continued use of fragile soils caused loss of fertility. This led to food shortages and eventually a switch to less-intensive farming systems. This is probably an over-simplification, however, since the discontinuity of settlements and tombs suggests that rather more deep-rooted problems connected with the political and ritual organization of society were at least contributory if not wholly to blame for what happened.

New patterns and new traditions

In the wake of these changes new patterns emerged. The traditional pottery styles were replaced by new types of round-bottomed bowls called Peterborough wares. Generally, Peterborough wares are coarse vessels made with liberal use of stone grits for tempering and the heavy application of impressed decoration, which in most cases covers much of the exterior surface of the vessel. Isobel Smith has traced the ancestry of the Peterborough series to the early third-millennium BC decorated wares of Wessex. Accompanying these new potting traditions were changes in the flintworking and boneworking, which in general became rather crude by comparison with the products of earlier centuries.

Settlement patterns, such as they can be reconstructed, changed slightly. Previously well-populated landscapes such as the Cotswolds and the Sussex Downs were abandoned in favour of adjacent lowland areas. Elsewhere, lower situations close to light soils were favoured too.

Burial rites and burial monuments became diverse. Long barrow traditions lived on in a few areas but in a very much reduced and debased form. At Alfriston, Sussex, an oval barrow some 24 metres (79 feet) long, was built about 2360 ± 110 BC over the inhumation of a female aged about 35 to 40 at death. At Barrow Hills near Abingdon, Oxfordshire, excavations directed by Richard Bradley revealed a rectangular barrow covering the grave of two adults,

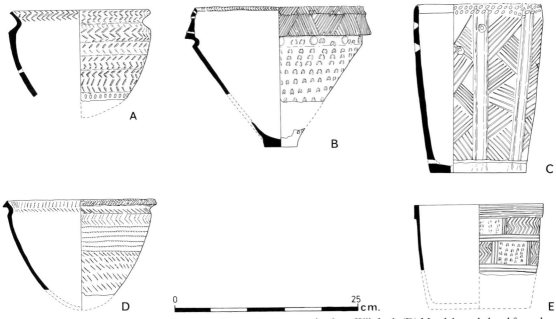

39 Peterborough series and grooved ware style pottery from sites in Wiltshire. (A) Mortlake style bowl from Wilsford; (B) Fengate style bowl from the blocking deposits in the West Kennet Long Barrow; (C) grooved ware jar from Wilsford; (D) Mortlake style bowl from the blocking of the West Kennet Long Barrow; (E) grooved ware bowl from Woodhenge. [*After Annable and Simpson 1964, 83 and 84*]

77

40 Mid third-millennium BC burial monuments.
(A) Multiphase ring-ditch monument at Four Crosses,
Powys. The earliest barrow was built about 2490 ± 70 BC
and is represented by the central pit, which contained a
single inhumation in the centre and a further inhumation
in each of the two smaller oval pits dug into the floor, and
an irregular oval ditch which provided material from
which a mound was built. The two concentric ditches
represent later reuse and enlargement of the site.
(B) Two adult inhumation burials found in the central
grave of a rectangular barrow at Barrow Hills, Abingdon,
Oxfordshire. (C) Entrance grave at Chapel Euny, Brane,
in West Penwith, Cornwall. (D) Entrance grave at
Bosiliack, West Penwith, Cornwall, after excavation. The
entrance is blocked by the small stone in the centre of the
kerb. [*(A) Photo: Christopher Musson for Clwyd Powys*
Archaeological Trust; copyright reserved. (B) Photo by
permission of Richard Bradley; copyright reserved. (C)
Photo: author; copyright reserved. (D) Photo: Craig
Weatherhill; copyright reserved]

one accompanied by a polished flint blade, the other accompanied by a shale belt-slider. A large leaf-shaped arrowhead was also loosely associated with the grave but could not be assigned to either individual.

Round barrows gradually took over as the principal burial monuments in the second half of the third millennium, even in areas where long barrows had previously been popular. At Stanton Harcourt, Oxfordshire, a grave within a circular ring-ditch contained the skeleton of a young woman accompanied by a polished flint knife and a shale or jet belt-slider very similar to the example already noted from Abingdon. Similar barrows are known in Dorset; two or more lie very close to Wor Barrow. In the Welsh Marches similar changes were taking place too. At Four Crosses, Powys, a ring-ditch surrounded a round mound under which was a single grave dated to about 2490 ± 70 BC. Three separate burials lay within this grave pit, the central one associated with a squat bowl. On the Isles of Scilly and around Land's End a new class of tomb known as entrance graves began to be built. They comprised circular stone cairns with a passage-like chamber opening into the mound and forming the repository for burials. About 50 examples are known, but few burials have been recorded from them because of the acidity of the soil and the activities of tin miners despoiling chambers within the last few centuries. In the case of the fairly intact tomb at Bosiliack, Cornwall, excavations by Charles Thomas in 1984 revealed that here the primary burial deposit comprised a partial cremation with a small pot.

The break with earlier traditions was not, however, absolute. Although causewayed enclosures ceased to perform their traditional roles around the middle of the third millennium many were visited and variously reoccupied even after the ditches had substantially filled up. At Windmill Hill, Wiltshire, Hambledon Hill, Dorset, and many others too, shallow scoops were dug in the top of the ditches as if to revive the old boundaries. Exactly why this should have been done remains unclear. A preoccupation with long mounds also persisted in a few areas and two new types of sinuous linear monuments appear at this time.

New linear monuments

Bank barrows, or long mounds, may owe their inspiration and in some cases their origin to earlier long barrows. Less than ten are known in southern England, usually on hill-tops, and few have been investigated. Each comprises a long narrow mound invariably in excess of 100 metres (328 feet) long. At Maiden Castle, Dorset, and Crickley Hill, Gloucestershire, long mounds were constructed over the razed remains of earlier enclosures. Excavation of the example at Crickley Hill revealed a complex history during which the mound was enlarged and extended several times. Deposits of animal bones placed under flat stones were set at intervals along the long sides. At the western end was a circular platform and at the eastern end an upright post. Traces of worn cobbling around the eastern terminal suggested to the excavator that the monument was used for rituals involving processions round the mound, although whether this can be applied to other bank barrows is not yet known.

Cursus monuments comprise a pair of linear ditches with internal banks, or bank, and closed ends. They are in many ways similar to bank barrows, although in general longer, and again may owe their inception to the long mound ideas of the early third millennium. Over 30 examples are now known in southern England, often on low ground where they have been identified from aerial photographs. The largest is the Dorset cursus which stretches for nearly 10 kilometres (6 miles) across the grain of the chalk downlands of Cranborne Chase and dates from 2490 ± 100 BC, if not a little earlier. The ditches are about 90 metres (295 feet) apart, but rather than being of one unitary construction, this cursus is really two monuments set end-to-end, a feature which can be paralleled at other sites. The Springfield, Essex, cursus is more modest in scale but typical of many. It is nearly 700 metres (2300 feet) long and the width between the ditches is about 40 metres (130 feet). Peterborough style pottery was found in the ditches during the excavation of the eastern terminal in 1979. Many cursus monuments incorporate earlier long barrows into their design. The Dorset cursus incorporates two long barrows, while the cursus at Dorchester-on-Thames, Oxfordshire, crossed a small rectangular enclosure—probably a mortuary enclosure.

The name cursus is a curious one and derives from the eighteenth-century idea that they were prehistoric racing tracks. Whether they were in some senses processional ways, as has been suggested for the Crickley Hill long mound, is not clear. Recent work has shown that within the class of cursus monuments there are in fact several rather diverse kinds of structure which can be differentiated on the basis of their lifespan and the way in which they were used. Francis Pryor has tentatively proposed three

A

B

41 Springfield Cursus, Essex. (A) View of the eastern terminal of the cursus under excavation; the cursus ditch has been half emptied in alternating sections. One corner is in the foreground, the ditch along the short side of the east end runs parallel to the left-hand side of the photograph. (B) Reconstruction drawing of the cursus by Frank Gardiner. [*Photo and drawing reproduced by kind permission of Essex County Council Planning Department; copyright reserved*]

categories for future assessment in the light of evidence from excavations: monumental or continuously used cursus monuments such as the Dorset cursus; short-lived or single-period cursus monuments such as Springfield; and long-lived episodic ditched alignments such as the example at Maxey which was dug and used in a series of short lengths sharing a common alignment but not necessarily involving both of the parallel ditches at the same time.

Henges

Alongside the development of bank barrows and cursus monuments was the appearance of quite different monuments, known as henges. These are circular enclosures which generally have a bank set outside the ditch thus making them useless as

defensive works unless the idea was simply to provide a barrier or to keep things in rather than out. Various types can be recognized according to the number of entranceways, and some have a bank on both sides of the ditch. Small henges (or hengi-form monuments) can look very like ring-ditch burial monuments, and indeed a number were used, or in some cases reused, as cremation cemeteries. At Dorchester-on-Thames, Oxfordshire, several such sites were located and excavated adjacent to a cursus, emphasizing the close connection which existed between different types of monument at this time.

Upon excavation, larger henges, which can be anything from 50 up to 200 metres in diameter (164 to 656 feet), are usually found to contain very little, simply a flat open area. Barford, Warwickshire, constructed about 2416 ± 64 BC, and Arminghall, Norfolk, built about 2490 ± 150 BC are at present the earliest known sites in southern England, but many were built during the years between 2500 and 2000 BC. The most famous henge in Britain must be Stonehenge in the heart of Salisbury Plain, Wiltshire, which began its long history about 2440 ± 60 BC, according to a radiocarbon date from the lower fill of the ditch.

Like causewayed camps before them, henges in southern England may have performed a variety of

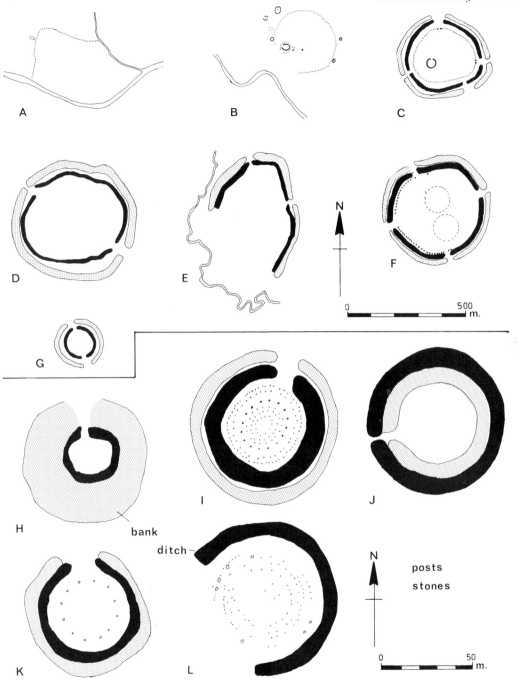

42 Early second-millennium BC enclosures (A and B), henge enclosures (C–E) and henges (F–L). (A) Meldon Bridge, Borders; (B) Forteviot, Tayside; (C) Mount Pleasant, Dorset; (D) Durrington Walls, Wiltshire; (E) Marden, Wiltshire; (F) Avebury, Wiltshire; (G) Thornborough (central henge), North Yorkshire; (H) Gorsey Bigbury, Somerset; (I) Woodhenge, Wiltshire; (J) Llandegai A, Gwynedd; (K) Stennes, Orkney; (L) Balfarg, Fife. [*(A) and (B) after Burgess 1980, 47; (C)–(F) after Wainwright 1979 figure 95; (G) after Thomas 1955 figure 2; (H) after Jones et al. 1938; (I) after Wainwright and Longworth 1971, 85; (J) after Houlder 1968 figure 1; (K) after Ritchie 1976 figure 2; (L) after Mercer 1981 figure 40*]

functions and most probably changed their role over the course of time. The majority were probably somehow utilized as ritual monuments (see below p. 86), but three large sites in Wessex—Mount Pleasant, Dorset, Marden, Wiltshire and Durrington Walls, Wiltshire—stand apart from the others in having abundant evidence for occupation within them, including timber buildings, middens and large amounts of occupation debris. Indeed, Mount Pleasant contains within its bounds a conventional henge, and Durrington Walls has a similar structure just outside its perimeter at Woodhenge. The site at Waulud's Bank, Luton, Bedfordshire, may also belong to this group of henge enclosures.

Northern Britain and north Wales

The pattern of change in the north is broadly similar to that already described for the south. Enclosures are few, but Briar Hill, Northamptonshire, fell out of use shortly after 2600 BC. In Yorkshire and Lincolnshire no new long barrows were constructed after about 2500 BC; one of the lastest to be built was probably Giant's Hills I near Skendleby, Lincolnshire, with a radiocarbon date of 2460 ± 150 BC. In North Wales tombs in the long mound tradition were blocked or abandoned around the middle of the third millennium. At Trefignath, in Anglesey, Gwynedd, Peterborough style pottery was found in the blocking of the latest chamber. Capel Garmon, also in Gwynedd, was probably blocked at about the same time. In their place new types of tomb were adopted—developed passage graves each comprising a large round mound with a central stone chamber approached by a long passage. Classic examples include Bryn-celli-Ddu and Barclodiad-y-Gawres, both in Anglesey. Further north still, chambered tombs round the Clyde area of southwest Scotland also fell out of use at this time. Monamore on Arran had been blocked by 2240 ± 110 BC. As in the south, there is evidence for the regeneration of woodland clearances in pollen sequences from the north. At Red Moss, Lancashire, for example reafforestation was complete by about 2400 BC and the same applies at Nant Ffrancon, Gwynedd, in North Wales.

Flintwork and pottery also changed. The Peterborough styles of the north can be distinguished from those of the south on the basis of form and favoured decoration. In Yorkshire, Rudston wares are the equivalent of Peterborough wares and in south-west Scotland Beacharra wares follow the same course of development. In the north east of England the strong round barrow tradition of the early third millennium continued after 2500 BC, but with a tendency for single, rather than multiple inhumation. At Whitegrounds, North Yorkshire, a pit grave dated to about 2570 ± 90 BC cut an earlier monument and contained an adult buried along with a fine flint axe of distinctive Seamer type and a jet belt-slider. At Duggleby Howe, also in North Yorkshire, a shaft-grave contained an adult male buried with a Duggleby type flint adze, a lozenge shaped arrowhead and an antler macehead. Other similar burials include Crosby Garrett, Cumbria, and Liff's Low, Derbyshire. Some of the many simple cist graves without accompanying objects known from northern Britain may well belong to this period.

Bank barrows are very scarce in the north, the most well-known examples being Long Low, Staffordshire, and Scorton, North Yorkshire. In contrast, henges and cursus are well represented. At Llandegai, Gwynedd, on the coastal plain of northwest Wales, two henges and a cursus or bank barrow form a small cluster of ritual sites. A similar set of monuments is known at Milfield, Northumberland, while at Rudston, Humberside, no less than three cursus monuments surround the present village. Similar clusters of monuments are known in Scotland, too, and at Balfarg, Fife, excavations have brought to light a ceremonial centre comprising henges and post settings. One of the henges dates to between 2500 and 2300 BC, and contains two concentric rings of upright posts.

Something of the social unrest at this time of change may be glimpsed at Meldon Bridge, Borders. Here a massive timber wall over 500 metres (1640 feet) long cut off a gravel promontory between two river valleys, enclosing ritual sites, burial areas and possibly also settlement areas. Radiocarbon dates suggest that the site was used towards the end of the third millennium BC. This site has many similarities with the large henge-enclosures in Wessex, and another similar site is known from aerial photographs at Forteviot, Tayside. At this last mentioned site a small henge lies within the enclosure, as at Mount Pleasant, Dorset.

Northern Scotland and the Islands

Change during the later third millennium BC in the very north of Scotland was less dramatic than

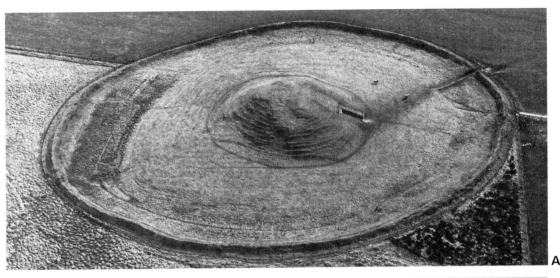

A

B

C

43 Late third- to early second-millennium BC large round burial monuments. (A) Maes Howe, Orkney. Chambered tomb probably built about 2000 BC. (B) Duggleby Howe, North Yorkshire. Multiphase chamberless burial monument used during the second half of the third millennium BC. (C) Inside the main chamber at Quanterness, Orkney, showing the fine wall construction and the entrance to one of the side chambers. The scale totals 2 metres in length.
[*(A) Photo: Bob Bewley; copyright reserved.*
(B) Photo: Mick Sharp; copyright reserved.
(C) Photo courtesy of Colin Renfrew; copyright reserved]

A

B

44 (A) Clava cairns, Balnuaran of Clava, Highland. General view of the south-western cairn showing the entrance, chamber, retaining kerb and part of the surrounding stone circle. (B) Recumbent stone circle at Loanhead of Daviot, Grampian. General view looking south-eastwards with the recumbent stone, its flankers and the graded stone circle with internal ring-cairn. [*Photos: Mick Sharp; copyright reserved*]

further south. Many of the traditions of earlier centuries were perpetuated. Peterborough wares are absent from the far north but a new type of pottery, known as grooved ware because of its distinctive incised decoration, appears alongside the local Unstan ware in the later third millennium BC. This class of pottery later became widespread in Britain. Tombs in the area also changed, from monuments with square or rectangular mounds which were so characteristic of the early third millennium, to developed passage graves rather similar to those already noted in North Wales. Quanterness, Orkney, is an early example of this class of tomb and excavations by Colin Renfrew revealed that it was built about 2640 ± 75 BC. Perhaps the finest tomb of this class is Maes Howe, situated on mainland Orkney overlooking the Loch of Harray. The mound, which is over 35 metres (115 feet) in diameter and 3.5 metres ($11\frac{1}{2}$ feet) high, is surrounded by a rock cut ditch. It was probably built about 2300 BC. A passage through the mound leads to a large square chamber with three smaller chambers leading off from it. In contrast to areas further south the burial tradition remained communal throughout the later third millennium BC. At Quanterness over 150 bodies were represented in the chambers explored, including men, women and children. Some of the earlier tombs continued in use; Isbister, Orkney, for example, received burials until about 2000 BC.

Around Inverness on the mainland is a small and geographically restricted group of distinctive tombs known as Clava cairns. These have round mounds with centrally set stone chambers approached by a passage. In contrast to other Scottish tombs the entrances to Clava cairns usually open to the south west, and many have a ring of upright stones set round the edge of the cairn. The only evidence for burial rituals is from Corrimony, Highland, where the chamber contained a single adult inhumation.

Nucleated settlements of the later third millennium are known at Skara Brae and Rinyo on Orkney and at other coastal sites. No cursus monuments or bank barrows are known, but henges have been recorded. At Stennes, Orkney, a henge was built about 2356 ± 65 BC, and at the Ring of Brogar closeby another was built about the same time. In northeast Scotland, particularly in Grampian, another series of monuments known as recumbent stone circles begin to be built from this time. These each comprise a ring of stones which are graded in height, the two tallest often in the south-west quadrant flanking a prostrate block. Inside the circle there

may be a ring-cairn in whose central space cremated human bone was deposited. Quartz stones are sometimes found scattered in front of the recumbent stone and on the basis of alignments and the orientation of the recumbent stones Aubrey Burl has suggested that these monuments may be connected with lunar rituals.

Ritual and prestige

Despite the regional diversity represented by pottery styles, types of monument, and local rates of change during the later third millennium BC, three themes can be identified. The first is the adoption of single grave burials with overt differentiation of individuals through variations in the number and quality of grave goods. The second is the development of circular enclosures for ritual and burial. The third is the development of greater inter-regional contact and the sharing of ideas and practices.

Burials and grave goods

In all parts of Britain except the very far north burials show greater evidence of differentiation, through association with different types of grave goods, from the mid third millennium onwards. About 75 per cent of burials from recorded contexts of this period are single graves. Grave goods are included with some burials, and a few individuals are accompanied by a considerable quantity of items. Phase 3 of the burial deposits at Duggleby Howe, North Yorkshire, serves to illustrate the point. Nine individual burials were present in this phase. The central grave was an adult male accompanied by no less than 33 objects including flint arrowheads, flint flakes, bone pins, boar's tusk implements and a beaver's incisor. The remaining eight graves, which included adults and children, contained no grave goods.

The meaning attached to the deposition of grave goods is uncertain. Analogy with present-day practices among primitive societies suggests a general correspondence between the number and type of objects buried and the wealth or status of the deceased. There are, of course, exceptions but it remains a reasonable assumption that, by and large, similar symbolism was involved in the observable prehistoric patterns. Many objects found in later third-millennium BC graves are relatively simple everyday forms given a rather better finish during production. Examples include arrowheads, scrapers,

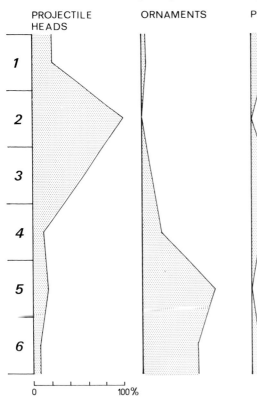

PROJECTILE HEADS ORNAMENTS POTS

0   100%

45 Changing associations of grave goods with burials in six successive stages spanning the period 3000–2000 BC. The percentages show the number of recorded associations containing one or more of the specified objects. [*After Kinnes 1979 figure 6.4*]

bone points, shale beads, antler tines, stone or flint axes, polished edge knives, serrated blades, stone rubbers and boar's tusk blades. But several types were new innovations. Antler maceheads—shaped pieces of antler perforated for hafting—have no antecedents and no obvious function. Likewise the jet belt-sliders common throughout Britain are inventions of the period around 2500 BC. Transverse arrowheads, thought to be especially useful for hunting birds, represent another new type, and bone skewer pins, sometimes with elaborated heads, first make an appearance at this time too, although they are common in Ireland slightly earlier.

In addition to the fine objects from graves, other items of unusual character circulated widely. Large stone axes, sometimes over 35 centimetres (14 inches) long, and rather cumbersome for ordinary woodworking or forestry, emanated from the Lake District axe factories and from sources in Wales. Large flint axes are also known, and at least ten

groups, or hoards, of large axes have come to light, mostly in eastern and southern England. Over 35 flint axes from Scandinavia have been found in Britain, some in hoards but including one from the barrow known as Julliberrie's Grave, Kent. Flat copper axes of distinctive Irish form, so called Lough Ravel types, are known from Moel Arthur, Clwyd, and other sites in Wales and England. These were the earliest metal objects used in Britain, and Peter Northover has shown that most are made from Irish metal and are therefore imports.

Clearly the circulation and use of these objects were subject to complicated rules governing both access to them and their ultimate disposal. Unusual and fine objects were exchanged between groups and were seemingly assigned various symbolic meanings which led some to be deposited as grave goods. In order to account for these patterns, Richard Bradley has postulated the existence of several exchange spheres operating at different levels within society. These ranged in scale from local networks distributing everyday items like pottery, flint and quernstones through to long-distance alliance structures which served to disseminate valuable goods and knowledge over great distances. The acquisition of goods and their deliberate placement in graves may have played a key role in reinforcing and emphasizing prestige both during the life of an individual and in death. It is therefore no surprise that many of the objects involved were personal items connected with dress (eg. pins, belt fittings, beads, pendants etc.) since appearance is one of the most frequently used, intimate and visual ways of displaying and symbolizing power, rank or status.

Circular monuments

The second major theme to emerge from changes during the later third millennium is the development of circular monuments—henges and barrows. This may again be closely linked with the overt differentiation of individuals because the very geometry of circular monuments creates a single focus at the centre with any number of lesser, but otherwise equal, positions round the circumference. Close association of many circular monuments such as henges and ring-ditches with linear monuments such as cursus and bank barrows reinforces the idea of order within society, since by their very nature processions imply an ordering of these taking part.

Sorting out the function of the great variety of circular monuments characteristic of this period is not easy, and is far from complete. Barrows covering

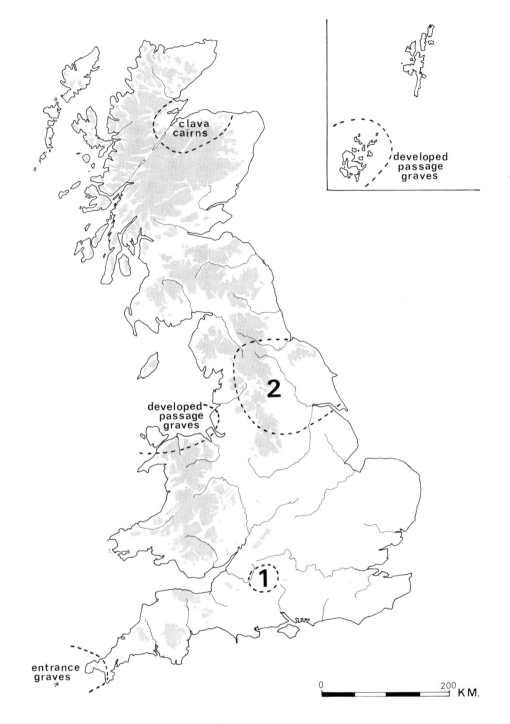

46 Distribution of late third-millennium BC tomb
types. 1 = Large round burial-less mounds; 2 = large
round unchambered mounds with burials.
[*Source: author*]

burials, and henges enclosing flat open spaces are relatively easy to separate, but many sites lie between these extremes. Moreover function may have changed over time: henges tending towards being ritual enclosures rather than burial monuments and ring-ditches becoming cemeteries rather than monuments for single burials.

When excavated, early henges usually reveal very little structural evidence—flat areas with perhaps a few postholes and depressions. At Llandegai, Gwynedd, one of the two henges excavated in 1966 proved to contain ritual deposits of stone axes. An axe of Lake District origin, in mint condition, was found buried blade downwards at the edge of the bank. Nearby a large unfinished axe from Pembrokeshire, which had at some time been used as a polisher, accompanied a cremation burial. This led the excavator, Christopher Houlder, to postulate a connection between axe exchange and henges. At Barford, Warwickshire, several quernstones were found in pits inside and outside the henge, and these could again be seen in terms of objects relating to exchange activities. Indeed it is tempting to interpret the function of henges as focal points in the complicated exchange systems which were obviously developing at this period. Perhaps they served to define neutral territory where two or more groups could meet for exchange rituals and in this respect took over some of the supposed roles of the causewayed enclosures of an earlier period. The odd reversal of the ditch inside the bank may, within such a context, reflect a deliberate inversion of the defensible position of the ditch outside the bank.

Closely, although be no means universally, associated with the development of henges in Britain is the spread of grooved ware pottery. Grooved ware probably originated in the far north around the middle of the third millennium, but by about 2200 it had become widespread. Detailed studies of decoration and form by Ian Longworth failed to identify any marked regional grouping of styles within the grooved ware tradition. Its widespread adoption may therefore have been partly or wholly due to fashion.

Inter-regional contact

The western seaways were important in developing and promoting inter-regional contacts, especially in northern and western Britain. Stone axes from Tievebulliagh in County Antrim, Northern Ireland, have been found in the west of England, Wales and widely in Scotland. Bronze tools from Ireland have already been mentioned. From about 2300 BC Ireland also influenced the development of tombs in western Britain. In Anglesey, Barclodiad-y-Gawres and Bryn-celli-Ddu represent direct copies of Irish passage graves found especially in the Boyne valley at this time. Even the distinctive curvilinear passage grave art used for decorating stones within passage graves in Ireland can be found replicated in the tombs of Wales and Orkney. The Calderstones from Liverpool, Merseyside, may be from another similarly ornamented tomb in the vicinity.

By maintaining an interest in communal tombs, the inhabitants of northern Scotland and North Wales kept alive earlier traditions, even though the form of the monuments altered. By about 1900 BC, however, even these outposts had been drawn into events taking place elsewhere in Britain, and became part of accelerating changes in ritual and the reorganization of power which characterized the centuries following 2000 BC.

The age of beakers

By about 2000 BC the tradition of acquiring and disposing of a variety of fine goods was widespread in Britain, and increasing in intensity. The simple goods of the late third millennium, many of which drew upon inspiration or sources in the north and west, were becoming widely copied and emulated so that new types had to be sought. For this attention shifted towards the Continent of Europe. The first new objects used in burial rituals over a very wide area were beakers. These are finely finished red coloured vessels with carefully executed decoration. The early examples have a bell-shaped profile and are usually decorated all over with cord impressions. The quality of these vessels is far superior to the Peterborough and grooved ware pots which were in use contemporaneously with the early beakers.

Beakers are found in most parts of Europe from Scandinavia to Italy and from Germany to Spain. The inspiration for, if not the origins of, the British beaker series lay in the Netherlands; indeed this may have been the source area for all beakers. At one time it was thought that the introduction of beaker pottery to Britain was the visible effect of an invasion of Continental people. Crucial to this argument was the recognition that the 'invaders' were, biometrically, more round-headed than the people who were buried in long barrows and chambered tombs. The Beaker Folk became well known in the literature as agents of change around the beginning of the second millennium BC, but recent work has called this interpretation of the evidence into question and the idea of beaker invasions as such is now no longer tenable. In the first place the Beaker Folk represent a classic example of where archaeologists have turned a group of artefacts, in this case mostly pottery, into a group of people, whereas in reality , of course, it was people who made and distributed the pottery. Most important of all is the realization that many of the traditions supposedly introduced by the Beaker Folk were in fact indigenous to later third-millennium BC communities in Britain. Single-grave burial, round barrows, and the use of metal objects all pre-date the introduction of beaker pottery. Even the supposed biometrical distinctions are no longer so clear since most long barrows were out of use long before 2000 BC and simple population genetics could easily account for the supposed changes over a period of perhaps five centuries.

There are now two schools of thought on the Beaker phenomenon. One adheres to the invasion idea, although admits a rather reduced influx of newcomers with less overall effect on the native population. The other follows the suggestion made by Colin Burgess and Stephen Shennan that beakers were part of a package of fasionable artefacts and ideas adopted by a population hungry for new symbols through which to emphasize social inequal-

47 Beaker burial at Ashgrove, Fife, seen obliquely during excavation in July 1963. Analysis of pollen from around the beaker suggests that it contained mead when first deposited. [*Photo: Kirkcaldy Museums; copyright reserved*]

ities and prestige. If this second idea is correct then the mechanisms behind the initial spread of beakers owe more to trade and exchange between the upper orders of society over a wide area than to the movement of population. A detailed appraisal of social change in the late third millennium by Alasdair Whittle shows that available evidence fits the latter explanation rather better than the former, but the issue is not yet fully resolved.

The reason for the widespread popularity of beakers is unclear. Their shape and size makes them suitable for use as drinking vessels and there is some evidence that this was indeed their function. At Ashgrove, Fife, for example, analysis of residue in a beaker from a burial cist suggested that it contained mead when first deposited. Whether or not they were part of a 'cult package' which included drinking rituals, beakers were often deposited with burials and clearly had some symbolic meaning in such contexts.

The earliest beakers were by far the finest. They are found mostly in eastern Britain, eastern Scotland, East Anglia, the upper Thames valley and Wessex. An example from Newmill, Tayside, is almost identical in form and decoration with the so-called All Over Ornamented (AOO) vessels of Holland. Copies were soon made locally and naturally slight changes in form resulted. Continued contact with the Continent provided new inspiration for form and decoration. J. N. Lanting and J. D. Van der Waals have identified seven distinct steps in the evolution of beakers in Britain, during which time the basic bell-shaped vessel first adopted a short-necked form and later a long-necked form.

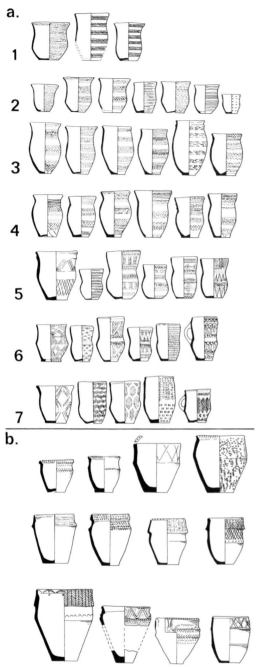

In addition to beakers, several other classes of object were adopted in Britain. Triangular-shaped arrowheads with tangs and sharp barbs became very common, and replaced the leaf-shaped forms which had been used for over a millennium. Rectangular stone wristguards to protect archers from the backlash of the bow string when an arrow was shot were also taken up. Shale and jet buttons, and belt rings represent additions to the items associated with dress. Most characteristic were new metal objects— not the thick chunky objects of native design, like the copper axes, but fine European types including tanged triangular daggers and knives, awls and pins. Gold was also used for earrings and button caps. Small whetstones to sharpen the daggers/knives, and stone battle-axes copying Continental bronze battle-axes also appear during the currency of beaker pottery.

Beaker graves and grave goods

The various objects closely associated with the introduction of beakers do not all appear at once, rather they were introduced over a period of perhaps three centuries. As they appear they were used as grave goods, sometimes with objects such as boar's tusks, flint knives, antlers and axes, more traditionally associated with late third-millennium BC burials. Clearly defined sets of male and female associated objects emerged. Other than pottery, the grave goods fall into three classes: weapons, personal/dress adornments and craft tools, although more often than not items from more than one class occur in the same grave.

Weapon graves are exclusively male. At Dorchester-on-Thames, Oxfordshire, a grave contained a wristguard, two daggers/knives and a beaker, while at Roundway, Wiltshire, there was a large dagger, a wristguard, a barbed and tanged arrowhead, a copper pin and a beaker with the deceased. Dress fittings and ornaments occur with both males and females. At Devil's Dyke, Sussex, shale and copper beads from a necklace accompanied a small beaker in the grave of a (?)female, while at Winterbourne Stoke, Wiltshire, a beaker, two stone whetstones, a flint blade, a jet button and a jet belt ring accompanied a burial of unknown sex. Craft tools were placed with both males and females; one of the most celebrated was found in the central position below a barrow at West Overton, Wiltshire. Here, an aged adult male was accompanied by a beaker, a bronze awl, two long thin slate strips (descriptively called 'sponge fingers'), an antler

48 Early second-millennium BC pottery. (a) Beaker pottery arranged in groups according to developmental steps or stages. (b) Food vessels and collared urns. [*After Burgess 1980 figures 2.12, 3.1 and 3.3*]

Objects	% of known examples with males	% of known examples with females
Flint arrowheads	100%	
Tanged copper daggers	100%	
Wristguards	100%	
Belt rings	100%	
Gold button caps	100%	
Antler spatulae	100%	
Flint daggers	100%	
Bronze daggers	100%	
Stone battle-axes	100%	
Slate polishers	100%	
Flint and stone axes	100%	
Pyrites nodules	100%	
Strike-a-light flints	100%	
Amber buttons	100%	
Flint scrapers	90%	10%
Flint flakes	73%	27%
Flint knives	82%	18%
Jet buttons	75%	25%
Bone awls/pins	85%	15%
Single rivet bronze daggers	66%	34%
Flint blades	50%	50%
Earrings (gold and bronze)	50%	50%
Pebble hammers	50%	50%
Shale/jet beads		100%
Antler pick or hoe	34%	66%
Bronze awls	27%	73%

[*Data from Clarke 1970 Appendix 3.3*]

Table 4 Grave goods deposited in Beaker graves by sex

spatula, a flint strike-a-light, a nodule of iron ore and a flint knife. The excavators suggested this was a leatherworker's grave.

Not all graves contain grave goods. At Eynsham, Oxfordshire, a cemetery of 21 graves was excavated in advance of gravelworking, but of these only ten contained grave goods, the remainder being un-accompanied inhumations. The same picture is reflected elsewhere. At Barnack, Cambridgeshire, the central grave contained the body of an adult male accompanied by a fine beaker, a bronze dagger, an archer's wristguard and a bone pendant. Around about were no less than 15 other graves, some cutting the primary grave, of which only three others contained grave goods. All the graves lay within a ring-ditch about 11.5 metres (38 feet) in diameter. A mound was constructed over the burials as a final ritual act.

A slight variation on the ring-ditch pattern can be seen at the West Overton barrow already referred to. Here, instead of a ditch, a kerb of stones delimited the focal area in which six burials were made, including the central grave. Two separate child graves had been dug before the circular bank was built. The burials had clearly been deposited during several episodes of use spread over a considerable time. Other than the central grave, only one of the children had any grave goods. A mound was built over the cemetery, but what dictated when it should be constructed is unclear. Together, the Barnack and West Overton cemeteries illustrate the complexity and diversity of burial deposits. Some graves were given a round barrow of their own, but many barrows cover small cemeteries. In general ring-ditches and barrows are more common in eastern Britain, while ring-cairns are more common in the west.

a.

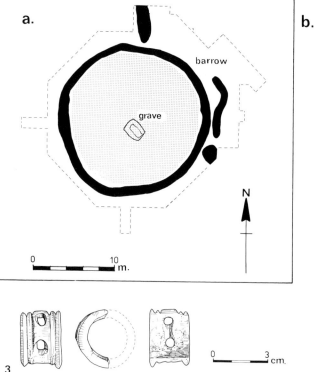

b.

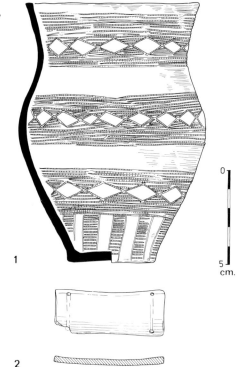

49 Beaker grave at Hemp Knoll, Avebury, Wiltshire. (a) Plan of the burial within its ditched barrow. (b) Grave goods from the primary grave accompanying an adult male aged between 35 and 45 years: 1 = beaker pot; 2 = stone wristguard; 3 = bone toggle/belt fitting. [*After Robertson-Mackay 1980 figures 2 and 11*]

Monuments and power

Displays of wealth through personal ornaments and fine objects were supplemented by displays of power through monument building, both ritual and domestic. Most distinctive are the massive henge-like enclosures surrounded by great continous earthworks at Durrington Walls and Marden, Wiltshire and Mount Pleasant, Dorset. Durrington Walls and Marden each cover over 12 hectares (30 acres), and Mount Pleasant is only slightly less. It has been estimated that Durrington Walls required at least 900,000 man-hours to construct, involving the removal of about 50,000 cubic metres (65,000 cubic yards) of chalk rubble with antler picks, baskets and ropes. At Durrington Walls two large timber buildings were located through excavation, the larger over 38 metres (125 feet) in diameter with five concentric

rings of posts. Whether they were ever roofed is a matter for debate, although the excavator, Geoffrey Wainwright, believes they were. A geophysical survey of Durrington Walls suggests that more similar structures lie in the areas of the enclosure not examined by excavation. Similar timber structures were found at Marden.

Grooved ware pottery is associated with the use of these large henge enclosures, and Alasdair Whittle has noted that early beaker burials are not found in their immediate vicinity. This he explains as resulting from conflict or competition between beaker-using and grooved ware-using groups. More specifically ritual henges of large size may also have been built to symbolize power and prestige. Avebury, Wiltshire, is perhaps such a site, almost as large as the henge enclosures just discussed, but rather more circular in plan and lacking the large quantities of domestic debris in its interior and ditch fills. It has been estimated that Avebury may have taken 1.5 million man-hours to build.

The construction of large mounds may have fulfilled a similar or additional function in symbolizing power and the control of resources. Silbury Hill, near Avebury, Wiltshire, was also built about 2000 BC or a little after and ranks as the largest prehistoric

A

B

50 Henge monuments. (A) Avebury, Wiltshire, looking south towards Silbury Hill. One of Avebury's two avenues can be seen leading from the henge towards the top left. (B) Ring of Brogar, Orkney, showing excavation through the ditch. The scale totals 2 metres in length. [*(A) Photo: West Air Photography, Weston-super-Mare; copyright reserved. (B) Photo courtesy of Colin Renfrew; copyright reserved*]

man-made mound in Europe. Its construction took place in three stages. First a small primary round barrow of turf and gravel about 36 metres (118 feet) in diameter was built, probably about 2145 ± 95 BC. Subsequently this was covered in a mound of chalk rubble and earth quarried from a surrounding ditch. Before the ditch had silted-up a change of plan was implemented and a much larger ditch provided chalk for the enormous monument seen today. The last phase of the mound was constructed as a series of steps, presumably to prevent collapse, each step then being filled with soil to provide a smooth conical outline. The top step was never filled and is still visible. Excavations have failed to reveal traces of any burials, but the mound covers an area of 2.2 hectares ($5\frac{1}{2}$ acres), and is 40 metres (131 feet) high. Its construction would have involved the equivalent of 500 men working every day for 10 years.

The work involved in constructing all these monumental sites was clearly enormous, not just in terms of the effort of building but also in providing food for the workers and materials (it is estimated that over 3.5 hectares ($8\frac{1}{2}$ acres) of woodland would have had to have been felled to provide the timber for each of the buildings at Durrington Walls). Clearly some authority must have been powerful enough to control such labour forces. The Wessex evidence must, however, be seen in context. The southern English downlands were probably among the most densely populated areas at this time. Elsewhere efforts were probably commensurate with the available labour. At Waulud's Bank on the outskirts of Luton, Bedfordshire, is a monument of similar design to Mount Pleasant although of slightly more modest scale. The Devil's Quoits henge near Stanton Harcourt, Oxfordshire, is over 110 metres (360 feet) in diameter and required over 26,000 man-hours to build. Further away still the group of four henges at Priddy on the Mendips in Somerset, the cluster of five or more henges in the Milfield basin of Northumberland, the group of five henges beside the River Ure around Ripon, North Yorkshire, and the pair of henges overlooking the Loch of Harray on Orkney, to name but a few, each represent feats of monument building which must have cost their respective local communities dearly in terms of sheer hard work.

51 Stone circles and rows. (A) The Merry Maidens stone circle, near Land's End, Cornwall. (B) The Merrivale stone row, Dartmoor, Devon. The row crosses a small cairn about mid-way along its length. (C) Circle and converging rows at Callanish, Western Isles, Scotland. [*(A) and (B) Photos: Mick Sharp; copyright reserved. (C) Photo: Royal Commission on Ancient Monuments, Scotland; Crown copyright reserved*]

Sticks to stones

After about 1700 BC a new type of stone circle appeared: not the small rings with closely spaced stones that were already common in the far north and west, but large circles with widely spaced stones giving the impression of a bounded space. Some were constructed inside henge monuments, as at Avebury, Wiltshire, The Devil's Quoits, Oxfordshire, Arbor Low, Derbyshire and Ring of Brogar, Orkney. In the case of Woodhenge and The Sanctuary, Wiltshire, stone circles replaced earlier wooden structures, and this pattern is repeated at many other sites too. It is notable that none of the large henge enclosures contained stone circles.

Many great open stone circles were built in new situations, especially in the west where the spread of settlement into the uplands during the early second millennium BC gave scope for new monuments in newly settled areas. Single circles such as the Rollright Stones, Oxfordshire, or Castlerigg, Cumbria, as well as groups of circles as at Stanton Drew, Avon, or The Hurlers, Cornwall, are widespread. A few, including Stanton Drew, Arbor Low and Avebury, contain U-shaped stone settings called coves.

Stone rows and stone alignments also began to be built from the early second millennium, perhaps doing the same for stone circles as cursus monuments and bank barrows did for henges.

A

B

C

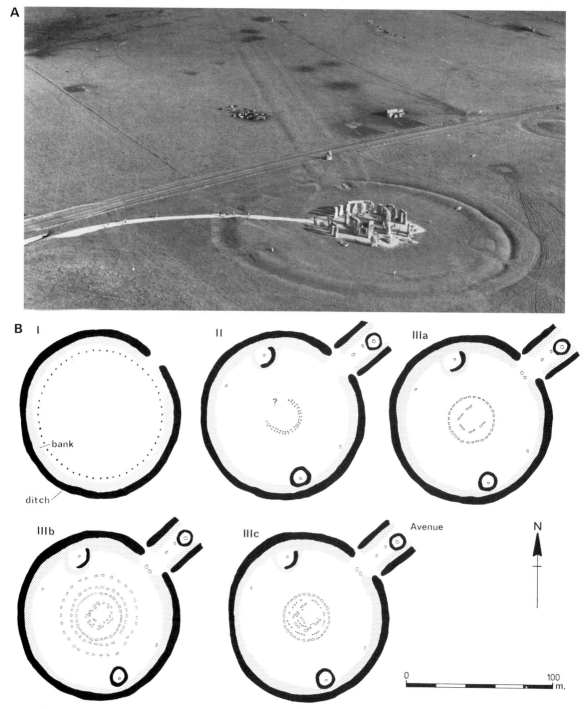

52 Stonehenge, Wiltshire. (A) Aerial view of the monument from the south-west. The avenue can be clearly seen leading from the earthwork surrounding the central circles towards the top of the picture. A large round barrow lies north-east of Stonehenge. (B) Plans of Stonehenge at successive phases during its long history of change and remodelling. [*(A) Photo: West Air Photography, Weston-super-Mare; copyright reserved. (B) After Royal Commission on the Historical Monuments of England 1979 figure 4*]

Stonehenge

The most famous stone circle in Britain lies in the centre of the henge monument at Stonehenge on Salisbury Plain, Wiltshire. This monument began life as a simple cremation cemetery and henge with an outlying stone (the heel-stone). After a period of abandonment the site was remodelled about 1700 BC. An avenue was added and a double circle of 82 undressed bluestones, brought from the Prescelly Mountains of South Wales, was built within the henge, although probably never finished. Further remodelling led to the dressing and erection 30 upright sarsen stones linked by mortice and tenon joints to a continuous ring of lintels and enclosing a horseshoe shaped setting of five trilithons. Two more remodellings followed involving the reincorporation of the bluestones.

Circles as observatories

There have been many claims that stone circles have astronomical alignments and were used as observatories; certainly general alignments on the extreme risings and settings of the sun and moon can be detected. Regularities in the spacing and number of stones suggests rudimentary mathematical skills, but more than this is pure speculation. No evidence exists for the use of stone circles as mathematical computers or for other scientific purposes. Rather, the evidence can be economically explained as relating to the construction of a simple calendar to aid the timing of rituals and the regularization of the seasons.

Fighting with goods

The overall impression given by the evidence for society in the early second millennium BC is of a balancing act where prestige and power counted for survival. At Mount Pleasant, Dorset, there are hints of what happened when this balance was upset. About 1687 ± 63 BC a massive palisade was constructed around an area of about 4.5 hectares (11 acres) within the earlier giant henge enclosure. The palisade was built from massive tree trunks set in a bedding trench about 3 metres (10 feet) deep, and it is hard to imagine that it was anything other than defensive. It was burnt down at some unknown date, and then partially dismantled.

53 Simplified prestige goods replacement model applied to late third- to early second-millennium BC pottery. Through time new types are used first as prestige goods then as domestic/everyday goods with consequent changes in the status their ownership and use confers. [*Based on Bradley 1984 figure 4.2*]

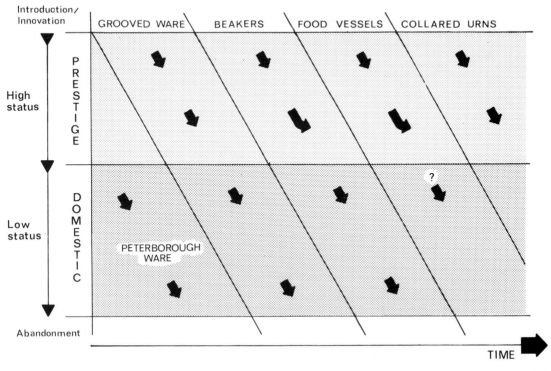

Elsewhere much of the fighting seems to have been more symbolic, using objects as indicators of power. A simple pattern had developed whereby goods were made or acquired for their prestige value until such time as they became debased by copying, faking and reproduction, at which point new types were taken to symbolize power and the old types became acceptable domestic items in everyday circulation. This is most clearly seen in the changes to pottery styles. Thus at first beaker pottery is rarely found outside of burial contexts whereas two centuries or so later it forms a recognizable domestic assemblage with new styles being chosen as grave goods. In many northern and western areas of Britain so-called food vessels replaced beakers as the fashionable pottery vessel to accompany the dead. Cremation increased in popularity during the early second millennium BC, and was accompanied by the widespread use of collared urns as containers for ashes. In many areas miniature pots were made to accompany the dead. The same pattern can also be glimpsed in the development of other classes of object, for example daggers and ornaments.

Round barrows remained the principal burial monument and large cemeteries of barrows developed, often clustering around an earlier long barrow or an early beaker burial. At Lambourn, Berkshire, a large cemetery of 45 round barrows and ring ditches developed, while at Barrow Hills, near Abingdon, Oxfordshire, 18 round barrows and an assortment of flat graves are known through excavation and aerial photography. In many cases henges provided a focus for round barrow cemeteries; around Stonehenge, for example, there are over 260 barrows within 3 kilometres ($1\frac{3}{4}$ miles) or so, while at Condicote, Gloucestershire some 20 barrows are known within 3.5 kilometres ($2\frac{1}{4}$ miles).

Burial rituals became complicated and elaborate. Cremation pyres are sometimes detected, while in other areas log coffins were sometimes used. Rich burials tended to be covered by a new barrow, but more often small cemeteries were covered by barrows in a final ritual act. The form of round barrows became diverse in the early second millennium BC. On the basis of surface features it is possible to identify bowl barrows, bell barrows, disc barrows, saucer barrows and pond barrows, depending on the shape and size of the mounds. The soils and geology of different areas played an important role in determining form; ditch digging, for example, is precluded in areas of hard rock.

In Wessex and central southern England a particularly rich series of graves characterized elite burials from the sixteenth century BC. In 1938 Stuart

54 Barrow cemetery at Oakley Down, Cranborne Chase, Dorset. Bell barrows, bowl barrows and disc barrows can be seen. There were originally at least 26 barrows in the cemetery. [*Photo: Cambridge University Collection; copyright reserved*]

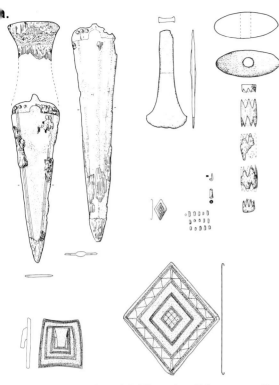

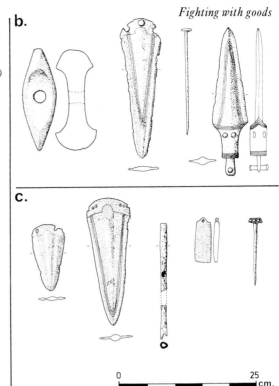

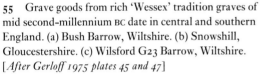

55 Grave goods from rich 'Wessex' tradition graves of mid second-millennium BC date in central and southern England. (a) Bush Barrow, Wiltshire. (b) Snowshill, Gloucestershire. (c) Wilsford G23 Barrow, Wiltshire. [*After Gerloff 1975 plates 45 and 47*]

Piggott proposed that these burials formed a distinct Wessex culture, since when they have assumed a prominent place in the prehistory of Britain. However, their place within the wider context of burial ritual during the early second millennium BC suggests that they simply result from communities having easy access to a wide range of resources. The goods deposited with the dead are of better quality than those with beaker burials, having benefited from the development of craft skills both in Britain and on the Continent. About 100 graves of this series can be identified, almost all under individual round barrows in linear or nucleated barrow cemeteries. Among the richest is the Bush Barrow burial in the Wilsford cemetery near Stonehenge, Wiltshire. This burial was that of an adult male, unusual in that the body was laid directly on the ground rather than in a grave pit. The body was accompanied by three daggers, one with its hilt inlaid with gold wire, copper and bronze rivets possibly from a leather helmet, a lozenge-shaped sheet of gold with impressed decoration, a gold belt hook, a small gold

lozenge, a stone macehead with bone fittings from the handle, and a bronze axe. The range of objects from other graves in Wessex includes crutch-head bronze pins, bronze awls, bone pins, gold and amber ornaments, perforated whetstones, and at Wilsford, Wiltshire, a bone whistle.

Around 1500 BC the contents of the rich graves changed slightly. Gold became rare, but polished stone axe-hammers and battle-axes, bone tweezers, new ogival-bladed daggers, amber and faience beads and bulb-headed pins appear for the first time. There was also a shift towards greater use of cremation.

Outside Wessex rich burials and dagger graves are more common than often supposed. At Rillaton, Cornwall, a beaten gold cup accompanied an inhumation under a large round barrow. At Mold, Clwyd, an individual was buried with a pectoral or cape of beaten gold and a necklace of amber beads. At Pen-y-Bont, Anglesey, a cremation was accompanied by a shale bead necklace, a jet button, a bronze armlet and two collared urns. At Kellythorpe, Humberside, an adult male was accompanied by a late beaker, a wristguard with gold-headed rivets, a copper knife/dagger and amber buttons. Rich graves are also known at Hove, Sussex, and Snowshill, Gloucestershire. The importance of the Wessex graves, however, is that they show a concentration of wealth over several centuries whereas in other parts of Britain rich graves appear to represent short-lived access to wealth in otherwise rather impoverished communities.

Foreign relations

Fundamental to the acquisition of goods during the late third and early second millennia BC were trade and close foreign relations with the Continent, northern Europe and Ireland. How much was directly imported and how much simply copied is impossible to determine, but the relative importance of different areas at different times can be glimpsed. During the late third millennium BC contacts with the west and north were important. Ireland especially provided the inspiration for passage graves and passage grave art, and directly contributed to the supply of goods in circulation with stone axes, copper axes, gold lunulae and possibly bronze halberds. From northern Europe came Scandinavian flint axes and Baltic amber. At least six stone battle-axes imported directly from central and northern Europe have been recognized among hundreds of British copies.

In the early second millennium BC the source of imports and inspiration shifted to the English Channel coastlands. Beaker influences have already been discussed, but it is worth emphasizing that after about 2000 BC beaker pottery and metalworking traditions ran roughly parallel on either side of the Channel. Evidence for direct imports is slight, but there must have been considerable travel between the two areas. Fragments of Niedermendig Lava quernstones from the Rhineland have been found at several sites near Avebury, Wiltshire, and may have been imported to Britain at this time.

Foreign connections after 1700 BC were especially strong with central Europe and northern France. Metalworking traditions, particularly the development of pins, spears and daggers, follow central European fashions. Cornish tin and Welsh copper and gold were being exploited by this time and presumably exported to Europe. Daggers from rich Wessex graves are closely related to the Armorican series of daggers in Brittany.

More distant connections have been claimed for the period 1700–1500 BC, but the evidence is scant and does not stand up to close scrutiny. Faience beads seem to have been manufactured in several parts of Europe and the Mediterranean, and although it is possible that some or all of the beads

from central southern England originate in the east Mediterranean, more local sources are possible. Keith Branigan has claimed links between the Aegean and southern England on the basis of four bronze double-axe heads of Aegean style from Britain. However, since none have demonstrably been found in archaeological deposits they could all be recent imports by collectors.

Economic growth

Technical studies of objects known from late third- and early second-millennium BC contexts suggest a technological revolution. New inspiration from Continental sources and constant demand for new types of goods as old ones became unfashionable stimulated this growth. Furthermore, as goods were customarily deposited in graves there was always a demand for new ones. Those who could not acquire the real thing often settled for good copies. Thus bronze daggers were replicated in flint or bone, and bronze axes with flared blades in stone or flint. Jet bead necklaces, splendid as they are, may simply be imitations of the more valued amber versions or gold lunulae.

The quality of flintworking degenerated around the mid third millennium BC, but underwent considerable refinement from 2000 BC onwards. Arrowheads, scrapers, axes and knives dominate assemblages, but other tools such as awls, sickles, points, notched flakes and discoid knives were also made. Pressure flaking became widely used to achieve a fine finish and polishing and grinding became more common for finishing knives and axes. Flint sources generally remained the same as a result of geological constraints, but Sussex was less important than in previous centuries, while East Anglia came to the fore. Flint mining at Grimes Graves, Norfolk, started on a grand scale about 2100 BC, although small-scale activity may have begun several centuries earlier. Several hundred mine shafts are known and each could have yielded up to about 8 tonnes of flint. Some was shaped into tools on site, the rest was taken away and either worked-up in nearby settlements or transported to distant communities all over southern and midland England as raw nodules. That ritual was important to the flint miners is evident from a small shrine comprising a heap of chalk surmounted by a carved figurine of a pregnant woman. In front was a heap of flint blocks and seven antler picks. Since the shaft in which this was found did not yield much flint it can reasonably

56 Grimes Graves flint mines, Norfolk. Shaft under excavation in 1971. [*Photo: Roger Mercer; copyright reserved*]

be assumed that better fortune was being hoped for by building the shrine.

In northern and western Britain fine igneous and metamorphic stone continued to be worked for axes and other tools. New sources came into use, including the Cwm Mawr picrite from Corndon Hill on the Welsh borders near Montgomery, Powys. Pecking and grinding were used extensively during the manufacture of stone tools and new forms included maceheads, battle-axes, axe-hammers and shaft-hole adzes. Some of the finest found their way into graves.

Evidence for pottery manufacture is slight. Local clays were mostly used, and bonfire firing would have been more than adequate. Beaker vessels were mostly made by the coil-building technique and fired in an oxidizing atmosphere. Decoration was applied with twisted cord or a notched bone comb, an example of which has been found at Gwithian, Cornwall. Boneworking became more widespread and the range of products diverse. Belt fittings, pins,

toggles, and imitation daggers were among the items produced. Although none has been found, clothes were probably largely made of leather, to judge from the number of scrapers and awls from settlement sites. Woodworking was very important and possibly the single most widespread craft, but again very little trace has survived. A few scraps of woollen cloth have been recovered on objects from early second-millennium BC contexts and spindle whorls first make an appearance at this time. Basketry was also common.

The single largest growth industry was metalworking. Early metal tools were imports, but native copperworking, goldworking and bronzeworking traditions soon developed in Wales and the west, and subsequently elsewhere including northern Scotland. Early metalworking equipment is so scarce that the technology involved is better known through the products than the workshops. Some idea of developments in technology can be gauged from the skills displayed by the products of each of five identifiable stages in metalworking between about 2100 and 1500 BC. Simple one-piece open stone moulds were used for casting axes, dagger blades and other items in copper or bronze, and these have been found in

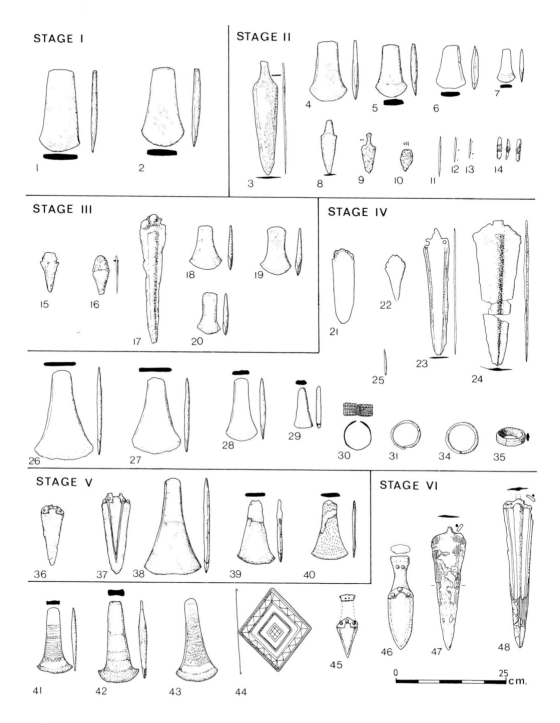

57 Typical products of metalworking stages I–VI from Britain and Ireland. Stages I–III copper, including axes (1, 2, 4–7, 18–20), knife/daggers (3, 8–10, 15–17), awls (11–13) and gold earrings (14). Stages IV–VI bronze, including daggers (21–24, 36, 37, 45–48), axes (26–29, 38–40, 41–43), awl (25), and gold ornaments (30–35, 44). Scale only approximate. [*After Burgess 1980 figures 2.13, 2.14, 3.7*]

Wales at Betws-y-Coed, Gwynedd, in the Welsh Marches at Walleybourne, Shropshire, and in north-east Scotland. Clay crucibles were used for melting metal in. Once cast, objects were hammered into shape with stone hammers. Sheet metalworking is evidenced by the bronze and gold objects, including earrings, tubular beads, button covers and plates. The Rillaton cup from a grave on Bodmin Moor, Cornwall, and the pectoral from Mold, Clwyd, illustrate the skills developed in sheet metalworking. Flat stone anvils and hammerstones are known from the graves of craftsmen, and as stray finds. As the technology and experience developed, larger and more complicated pieces could be cast and hammered. Two-piece moulds for casting daggers and spearheads were developed from about 1600 BC. Much early metalwork, like the flintwork, required other materials to make the complete item. Bone and wooden handles for daggers, wooden handles for axes and leather sheaths would have been common, although largely now lost to us.

Politics and small-time elites

The break-up of society in the mid third millennium BC, evidenced by changes in the blocking of tombs, the abandonment of enclosures and the regeneration of clearances, marked the end of the ancestor cults and community-based ideologies characteristic of the early third millennium. New structures developed, and, as we have seen, the evidence from the burial record and the existence of massive enclosures and displays of power indicates the emergence of a stratified society. Ian Hodder has suggested that at times of social stress group affinity may be symbolized through such devices as the introduction of decoration on pottery or personal ornamentation. This is exactly the type of evidence which appears with the development of the highly decorated Peterborough pottery and increased use of personal ornaments as grave goods. The new order appears to focus on the individual rather than the community and the most powerful individuals, according to the evidence of the graves, are probably those who acquired the most wealth in terms of personal objects. These people have the largest barrows and the most elaborate rituals. Whether they were the heads of families or of some larger grouping is not clear, nor indeed is whether power devolved through fixed descent patterns, or was regularly contested.

Colin Renfrew has characterized the early second-millennium BC societies in Wessex as group-orientated chiefdoms. Personal wealth was accumulated by the head of the group, or chief. This person in turn controlled the redistribution of goods and services, possibly through ritual of some kind. Skills may have been pooled in large communal endeavours, and in this the chief would control the deployment of labour. Within such a society the redistribution of goods and perhaps also foodstuffs might be expected to take place at fixed and regular intervals, perhaps at feasts or other public gatherings. The identification of individual chiefdoms is not easy given existing knowledge of the distribution of sites. For Wessex, Colin Renfrew has suggested the existence of perhaps four or five major units or territories, each served by a focal monument or group of monuments, for example Avebury/Silbury Hill or Stonehenge/Durrington Walls. Elsewhere in Britain similar clusters of monuments can be identified (see p.94) and may betray the existence of discrete territories in heavily populated areas. In North Yorkshire the presence of henges on the lower reaches of all the main rivers flowing eastwards from the uplands may suggest the existence of territories spanning more than one landscape type. At a more detailed level of analysis local settlement patterns can be identified within a few of these territories on the basis of barrow groupings. In the upper Thames valley, for example, barrow clusters occur every 4 kilometres ($2\frac{1}{2}$ miles) or so, while work by Stephen Green in the Great Ouse Valley suggests that here the interval between clusters was about 10 kilometres (6 miles). By 1500 BC the population of Britain was probably much higher than a millennium earlier, to judge from the number of monuments and the distribution of settlements. Average densities may have been in the order of ten persons per square kilometre in the south and east, less in the north and west.

Settlement and subsistence

Despite the abundance of evidence for monuments and rich burials, knowledge of the subsistence base which supported these societies, and the settlements in which they lived, is rather poor. For much of the period 2500–1500 BC the main form of settlement in the south was the small isolated farmstead, although clusters of pits and postholes are all that survive of most sites. In the far north of Scotland nucleated settlements dated to 2500–1800 BC are well known.

After the initial contraction of settlement in the mid third millennium BC there was renewed expan-

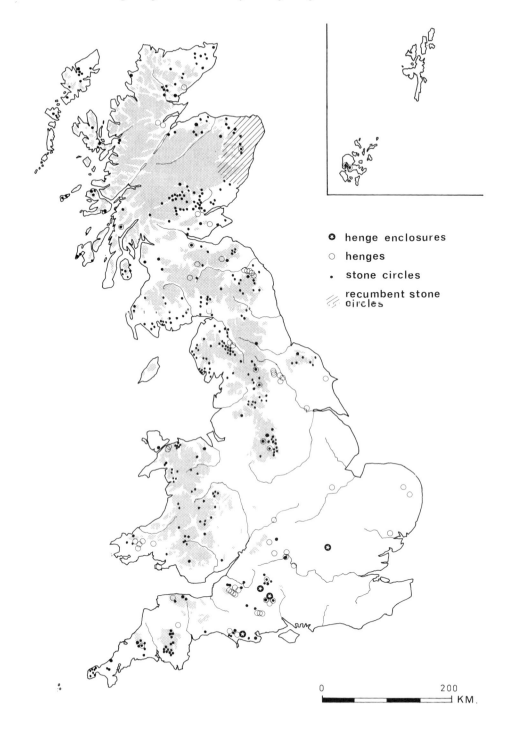

58 Distribution of major henge monuments and stone
circles in Britain. [*Based on Burl 1976 figure 1, and
Wainwright and Longworth 1971 figure 94 with additions*]

sion to the extent that by 2000 BC pollen diagrams show greater evidence of clearance than ever before. Use of the ard or light plough may be partly responsible for this, and plough marks have been recorded at a number of sites including Amesbury, Avebury; South Street, Wiltshire, and Simondston, Glamorgan. Arable cultivation was clearly widespread, and grain has been recovered from pits on many settlements, some associated with grooved ware at Barton Court Farm, Oxfordshire, Mount Farm, Dorchester-on-Thames, Oxfordshire and Down Farm, Woodcutts, Dorset. Wheat (*Triticum dicoccum*) and barley (*Hordeum sp.*) have been recorded from numerous pits containing beaker pottery, and most settlements yield grain processing equipment. Animals were also important. In the Midlands and north of England cattle and sheep numbers are surpassed at most sites by the amount of pig bone recovered. At Puddlehill in Bedfordshire, for example, grooved ware pits contained 60 per cent pig, 23 per cent ox and 17 per cent sheep/goat. Very similar frequencies were recorded at North Carnably Temple, and Low Caythorpe, Humberside. Further south the picture is not so clear. At Poors Heath, Risby, Suffolk, a mixed deposit containing beaker and food vessel pottery comprised 22 per cent pig, 43 per cent ox, 26 per cent sheep/goat and 8 per cent horse. At Snail Down, Wiltshire, a site dated to 1540 ± 90 BC yielded 10 per cent pig, 38 per cent ox and 26 per cent sheep/goat.

The importance of livestock can be seen most clearly at Fengate, Cambridgeshire, where excavations have brought to light the complete plan of a settlement dating to between *c.*2030 ± 100 BC and 1860 ± 150 BC and associated with grooved ware pottery. The focus of the settlement was a ring-ditch (indistinguishable from a burial monument before excavation) within which was a house. Adjoining the settlement proper was a small field-system comprising two long rectangular paddocks separated by a droveway. Ditches and hedges defined the paddocks, and the entrances were designed to facilitate stock control. Grazing was available on the surrounding fen-edge. Hunting was also undertaken by the inhabitants of this settlement, to judge from the bones of wild cattle (*Bos primigenius*) and deer. Curiously, about 400 years after this settlement had been abandoned, a barrow was constructed within the ring-ditch. Similar settlements have been noted under barrows elsewhere in Britain, for example at Playden, Sussex, Chippenham, Cambridgeshire and Newton Mumbles, Glamorgan. In all cases the house at these settlements was round in plan.

In the far north nucleated settlements predominate. The most completely known site is Skara Brae, Orkney, which dates to between 2480 ± 100 BC and 1830 ± 110 BC. Here, ten or more houses cluster together, linked by means of dry-stone-walled passages. The whole settlement was semi-subterranean, having been built into a vast midden. The houses have a uniform plan with a square stone hearth at the centre, stone beds on either side of the entrance and a dresser facing the door. Stone boxes were sunk into the floor, possibly as water containers or tanks in which to keep shellfish fresh. In addition to the exploitation of marine resources, including whales and shellfish, domestic animals were husbanded (mostly sheep and cattle) and cereals were cultivated nearby on the coastal fringe. Similar settlements are known at Links of Noltland and Rinyo on Orkney. Most of the other outer islands, including Shetland, were settled by this time.

Coastal settlements are well known all around Britain, often associated with beaker pottery. Extensive spreads of pottery, flintwork and shell-middens are known at Newborough Warren, Anglesey, Merthyr Mawr Warren, Glamorgan, Northton, Harris, and Ross Links, Northumberland.

In upland areas of northern and western Britain activity became more intensive after 2000 BC. Pollen diagrams suggest some clearance, and the spread of stone circles and burial cairns shows widespread colonization of Dartmoor, central and North Wales, the Pennines, the Lake District and the North York Moors. Settlement in these areas may not have been permanent, however, The evidence suggests seasonal occupation, possibly within a transhumance pastoralist economy based on the surrounding lowlands and nearby coastal fringes. A number of upland cave sites show traces of periodic occupation and small settlements have been located beneath some upland barrows such as Cefn Caer Euni, Gwynedd. Among excavated sites is Trelystan, Powys. Here, two small roughly square huts dating to between about 2310 ± 70 BC and 2035 ± 70 BC were located beneath later burial monuments. Each hut had a central hearth and several pits dug into the floor. Analysis of the flintwork and pottery (grooved ware) suggested that it had been introduced to the site from adjoining lowland areas. The rather flimsy nature of the huts, together with the fact that the only plant remains recovered were wild species, rather points to seasonal occupation of the site.

Standing stones and landscape divisions

Single standing stones are scattered widely in western and northern Britain, and in some cases these too may relate to a transhumance system. In north Wales Emrys Bowen and Colin Gresham have shown that standing stones occur along the principal routeways into the uplands. Few have been excavated, but at Rhos-y-Clegyr, Dyfed, on the coastal plain of south-west Wales, the wall-bases of no less than seven structures were located around the standing stone. These huts had clearly been constructed and used over a considerable period of time and it is tempting to interpret this evidence as indicative of successive seasonal visits to a winter base camp.

Other than the small-scale landscape subdivisions at sites such as Fengate there is little evidence for formal land apportionment until about 1500 BC. At this time pit-alignments and boundary features begin to appear in areas as far apart as the Milfield basin of Northumberland and the high moors of Dartmoor. These developments mark the beginning of a new episode of settlement and land-use, however, and are the precursors of events after 1500 BC.

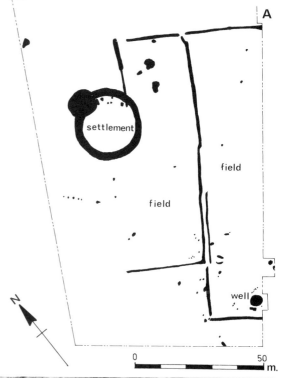

C

59 Houses and settlements of the late third and early
second millennia BC. (A) Plan of settlement and fields as
revealed by excavations at Fengate, Cambridgeshire.
(B) Stake- and post-built house dated to about 2000 BC at
Trelystan, Powys. White pegs show the positions of the
postholes forming the wall-line of the building; a central
hearth and two internal pits can be seen. Scale totals
1 metre. (C) View of the interior of house 7 at Skara Brae,
Orkney, showing the stone dresser, seat, central hearth,
tanks in the floor (for keeping shellfish in?) and beds.
[*(A) After Pryor 1978 figure 6. (B) Photo: Bill Britnell
for Clwyd Powys Archaeological Trust; copyright reserved.
(C) Photo: Mick Sharp; copyright reserved*]

5 After the Gold Rush

Agrarian Societies 1500–600 BC

Opportunities and adaptations

In the centuries following 1500 BC many of the patterns of life which had emerged in the early second millennium continued to develop. Those occupying leading positions in society formalized and strengthened their roles, and while gold declined as an indicator of power, new symbols were adopted, notably fine bronzework and weaponry. This was not, however, a period of stagnation. Change was continuous and deep-rooted. By 600 BC the pattern of society prevailing a millennium earlier had completely altered, so much so that some writers have sought to identify discontinuities in the development of society through this period, largely without success. The key to changes during the period as a whole would seem to be society's adaptability to available opportunities.

In the middle of the second millennium the climate of Britain was favourable for the expansion of settlement onto poorer soils and into upland areas. Pollen records indicate further clearance of woodland in most areas from 1700 BC onwards. Adaptation to this opportunity was clearly successful, since the later second millennium represents the zenith of prehistoric settlement in terms of the extent and intensity of occupation. But success was relatively short lived for two reasons. Firstly the soils in many newly colonized areas could not withstand continuous intensive exploitation and quickly deteriorated, and secondly a climatic amelioration in the late second millennium meant that upland settlement was no longer practical.

In the early first millennium, following the contraction of settlement, new adaptations had to be made. These will be considered more fully later in

this chapter, suffice it to say here that they set the course for the development of society over much of the following millennium.

Land management, settlement and subsistence

The single most dramatic change to the British landscape took place in the period around the middle of the second millennium BC. Clearance and expansion had been in progress for several centuries but after about 1500 BC major areas of relatively open landscape were enclosed as fields with stone banks or hedges and ditches. Superficially the settlements and fields of this early enclosure movement look similar the length and breadth of Britain. Circular houses built of wood or stone, either spread among the fields or clustered together within compounds or ditched enclosures, droveways linking settlements and fields, and small square or rectangular fields were certainly widespread, but beneath these similarities lie marked differences in local subsistence practices.

Dartmoor and the south west

Some of the most complete evidence for land-use at this period comes from Dartmoor where there has been relatively little later interference with the landscape and where a number of detailed studies have been undertaken. It seems that by about 1300 BC Dartmoor had been divided up into ten or so unequally sized units. Each unit contained valley land, hill-slope land and high open moorland which Andrew Fleming suggests was used communally,

A
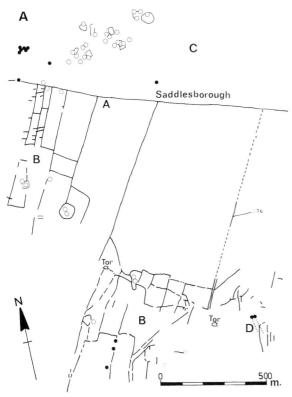

B

60 Field-systems on Dartmoor. (A) Plan of the field system on Shaugh Moor and Wotter Common.
A = terminal reave, B = parallel reave systems,
C = unenclosed moorland (grazing?), D = stone row.
Houses are shown by open circles, barrows and cairns by dots. (B) Aerial view of part of Mountsland Common, near Horridge. The well-preserved boundaries and associated houses here are part of what is probably the largest field system on Dartmoor, the Rippon Tor system which covers at least 3000 hectares. [*(A) After Smith* et al. *1981 figure 2. (B) Photo: Cambridge University Collection; copyright reserved*]

probably for grazing. Dividing the common land from the settlement units were stone banks or reaves. Natural watersheds, rivers, and other reaves marked the sides of each unit, and within the units were settlements and more reaves defining field-systems. Perhaps the most surprising thing about the way the landscape was organized is the fact that it seems to have happened as the result of a single decision rather than through piecemeal extension and elaboration around a core area.

The largest identifiable unit is around Rippon Tor on the eastern side of Dartmoor. It covers some 3300 hectares (about 6 by 6 kilometres) (8150 acres [$3\frac{3}{4}$ by $3\frac{3}{4}$ miles]) and includes several settlements.

On Dartmoor as a whole over 200 kilometres (125 miles) of reaves have so far been identified enclosing a total of over 10,000 hectares (25,000 acres). Clearly such landscape organization represents considerable investment of time and energy, and considerable political power to instigate. Most important is the fact that this landscape organization post-dates the first expansion of settlement onto the moor, since reaves overlie, and sometimes cut through, earlier cairns and stone rows.

Settlements on Dartmoor are varied. In many areas single houses lie scattered among the fields, as at Holne Moor where excavations directed by Andrew Fleming revealed a large circular dwelling built just inside one of the main terminal reaves dividing common land from enclosed land. Elsewhere enclosures predominate, as at Grimspound and Riders Rings, and at least some of these were probably herders' settlements. Excavations on Shaugh Moor have illustrated the complexity of some of these sites by demonstrating that the enclosure wall was a late addition to an unenclosed hut group. If the same sequence could be established for other sites it may point to an increasing concern for protection or defence in the early first millennium.

Elsewhere in the south-west peninsula a broadly

109

61 Mid second-millennium BC reaves, houses and settlements on Dartmoor. (A) Terminal reave at Holne Moor under excavation. The remains of the stone bank can be seen in the excavated area, and the line of the reave can be traced towards the horizon. Scale totals 1 metre. (B) House set on the terminal reave at Holne Moor under excavation. The line of the reave can be seen on the far side of the excavation. The door into the house is towards the rear left. The stone foundations would probably have supported a wooden superstructure and roof. (C) Enclosed multiphase settlement on Shaugh Moor under excavation. This site started life as one or more wooden round houses, but by about 1200 BC stone houses were being constructed and the rubble enclosure bank had been constructed. Radiocarbon dates suggest that some of the houses may have been in use for 400 years or more. [*(A) and (B) Photos: Andrew Fleming; copyright reserved. (C) Photo: Central Excavation Unit of the Historic Buildings and Monuments Commission; copyright reserved*]

C

similar pattern of settlement can be detected. At Trevisker on the north Cornish coast near St Eval, a small agricultural settlement comprised two timber round houses and ancillary buildings. The subsistence base of this settlement was cereal agriculture and animal husbandry. No field-system was identified at Trevisker but nearby, on Stannon Down on the fringes of Bodmin Moor, round stone houses amid a field system were excavated in 1968. The fields here were of two types: strip fields presumably used as garden plots for growing cereals, and larger irregular enclosures probably used as stock corrals. Quernstones were found in the huts confirming the use of cereals, but because no bone survived in the acid soil of the site no indication of what animals were kept could be obtained. At Gwithian, again on the north coast of Cornwall, a settlement dating to about 1300 BC became covered in sand after its abandonment. The homestead lay within a circular enclosure; to the south were eight fields, all clearly used for agriculture since traces of ard marks and even spade marks were found as outlines in the soft sandy subsoil.

Extensive field-systems have also been found in Penwith and on the Isles of Scilly where some of them have since been drowned by the sea. Coastal settlements abound in the south west. At Nornour, Scilly, occupation started before about 1310 ± 280 BC and a series of stone built round houses probably

represents several successive rebuildings of a long-lived but small settlement. The occupants relied upon cultivated cereals, and sheep, cattle and pigs kept on nearby pasture. Their diet was supplemented by fish and shellfish, and grey seals were hunted. Evidence of potting and stoneworking alongside the subsistence remains suggests that this small community was virtually self-sufficient.

Wessex

On the chalklands of Wessex, from Dorset across to Sussex, and also on the surrounding heaths and vales, later second-millennium BC settlement was especially dense. Both enclosed and unenclosed sites are found, many undergoing enclosure late in their life. At Shearplace Hill, Dorset, the nucleus of the settlement, loosely dated by a single radiocarbon date to 1180 ± 180 BC, lay within a small enclosure and comprised two structures, probably a house and a byre, together with a working area and a pond. Adjacent to the living area was a stock pen and a larger enclosure for cultivation. Further fields lay beyond and were linked to the settlement by a trackway. Cattle, sheep and pigs were kept. The main house was roughly circular, about 7 metres (23 feet) in diameter, and built with two concentric rings of postholes. A weaving comb from the site attests textile manufacture.

Within Cranborne Chase, Dorset, a number of sites of this period have been investigated. At South Lodge Camp, a roughly square enclosure was constructed over an earlier unenclosed settlement within a field-system. The internal organization of this enclosure is especially noteworthy. At least two circular post-built structures were located, the largest one, some 5.5 metres (18 feet) in diameter, was probably a house. The southern half of the enclosure was largely given over to storage pits. In the south-west corner was a midden and near the main house was a mound of burnt stones, possibly resulting from the cooking of meat by boiling. Similar, although less well investigated, enclosures include Harrow Hill and Martin Down. These enclosures were not always fully enclosed: Martin Down lacked one side and Angle Ditch has only two sides. At Down Farm, three sides of the enclosure are represented by a bank and ditch while the fourth was closed by a fence. Among the buildings found at this last mentioned site was a rather unusual post-built rectangular structure some 4 metres (13 feet) wide and over 13 metres (43 feet) long.

In Wiltshire settlements of this period include Rockley Down and Fyfield Down, both associated with extensive field-systems. Further east at Chalton, Hampshire, an unenclosed site dated to about 1243 ± 69 BC comprised one large round hut and a smaller hut nearby. Grain storage is suggested by the presence of pits, and sufficient capacity existed to provide for a single family of perhaps four to six people.

Throughout Wessex field-systems, often called Celtic fields, have been recognized, and many date to the late second millennium BC. They are generally fairly regular arrangements of small square or rectangular units defined by low banks or lynchets. They now survive best on steep slopes where later agricultural activity has been minimal, but once they covered much wider areas of the downlands. Two types can be defined. The first, usually termed cohesive systems, look as though they were planned and laid out in one operation, rather like the Dartmoor parallel reave systems. Large blocks of land were first defined as clear strips, or axes, and then these blocks were subdivided into fields. Whether this subdivision was for mixed cropping or due to laws of inheritance is not known. The second type of field-systems are called aggregate systems for here fields were clearly added to one another on a piecemeal basis. Some individual field-systems cover 5 square kilometres (2 square miles) or more.

In Sussex some 12 settlements of this period are known, of which Itford Hill and Black Patch are the most fully investigated. At Black Patch, excavations by Peter Drewett between 1977 and 1979 revealed a series of four house platforms distributed among an extensive field-system along the side of a hill. Platform 4 was excavated in detail and found to contain five huts dating to between 1130 ± 70 BC and 830 ± 80 BC. The central structure was the largest and contained pits for storing barley. Analysis of the pottery and artefacts scattered around the platform allow it to be interpreted as the main house and it stood within its own fenced enclosure. Two of the other buildings were also possibly houses, one of them probably the kitchen, the other a residence for dependants of the main family. The remaining two huts were probably given over to storage, or animal shelters. The economy of the settlement was basically mixed farming, exploiting the surrounding downland and valley bottom. Cattle were the dominant species of animal represented by the animal bones and barley the main crop cultivated. Marine Mollusca on the site attested occasional trips to the coast.

Eastern England

In East Anglia, the Thames valley and the Midlands the number of sites known from this period is less than from central southern England. At Mucking on the north side of the Thames Estuary, Essex, an extensive field-system was set out in the thirteenth and twelfth centuries BC with a settlement nearby. A riverside occupation site, Aldermaston Wharf on the River Kennet in Berkshire, yielded evidence for two round huts with adjacent clusters of pits, fences and a pond. Spindle whorls and loom weights attest the manufacture of textiles and there were also traces of metalworking on the site. In the Fens, the site at Fengate near Peterborough, Cambridgeshire, provides a vivid insight into a relatively complete farm of the period, laid out about 1200 BC. The mainstay of the economy here was pastoralism, and the series of small rectangular fields, bounded by ditches and hedges, was probably for stock control and winter grazing. Wells were situated in some fields. Four structures were found during excavations, two probably houses, the other two probably stock shelters. No querns were found to suggest cereal cultivation and it is concluded that the rich summer grazing on the nearby fen edge was used to support the animals.

Enclosed settlements existed in this area too. At Springfield Lyons, Essex, a settlement comprising

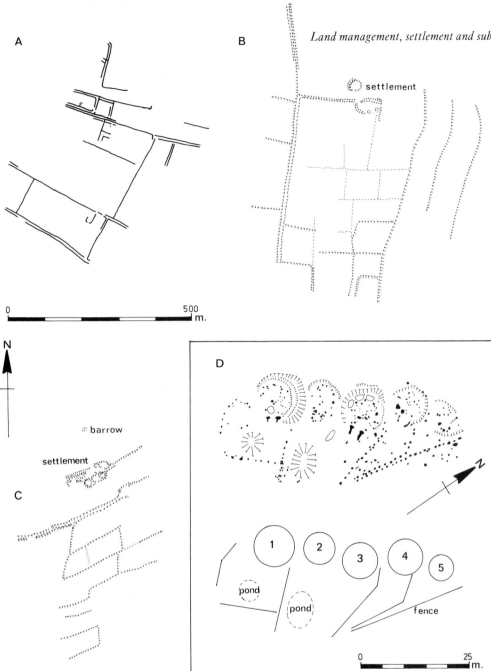

62 Late second- and early first-millennium BC settlements and field-systems in southern and eastern England. (A) Fengate, Cambridgeshire. Plan of ditches defining fields and enclosures as revealed by excavation. (B) New Barn Down, Sussex. A trackway flanked by small square fields and a settlement area recorded as earthworks during field survey. (C) Itford Hill, Sussex. Small square fields and a settlement area known through excavation and field survey. (D) Black Patch, Sussex.

Settlement area comprising five buildings as revealed by excavation (upper) and as interpreted by the excavator on the basis of finds and structural remains (lower). 1 = compound head's wife's house, also used for food preparation; 2 = animal shelter; 3 = compound head's house, also used for storage and crafts; 4 = reliant relative's house; 5 = animal shelter. [*(A) After Pryor 1980 figure 5. (B) and (C) After Drewett 1978 figures 1 and 2. (D) After Drewett 1979 figure 1*]

113

A

B

63 Enclosed farmstead at Springfield Lyons, Essex. (A) Aerial view of the site under excavation showing the enclosure ditch and numerous bedrock-cut internal features. (B) Reconstruction drawing of the site about 900 BC by Frank Gardiner. [*Photo and drawing reproduced by permission of Essex County Council Planning Department; copyright reserved*]

several round houses and the usual range of farm-yard features lay within a substantial enclosure over 65 metres (213 feet) in diameter and comprising a bank and ditch with no less than six entranceways. Further north, at Billingborough, Lincolnshire, a small square enclosure, somewhat similar to those noted above from Cranborne Chase, was the focus of a small farm. Recent ploughing had removed much of the evidence for structures, but sufficient survived to show that circular buildings had once been present. Further north still, at Thwing, Humber-side, a settlement dating to the eighth or ninth century BC lay within a defended circular enclosure. The rampart here was braced with timbers and the ditch was deep and wide. In the centre of the site was a large circular house some 28 metres (92 feet) in diameter. From this building came many objects of a domestic character including a quern, two rubbing stones, two complete loomweights, spindle whorls, pottery, and animal bones of cattle, pig, sheep and horse. Bronze weapons and personal ornaments were also found.

Wales and the west

Almost nothing is known at present of settlement during the late second and early first millennium BC in Wales and the Welsh Marches, despite the fact that numerous burial monuments and stray finds of bronze tools and weapons have come to light in the area. Recent excavations by the Dyfed Archaeological Trust on Stackpole Warren have revealed an enclosed settlement dating to about 820 ± 60 BC, but full details are not yet available. It is, however, likely that, as in other upland areas, many of the known but undated round houses and field-systems will prove to be of later second- and early first-millennium BC date when investigated.

Northern England and Scotland

In the north of England and southern Scotland upland patterns akin to those already noted from Dartmoor prevail. Arable cultivation is attested by the numerous clearance cairns characteristic of many northern upland areas. In the border counties, settlements often comprise platforms containing

64 Early first-millennium BC settlements in northern England. (a) Green Knowe, Borders. Houses number 1–9 running along the contour of the hill-slope. (b) Standrop Rigg, Linhope, Northumberland. Houses, numbered 1–6, amid fields/paddocks. [*(a) After Jobey 1983 figure 2. (b) After Jobey 1980 figure 2*]

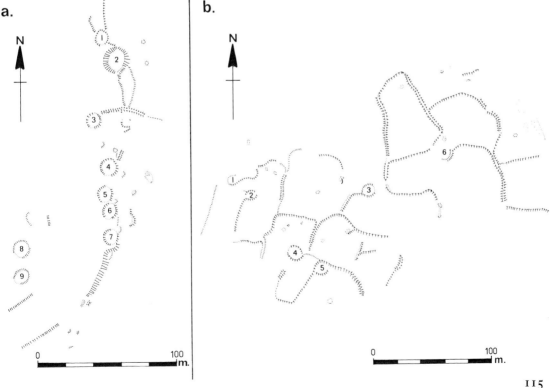

65 Burnt mound at Liddle Farm, Orkney, under excavation. The stone trough and cooking area lies in the centre of the picture with the stoney mound sectioned in the background top right. Scales each total 2 metres.
[*Photo : John Hedges ; copyright reserved*]

round stone houses arranged around the contour of the hill-slope. Aerial photography by Tim Gates and others has revealed 90 or more of these unenclosed settlements in Northumberland, and although only eight have been excavated most seem to be of early first-millennium BC date. Among those which have been excavated is Standrupp Rigg, Northumberland, which lies at 380 metres (1247 feet) above sea level in the Cheviots. Here five or six round stone houses had been built within a field-system of 2.75 hectares (7 acres) or more. Enclosed settlements are also known, as at Bracken Rigg, Northumberland, and there are also many agricultural features of this date such as the odd lengths of dyke and the L-shaped and C-shaped enclosures which were probably wind breaks for animals grazing the exposed northern hills. At Culbin Sands, Grampian, a coastal settlement broadly similar to those in south-western Britain dates from about 1259 ± 75 BC.

Perhaps the most northerly settlement known is at Jarlshof in Shetland. Here, solidly built oval houses were found, probably representing a succession of rebuildings by a small community. Each house had a central hearth with two partitioned cubicles and a larger oval chamber at the inner end. The occupants were primarily pastoralists, and some of their cattle were stalled inside one of the houses. Shellfish were also collected from the nearby shore.

Burnt mounds

One further class of site closely connected with settlement, and widespread in parts of southern England, the Midlands, Wales and the far north is the burnt mound. These comprise oval or more often crescent-shaped heaps of burnt stones with a trough or stone-lined pit at the centre. They are often situated beside streams or near water and have been interpreted as cooking sites. The burnt stones would be used to heat water in the trough, or perhaps the trough was used as an oven. Dating evidence is sparse, but structural features are similar between examples excavated at Lymington, Hampshire, and Quoyscottie in Orkney.

Burial rites and communal ritual

After 1500 BC there were major changes in the character of ritual monuments and in the treatment of the dead. Construction of round barrows over burials became less popular, and there was a swing away from inhumation burial towards a preference for cremation. Grave goods became less common and the rich series of Wessex style burials from central southern England ended. Among the last of these rich Wessex graves was one discovered at Hove, Sussex, deposited about 1239 ± 46 BC. The body had been placed in a hollowed treetrunk coffin, together with an amber cup, a polished stone battle-axe, a perforated whetstone and an ogival dagger. Interest in megalithic monuments such as Stonehenge waned too, and, as noted above, stone rows and cairns which happened to lie within areas taken into intensive cultivation were sometimes ignored and even slighted.

Burials dating to the later second millennium were sometimes added to earlier monuments, pre-sumably at least in part because of some lingering respect for the established sanctity of such places. At Dyffryn Ardudwy, Gwynedd, a cremation in a decorated urn was placed inside the chamber of a portal dolmen which had probably not been used for a thousand years or more. Likewise in Scilly, cremations were placed in the passageways of entrance graves as at Knackyboy Cairn, St Martin's. Round barrows also attracted attention, often being enlarged to take secondary burials which were simply dug into the surface of the mound. At Trelystan, Powys, a layer of turf was superimposed on the original cairn, rings of stakes were hammered in and at least five new burials were added some time shortly after 1590 ± 65 BC. Similar additions were made to the Sutton 268 Barrow, Glamorgan. Among the most spectacular must be the Knighton Heath Barrow, Dorset, where no less than 60 cremations, mostly in urns, were placed in the upper levels of an earlier barrow between 1205 ± 49 BC and 1102 ± 40 BC. Men, women and children were represented, and other than the pots containing their cremated remains there were very few grave goods.

Cremation cemeteries

In large areas of southern, central and midland England flat cremation cemeteries became common between about 1200 and 900 BC. Often these clustered round existing barrows, and were characteristically sited near to contemporary settlements.

66 Two round barrows under excavation at Trelystan, near Welshpool, Powys. Two stages in the development of the mound in the foreground can be clearly seen, with the primarily monument represented by the central stone kerbed structure and the later enlargement represented by the earth mound and concentric rings of stakeholes [*Photo: Bill Britnell for Clwyd Powys Archaeological Trust; copyright reserved*]

Thus South Lodge Camp, Dorset, has a cemetery of over 20 burials clustered around and cut into earlier barrows within 200 metres (656 feet) of the enclosure. At Itford Hill, Sussex, a sherd of pottery from the burial ground joins with a sherd from the settlement, thus confirming the intimate connection between these two sites.

It is possible that the practice of reusing old monuments owes something to a shortage of land upon which to build new barrows. Much of the farmed land in southern England was under cultivation, and barrows and ploughing do not easily mix.

Cremation burials in these flat cemeteries were usually contained in large coarse pots or urns, basically domestic vessels used for burial purposes. Regional variations in styles abound. In Cornwall the Trevisker style is common, in Hampshire, Dorset and Wiltshire the Deverel Rimbury styles, and further afield copies of the Deverel Rimbury urns are found. A number of these cemeteries have been excavated in recent years. At Kimpton, Hampshire, a cemetery dating to between 1610 ± 189 BC and 1020 ± 120 BC contained 158 urns and 164

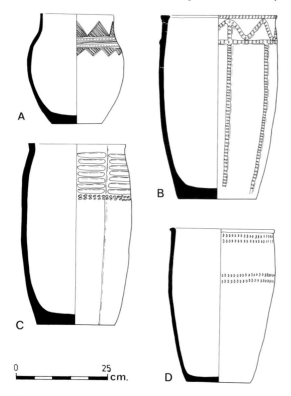

67 Globular and bucket-shaped urns of middle–late second-millennium BC date from burials in Wiltshire. [*After Annable and Simpson 1964 figures 566–569*]

cremations. Within the spread of graves were five distinct clusters, plus peripheral burials, and this is interpreted as resulting from the growth of the cemetery over time. Some 15 separate clusters of burials were recovered at Simons Ground, Dorset, where urnfields containing over 300 burials were clustered round the southern half of several earlier barrows. These urnfields spanned the period 1250 to 650 BC. Further north, on the periphery of the distribution of this type of burial, at Bromfield, Shropshire, 14 graves were found in a single cluster dating to between 1560 ± 180 and 762 ± 75 BC. Analysis of the groups of burials within these cemeteries reveals very little differentiation between burials, and except for the central positions accorded to male burials at Itford Hill and Simons Ground site G, there is little segregation of the sexes. Each cluster may in fact represent a family group plot or burial area.

In the north and west of Britain the large Deverel Rimbury urn cemeteries are absent, possibly reflecting lower population density and partly because the traditions of reusing barrow burials continued longer. At Bedd Branwen, Gwynedd, a round barrow was used as a cremation cemetery between about 1403 ± 60 and 1274 ± 81 BC. Similar cemeteries are also found in the north of England and Scotland. One at Catfoss, Humberside, lay within a penannular ring-ditch. Also widely distributed in Scotland are the enclosed cremation cemeteries consisting of unfaced ring-banks surrounding rough low cairns piled over simple cremations in pits. The example at Weird Law, Borders, has been radiocarbon dated to about 1490 ± 90 BC, while one at Whitstanes Moor, Dumfries and Galloway, is a little later, dating to 1360 ± 90 BC.

In the west of Britain cremations around standing stones are not uncommon, the stone acting as a focus or marker for a small cemetery or ritual site. At Stackpole Warren, Dyfed, a standing stone surrounded by a trapezoidal setting of over 3000 smaller stones was erected some time after about 1395 ± 65 BC. A pit dug near the standing stone contained a cremation dated to 940 ± 70 BC.

Rivers, lakes and bogs

After about 1000 BC much of the traditional burial record in Britain disappears. Only the flat cremation cemeteries continue for a period, in some cases perhaps as late as 600 BC, when these too cease to be used. Coincident with this decline in burial sites is an increase in the amount of fine metalwork found in

68 Standing stone and stone settings at Stackpole Warren, Dyfed, set up some time between 1400 and 900 BC. Scale totals 2 metres. The clay-lined oval pit in the foreground contained a burial dated to the mid second century BC. [*Photo: Don Benson for Dyfed Archaeological Trust; copyright reserved*]

69 Deposition of bronze objects in the River Thames and River Kennet compared with finds from elsewhere in Berkshire, Buckinghamshire and Oxfordshire. (a) Objects by period. 1 = early second-millennium. 2 = middle–late second-millennium. 3 = early first-millennium BC. Emphasizing the swing towards deposition in rivers. (b) Objects of early first-millennium BC date by type emphasizing the predominance of weapon finds from the rivers. [*After Ehrenberg 1980*]

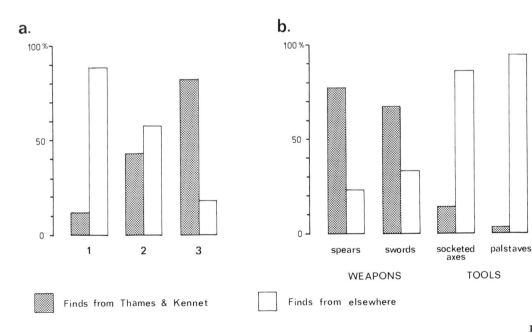

rivers, lakes and bogs. Colin Burgess has suggested that wet places became the focus of a new water cult in Britain around the turn of the first millennium, although springs and rivers may have held a special place in the beliefs of earlier societies. Of course, other explanations for the high incidence of metal objects from wet places have been offered, for example eroded river bank settlements, loss during transport and river battles, but none seems very satisfactory when it is realized that much of the metalwork recovered is not of the type usually found on settlements but rather high quality objects best seen as prestige goods. This point will be developed further later in this chapter. Weapons predominate, as they did in graves during the preceding millennium, and it seems likely that they relate to river burials and votive deposits. The Thames and Witham are particularly rich in such finds, but in the west, lakes and mires yield large quantities too. One typical example is the Broadward collection found during the drainage of a mire near Clun, Shropshire, in 1867. Many spearheads and other weapons were carried off at the time, but 70 or so items are still extant in the British Museum.

Foreign connections

Throughout the later second millennium and the early first millennium BC close ties linked Britain and her neighbours on the Continent and in Ireland, although naturally the orientation and the intensity of contact changed over the period. Particularly close ties between southern England and the Low Countries emerged between 1300 and 1100 BC. The metalwork in both areas is almost identical, suggesting considerable sharing of ideas. Pottery too shows similarities. The Wessex biconical urns found in south and south-eastern England are paralleled by Hilversum urns used at the same time in Belgium. Trevisker ware made in Cornwall has been found at Hardelot in the Pas de Calais and serves to underline the strength of the cross-Channel links. And similarities go deeper than the pottery and the metalwork. Stake circles beneath barrows are found on both sides of the Channel at this time, and the rectangular wooden building at Martin Down, Dorset, finds its best parallels at Deventer and Hoogskarspel in the Netherlands where such structures are characteristic of settlement sites during this period.

A second period of intensive European contact in the eight and seventh centuries BC introduced new inspiration for pottery styles in the form of angular bowls which replaced the post-Deverel Rimbury wares of the tenth to eight centuries. Exchange of metalwork between Britain and the Continent continued, although whether the users of bronze tools and weapons here in Britain were aware of the distant origins of some pieces we shall never know. Particular mention may be made of the so-called 'ornament horizon' of the twelfth century BC when, in southern England, there was a revival of interest in manufacturing ornaments. The inspiration for many of these items, mostly pins, armlets and torcs, lay directly across the Channel in northern France; some may indeed be direct imports.

It was not just high-status items such as ornaments and weapons which were exchanged over wide areas. One farmer who lived at Horridge Common in the heart of Dartmoor during the thirteenth century BC acquired a bronze palstave probably manufactured in Bohemia, but he appears to have lost it out in his fields some time later. Movement in the other direction is represented by a number of finds, among them a hoard of bronzes from the Dutch Voorhout which contained North Wales pattern palstaves made in metal from North Wales. Whether this hoard was deposited by an itinerant Welsh smith or a trader will never be known, but it does make the point that many bronze objects of the period have been found as hoards, some possibly deposited or hidden for safety in times of trouble. Another example is the group of gold objects from Islay, Strathclyde, western Scotland, probably an Irish tradesman's hoard.

Artefacts are the more tangible side of foreign exchange. So much contact between Britain and Europe and Ireland is attested that some common language must have been spoken even though we do not know what it was. Political and social unrest elsewhere in Europe can also be detected in Britain through clues in the patterns of foreign exchange. In the early twelfth century BC the Mediterranean world was thrown into chaos by raiders (known collectively as the Sea People or the Philistines of Biblical account) who probably came from or drew mercenaries from northern and central Europe. Whether anyone from Britain was involved is not clear, although adventurers on such raids would provide a convenient context for the arrival in Britain of Mycenean and Cypriot metalwork of thirteenth- to twelfth-century BC date. Sadly none of the pieces known to date has been found in a secure archaeological deposit, which makes evaluation very difficult. What is clear, however, is that the experience gained by European armourers in supplying weapons to mercenaries fighting in the Mediterranean promoted the introduction of new weapon types such as swords and shields to Britain before the eleventh century BC. With the emergence of the first warrior aristocracy in Europe, Britain was kept well supplied with new ideas for weapons and military equipment.

At present no ships which can be said to be sea-going vessels are known from this period, although they must have existed. Over 20 log-boat canoes have been found dating from the second millennium BC and earlier, and three plank-built boats, variously dating to between 1430 ± 100 BC for boat 1 and 750 ± 150 BC for boat 3, have come to light in the river mud at North Ferriby, Humberside. All these crafts were probably for riverine travel. Two wrecks of ocean-going boats of the period are known from their cargoes, however. The earliest probably dates to about 1100 BC and lies just off Dover. The cargo, which has been recovered by divers, includes over 95 bronze objects, many broken and all seemingly of Continental origin. Daggers, dirks, rapiers and

palstaves were among the objects found. The second cargo is more modest, comprising a mere seven objects: two palstaves, four blades and a sword. It was found off Salcombe, Devon, but the search for more pieces continues.

Crafts, industry and exchange

Arguably the most visible impact of foreign connections at this time was the effect on the manufacture of goods. Many studies have been carried out on the bewildering range of metal objects from the period, as for a long time metal objects were the only things that could be positively attributed to the early first millennium BC. With more radiocarbon dates and new excavations it is now possible to fill the picture out a bit more fully.

Domestic crafts

Domestic crafts provided the main items for everyday use, and many settlements were probably largely self-sufficient. Pottery, for example, was generally made from local clays even though regional styles betray wider community affinities. Pottery traditions, including the Trevisker series of the south west and the Deverel Rimbury wares of central England, can be traced back to their roots in the early second millennium BC among grooved ware, food vessels, and collared urns. After about 1000 BC new styles, with more angular profiles, generally called post-Deverel Rimbury wares, appear in the south as a result of Continental inspiration, while in the north flat-rimmed ware in a coarse thick fabric became popular.

Flintwork declined in importance and competence, and stone tools too found less use as metal tools for the craftsman became widespread. This change is nowhere less graphically illustrated than at Grimes Graves, Norfolk, where a metalworker set up a workshop in the twelfth century BC amid the hollows of the previously prosperous flint mines.

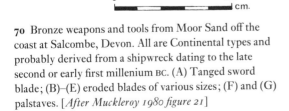

70 Bronze weapons and tools from Moor Sand off the coast at Salcombe, Devon. All are Continental types and probably derived from a shipwreck dating to the late second or early first millenium BC. (A) Tanged sword blade; (B)–(E) eroded blades of various sizes; (F) and (G) palstaves. [*After Muckleroy 1980 figure 21*]

Bronze, iron and gold

The development of the metalwork industry has been charted by Colin Burgess who recognizes five industrial stages between about 1500 and 600 BC, each conveniently named after a typical assmeblage. In chronological order these are the Taunton phase, the Penard phase, the Wallington/Wilburton phase, the Ewart Park phase and the Llyn Fawr phase.

Mike Rowlands has suggested that during the earliest of these, the Taunton and the Penard phases, metalworking took place at two distinct levels. Local industries geared up to making small items such as tools, small spearheads and ornaments were widespread. From visible similarities between individual products and occasional evidence for use of the same mould it seems that each smith was working to produce bronzes for communities within a radius of 15 to 20 kilometres (9 to 12½ miles). Whether there were fixed local workshops or whether the smith moved round to settlements within this area is not clear. Hoards of finished and part-finished tools, however, suggest that at least in the south smiths worked seasonally and cast a sufficient number of items to provide a stock for subsequent use and distribution.

At an altogether different level, regional industries can be recognized from similarities in product design and casting technique used over wide areas. These items are exclusively weapons: rapiers, large spearheads and, later, swords. Such items are rarely found in hoards alongside the more prosaic pieces, and they generally display more complex casting technology. The Thames valley emerged as one of the major production centres, but other centres too must have been active, probably one in East Anglia and one in the south west.

Metal ores were certainly being worked fairly widely in the west of Britain by the turn of the second millennium, and a radiocarbon date of 990 ± 80 BC from charcoal mixed with mining waste in a gallery deep within a copper mine on Great Ormes Head, Llandudno, Gwynedd, suggests that some workings were on a considerable scale. Bun-shaped copper ingots represent the form in which raw metal was transported to the eastern-based smiths. To what extent bronze objects were recycled at this time is unknown.

From about 1000 BC (the Wilburton industrial phase) the metalworking industry undergoes a period of change which gathers pace in the eighth century. Lead bronze, which although softer allows more complex castings to be made, became common first in the south and later throughout Britain. The two-tier system of production broke down, and all types of object were made locally, although the Thames valley remained in the vangard of developments, possibly because of its close ties with the Continent. Smiths obviously kept well abreast of changes in techniques and styles and it seems likely that they emerged as full-time specialists, possibly with patronage from a chief or leader.

Obtaining three types of raw material, copper, tin and lead, to make new castings implies a complicated distribution network, and it is perhaps a reflection of this complexity that hoards of scrap metal, sometimes associated with metalworkers' tools and moulds, became very common at this time. Sophisticated two- and three-piece moulds were developed and sheet metalworking was more widely practised, again through Continental inspiration, to produce buckets, cauldrons and shields which seem to have been added to the range of prestige items produced by the eighth century, if not earlier. Other new types included constantly changing weapon designs, socketed sickles, knives, new razors and horse harness fittings. It was also at this time that metal objects, particularly the larger and more complex items, began to be deposited as votive hoards in rivers, lakes and bogs. This conspicuous consumption of wealth created a continuous and ravenous demand for new goods and probably promoted innovation and experiment.

Whether because of difficulties in obtaining supplies of bronze, or for some other reason such as an increased demand for metal goods, British smiths began using iron from about 650 BC. Iron ores were much more widely available than copper, tin and lead, and would have involved fewer well co-ordinated exchanges to obtain supplies. The techniques of roasting and smelting were, however, much more difficult than for the softer non-ferrous metals and required higher temperatures. At first iron objects were direct copies of bronze ones, sickles, axes and edged tools and weapons being the most common. All early ironwork was forged, presumably because casting produced very brittle and therefore quite useless tools and weapons. Early products were hardly of better quality than their bronze counterparts, although iron would have provided a longer-lasting cutting edge. At Llyn Fawr, Glamorgan, a hoard of 21 objects was found in a lake high up in the hills. Among these items was an iron spearhead and an iron sickle as well as an assortment of bronze axes, sickles, spearheads, horse harness fittings and a cauldron.

Goldworking continued alongside bronzeworking and ironworking for the manufacture of ornaments such as bracelets, torcs and sleeve fastners. On the Dorset coast Kimmeridge shale also was worked into bracelets and other ornaments at Eldon's Seat, among other places, and Channel coal was worked at Swine Sty, Derbyshire. One of the most splendid items manufactured in shale is the Caergwle bowl found near Caergwle Castle, Clwyd in 1823. The

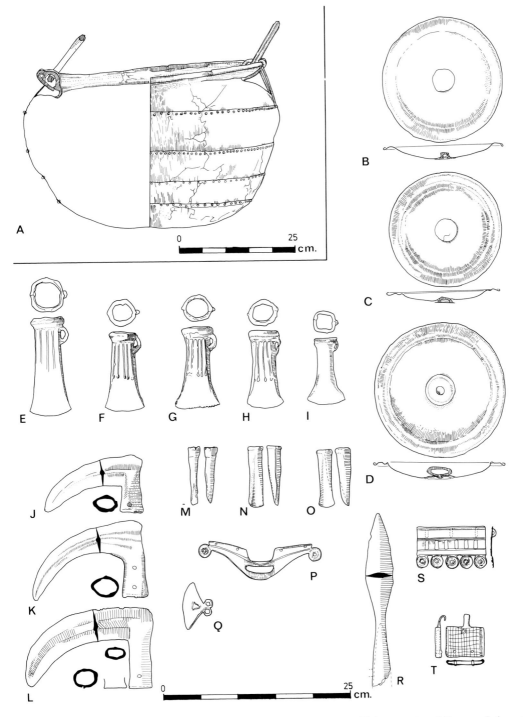

71 Finds from the Llyn Fawr hoard, Glamorgan.
(A) Sheet bronze cauldron; (B)–(D) bronze horse harness discs; (E)–(I) cast bronze socketed axes; (J) and (K) cast bronze sickles; (L) wrought iron sickle; (M)–(O) bronze socketed gouges; (P) bronze winged ?harness fittings; (Q) bronze razor; (R) wrought iron spear; (S) and (T) bronze harness fittings. [*After Savory 1976 figures 2, 10 and 11*]

123

A

72 Early first-millennium BC woodworking.
(A) Flag Fen, Peterborough, Cambridgeshire. Remains of wooden buildings and structures set on a wooden platform and dating to about 800 BC. Worked timbers can be clearly seen. Originally the site lay within a shallow lake or marsh. (B) Pieces of worked and jointed ash planks dating to about 700 BC from Withy Bed Copse, Somerset. [*(A) Photo: Francis Pryor (Fenland Archaeological Trust); copyright reserved. (B) Photo: Somerset Levels Project; copyright reserved*]

object is boat-shaped and is generally regarded as being a votive boat, the decoration representing shields, oars, waves and the ribs of the boat itself.

Woodworking was widespread and important although poorly represented archaeologically. Waterlogged deposits in a ritual shaft or well sunk 33 metres (108 feet) into solid chalk at Wilsford in the middle of Salisbury Plain, Wiltshire, yielded a wooden bowl and fragments of a bucket dated to about 1380 ± 90 BC, and provide tantalizing glimpses of the sort of objects which must have been commonplace. Wooden boats have already been mentioned, and trackways are known from this period in the Somerset Levels. Perhaps most impressive of all, however, is the timber platform at Flag Fen, Cambridgeshire, preserved in the silts and peat of the East Anglian Fens. Excavations by Francis Pryor have uncovered an occupation site which originally lay within a shallow lake or lagoon. The platform itself contains thousands of worked timbers, and there are also the foundations of timber buildings.

Textile production is attested from the later second millennium BC onwards by loom weights, spindle worls and weaving combs from a number of sites in southern England. After 1000 BC such finds are also known from northern Britain.

Exchange practices

How goods such as fine pottery, querns and metalwork were exchanged between areas and between communities is unclear. Some bronze hoards suggest itinerant traders, but over what area they operated or whether other explanations should be invoked to explain the evidence cannot be said. Communal meeting places may have existed over much of southern England in the late second millennium BC, and four possible sites have so far been identified: Rams Hill, Oxfordshire, Norton Fitzwarren, Somerset, Highdown Hill, Sussex, and Martin Down, Dorset. Other sites undoubtedly await discovery, perhaps in Kent and Devon. Only Rams Hill has been extensively excavated, although the others have similar features according to more limited excavations and surface traces. At Rams Hill a substantial timber-laced earthwork dating to the eleventh century BC bounded the occupation area but had several entrances leading off in different directions. There were very few traces of domestic occupation and it is notable that the site overlooks a range of different landscapes. Moreover, pottery from the site represented many different fabrics and was drawn from a wide hinterland. Ann Ellison has found that weapon and ornament finds cluster in the neighbourhood of these enclosure sites and suggests that each acted as a focus for the distribution of objects, and accordingly were located at the junction of several community areas. In this way they served to link small-scale interlocking exchange networks.

Horse riding and wagons

It is not known when horse riding was first practised in Britain, but it was possibly as early as the turn of the second millennium BC. From the tenth century BC, however, it apparently took on an extra importance because for the first time harness fittings appear in the archaeological record. The earliest pieces are cheek pieces and strip fittings, the former in antler or bronze, the latter always in bronze. British specimens are identical with Continental pieces of the same date. Other associated objects include nave bands, pendants and bronze *phalera*, all

73 Distribution of late second-millennium BC pottery
styles and main enclosures. 1 = Norton Fitzwarren,
Somerset. 2 = Martin Down, Dorset. 3 = Ram's Hill,
Oxfordshire. 4 = Highdown Hill, Sussex.
[*Source: author*]

of which are closely linked with horse riding in Europe. The large hoard of objects deposited in a cave at Heathery Burn, Durham, contained a variety of horse trappings as did the Llyn Fawr hoard from Glamorgan. Finds have also come to light on settlements including the eighth-century site beside the Thames at Egham, Surrey, which may have been operative as a trading site and boasts the earliest wooden waterfront yet known in Britain.

Some of the horse tackle suggests the presence of wagons or carts. When wheels were first introduced into Britain is as problematical as when horses were first ridden, but again wheels were used on the Continent from about 2000 BC and there is no reason to think that they were not known to those living in Britain too. Exactly how wagons or carts of this period were used is not known. There were no roads to speak of and it seems likely that, as with so many innovations of this period, they were simply for display. It is notable that horse gear is very rare in the north and west, presumably reflecting the more rugged terrain.

Environmental change?

It is always difficult to know how much emphasis to place on long-term environmental change as a factor in social change. A succession of bad harvests and even minor fluctuations in weather patterns can be disastrous for communities living in marginal areas, but around the turn of the first millennium BC environmental changes seem to have had a wide-ranging effect. Temperatures generally fell and rainfall increased. This was accompanied by widespread coastal inundation.

Cooler wetter conditions are also implied by a renewed episode of track building in the Somerset Levels, and many upland areas and marginal lowland areas like the New Forest, the Dorset heaths, and the Surrey heaths were abandoned. On Dartmoor and in many upland parts of Wales blanket bog began to form over abandoned fields during the early first millennium BC. Soil fertility in these areas did not recover and natural woodland did not regenerate. Paradoxically, although these areas are often considered 'natural' by today's visitors and tourists, most of our moors and heaths owe their origin to the phase of widespread settlement and intensive land-use in the second millennium BC. Another indicator of a wetter climate may be the interest in wet places shown by the apparently preferential deposition of metalwork in rivers, lakes and bogs.

Weapons, forts and ranches

The settlement expansion in the early second millennium and the intensification of land-use after 1500 BC implies an overall increase in population, and more particularly population density, over much of Britain. Thus the effects of soil exhaustion and climatic deterioration after 1000 BC would have created considerable stress as diminishing resources were expected to support the high population levels. Especially badly hit were areas flanking the marginal lands of western Britain. The changes which resulted from this social pressure are most clearly seen in southern Britain, but, as we shall see in a later section, the north did not escape unscathed.

Fields and boundaries

Perhaps the most visible sign of change in the early first millennium was in the organization of the landscape. It was not only the field-systems of upland areas which were abandoned, the Celtic fields of Wessex and the Midlands also fell out of use and in their place the landscape was divided up into large open areas by linear earthworks—ranch boundaries as they are sometimes called. These boundaries were not set out evenly and regularly as the field-systems had been, rather they are sinuous straggly lines of bank and ditch running for many kilometres across the countryside with every suggestion that their creation was a compromise boundary between the landowners on either side. In Hampshire and Wiltshire they are especially numerous, but are less common in Dorset west of the River Stour. Most are from 3 to 6 metres (10 to 20 feet) across and are sometimes aligned on earlier barrows and natural landscape features.

Outside Wessex linear boundaries are often badly preserved but are nonetheless present and can sometimes be found through aerial photography. Reconnaissance work by Jim Pickering has revealed many boundaries in the Midlands, some certainly of this period, and similar earthworks have been detected in Humberside, Yorkshire, Cumbria, Shropshire, Gloucestershire and Berkshire. In some cases they divide plateau land, elsewhere they cut off promontories.

Associating linear boundaries with a particular subsistence economy is more difficult. Few have been excavated, and they would not necessarily provide evidence of date and function anyway. It is noteworthy, however, that at Grimthorpe, Humberside, cattle bones accounted for 54 per cent of all bones recovered, and at Ivinghoe Beacon, Buckinghamshire, cattle bones represented 60 per cent of bones found in the eighth-century levels.

Settlements of the early first millennium BC show a general, although not universal, tendency to be enclosed. This probably stems from a trend towards enclosure in the late second millennium, exemplified at sites such as Shaugh Moor on Dartmoor and South Lodge Camp on Cranborne Chase, which both began life as open sites. In lowland areas rectangular and circular enclosures became common; examples of the latter include Grimthorpe, already referred to, and Mucking, Essex, where two such enclosures overlie the earlier field-system. Most show signs of a mixed economy, although cattle are the most numerous animal species. The range of crops is supplemented at this time by the introduction of rye, perhaps another indication of the need to produce food in less favourable conditions.

Defended enclosures and weapons

In a few areas, notably the Welsh Marches and other upland peripheries, hill-top settlements developed, as at Mam Tor, Derbyshire, where round huts were terraced into the upper hill-slopes around 1000 BC. None of these early hill-top settlements was defended, perhaps because their position alone provided safety. But by the seventh century hill-top enclosures certainly were being built. The principles of rampart building, such as were being used at sites on lower ground from the beginning of the first millennium BC, were applied to hill-top sites with great effect and heralded the start of several centuries of intensive and widespread hillfort building.

Three sites in the northern part of the Welsh Marches at Breiddin, Powys, Moel-y-Gaer, Clwyd, and Dinorben, Clwyd, illustrate this development very well. All were seemingly occupied in the eighth century BC, but none of them was undisputably enclosed or fortified at this time. Charcoal from postholes of the primary rampart at Breiddin provided a primary date of 740 ± 70 BC, while a second determination on charcoal from the core of the rampart yielded a date of 560 ± 60 BC. Together these suggest a sixth- or seventh-century date for the establishment of the defences. The same applies at Dinorben, where radiocarbon dates from excavations on the site by Hubert Savory suggest occupation during the ninth century, but from more recent excavations by Graeme Guilbert it is clear that the defences were not built until about 460 ± 30

BC. At Moel-y-Gaer the first phase of the defences, dated to about 620 ± 70 BC, comprised a palisaded enclosure, which was followed about 580 ± 90 BC by a more substantial rampart.

Further afield, the site of Crickley Hill, Gloucestershire, had emerged as a heavily defended hillfort with a timber-laced stone rampart by 640 ± 60 BC, according to radiocarbon dates on wood from the lowest tier of the rampart lacing. Mam Tor, Derbyshire, was another site defended early in the history of hillfort building, but probably not as early as the initial occupation of the hill-top.

The need for defence, illustrated by the emergence of the hillforts, is approximately coincident with the development of a greater range of weapons. The first swords in Britain were developed, with Continental influence, from rapiers. These were jabbing swords, however, and of limited use for fighting. From the ninth century BC slashing swords of leaf-shaped outline appear. The earliest examples were introduced from the Continent and are mostly found in the Thames valley and the south east of Britain. A British series soon developed and thereafter swords underwent almost continuous modification and refinement to their design, especially the hilts. Round metal shields appear in Britain before the ninth century, presumably imitations of more practical leather or wooden examples which simply do not survive. Some regional preferences can be detected in the types of weapon used: swords in the south, and to the north of the Thames spearheads. After the eighth century, however, swords became more widespread.

Horses were important to the warriors of the early first millennium. Evidence for harness arrangements has already been mentioned but their value for the swordsman is emphasized by the fact that winged chapes to grace the end of sword scabbards developed after the introduction of the slashing sword, presumably so that the sword could be drawn while riding by hooking the chape under the left foot.

There is good evidence to suggest that some of the weaponry known from this period saw action. From Tormarton, Avon, the remains of two young men were found buried in a pit or ditch. The first body had a hole through the pelvis caused by a bronze spearhead being thrust into his right side. The second body had a similar hole through the pelvis, traces of a severe blow to the head and the tip of a bronze spearhead embedded in his spine. A radiocarbon date suggests that this incident took place about 977 ± 90 BC.

Raiding may have been one component of war-

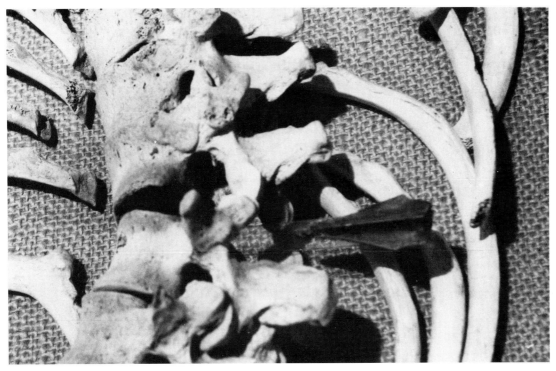

74 Burial from Tormarton, Avon, showing the tip of a bronze spearhead in the spine of a young adult male. The position where the tip lodged can be seen by the staining on the vertebrae. Dated to about 950 BC. [*Photo: author by permission of Bristol City Museum; copyright reserved.* BRSMG: *113/1968*]

fare, and Hubert Savory has rather speculatively suggested that some or all of the objects in the Llyn Fawr hoard from Glamorgan were booty obtained during a raid on Somerset or some other area of the south west by the hill folk of Glamorgan.

It is, however, important to distinguish between the functional weapons on the one hand and on the other those which are too ornate to be useful and which were presumably just for show. The importance of such parade weapons can be traced back to the battle-axes and copper daggers of the early second millennium, although by the first millennium the range and quality of such items was outstanding. The spearheads of Broadward type with their large flat blades and pointed barbs, the round beaten bronze shields and indeed some of the ornate swords could not have served in battle, and, not surprisingly, are rarely found in damaged condition. As Colin Burgess has remarked, the sensible warrior would have equipped himself with something more practical once the parading about stopped and the real fighting began.

Salt production

In the early first millennium the first firm evidence for the widespread production of salt from sea-water appears in the archaeological record. Much of the evidence comes from the east coast of England and the south west. Sea-water was probably first evaporated off in large open saltpans and then the remaining concentrated brine reduced by boiling. It is this phase of saltmaking which leaves archaeological evidence. Coarse ceramic vessels, made in a crude fabric called briquetage, were used in the boiling process together with various ceramic stands and supports. It is likely that saltmaking was seasonal, only practised during the summer when high temperatures permitted natural evaporation

At Walton-on-the-Naze, Essex, a saltworking site now on the foreshore has been dated to 1070 ± 90 BC, and other sites in the area are probably of very similar age. Saltmaking equipment has been found in a pit dating to about 600 BC at Mucking on the Thames Estuary and also in the part-filled ditches of the field-system at Fengate, Cambridgeshire, seemingly abandoned in the ninth century. It is possible that the brine springs of Droitwich, which are amongst the purest in Europe, were also being exploited by this time. Exactly why there should be an interest in large-scale salt production during the

75 Clay vessels and equipment used in salt production at Mucking, Essex, in the early first millennium BC. The circular object bottom right measures 65 millimetres in diameter. [*Photo: W. T. Jones APRS FSA; copyright reserved*]

first millennium BC is not at present clear. It is, however, tempting to associate it with the rise in ranching and the need to preserve meat and provide stock with vital salt intake.

Ripples in the north

Many of the changes already described in southern Britain during the first few centuries of the first millennium BC can also be detected in the evidence available from the far north. In general, however, things took longer to reach these remote areas and some short-lived traditions such as the carp's tongue type swords never spread beyond south-eastern England.

Regional and local traditions of metalwork developed and a metalworking area replete with a mould for a seventh-century Ewart Park type sword was excavated at Jarlshof in Shetland. Traditions of depositing metalwork in wet places were common, and are well illustrated by the five or six round bronze shields apparently found set in a regular ring in a bog at Luggtonridge Farm, Beith, Strathclyde. From the eighth century BC flat-rimmed pottery in coarse bucket-shaped vessels became widespread and is found on settlement sites.

Settlements, like their southern counterparts, tended to be defended, often with a palisade. Over 60 such sites are known on the Cheviots, in Northumberland and Borders, although not all are of the same

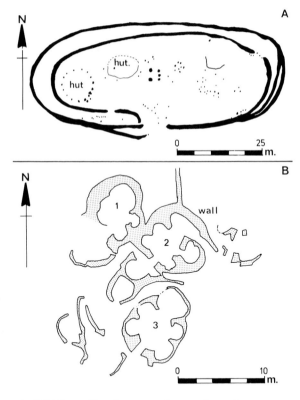

76 Mid first-millennium BC settlements in northern England and Scotland. (A) Staple Howe, North Yorkshire. Multiphase palisaded enclosure. (B) Jarlshof, Shetland. Clustered houses. [*(A) After Brewster 1963; (B) After Hamilton 1956*]

77 Distribution of regional metalworking traditions and
hillforts in the early first millennium BC. [*Based on
Cunliffe 1978 figure 4.1 with minor changes and additions*]

date. Similar settlements also occur in North Yorkshire, as at Staple Howe, which was founded by the sixth century if not earlier. Fenton Hill, another palisaded enclosure in Northumberland, was constructed in the eighth century. Some of these sites continued relatively unchanged into the later first millennium; others, like Fenton Hill, were later defended. In the far north open settlements predominated. Jarlshof has already been mentioned and nearby is the site of Clickhimin where a similar sequence is evident with the earliest phase being an oval cubicled house built entirely of stone. By the sixth–seventh century BC forts were being built in the far north, often with timber-laced ramparts which were fired to produce a vitrified wall. At Finavon, Tayside, a radiocarbon date of 590 ± 90 BC dates the charred beams of the first rampart.

Society and politics

After a millennium of continuous adaptation and change, the societies which covered most of Britain in the early first millennium were very different from their second-millennium BC predecessors. The early chiefdoms discussed in the last chapter had by this time become cemented into powerful political units, forming their own destiny and seemingly prepared to fight each other for power or resources.

Defining the territories of these societies is extremely difficult. Localized autonomous or semi-autonomous communities undoubtedly provided the basic social unit, but on a larger scale Colin Burgess has been able to discern three broad social areas each with a distinct repertoire of weaponry in the eighth–seventh century. The first extends over a great triangular area with its apex in South Yorkshire, extending down the Marches and spreading out into the south west and southern England and the Thames valley. Here there was a preference for

spearmen and much attention to the water cult. These Broadward tradition spearmen hemmed in the carps tongue weapon tradition province of south-eastern England where swords and spears were used together. To the north of the Broadward tradition area, stretching from Yorkshire to Aberdeen, was a third region characterized by swordsmen's hoards containing up to three swords with accompanying chapes and rings.

But there were other features of this society emerging in the early first millennium BC besides the warrior element and these deserve mention because of their implications for the later first millennium. First there is a hierarchy of settlement with small open settlements and larger enclosed or defended sites. Whether this corresponds to a hierarchy within society is not clear, but it does seem that not everyone had access to the fine metalwork so commonly deposited in wet places. The evidence available for metalworking suggests that the skilled smiths engaged in making weapons and fine sheet metal objects were closely tied to a chief or powerful leader. Horsemanship, combat and display were closely linked and clearly a fundamental part of the political system. European influence was strong and a common language can be suspected.

Feasting may have been a part of the ceremonial too. The large cauldrons and buckets found in Britain stand at the head of a long-lived tradition of eating and drinking ceremonies which were common over large parts of Europe throughout the first millennium. Accompanying some cauldrons are so-called flesh-hooks used to serve the contents of the container. If later analogies are correct then meat was cooked in these sheet bronze vessels and served with the flesh-hook in such a way that the precise standing of each warrior in the chief's retinue would be reflected in the particular portion of meat given to him. These things combined are the first signs of what may be identified as Celtic society in Britain.

6 Below the Salt

Tribes and Chiefdoms 600–100 BC

Amelioration, population and continuity

The events of the early first millennium BC set the stage for what followed. Fewer resources balanced against greater demands, whether because of environmental change, or social factors, or a combination of the two, led to a period of aggression, unrest, uncertainty and tension. Traditionally the emergence of a hillfort-based society after about 650 BC is interpreted as the response to these conflicts, and in some areas this is true. But taking Britain as a whole, the problems of the early first millennium were resolved in different ways in different places. Especially important were regional variations in subsistence economy and in political organization.

The deterioration of the climate which has been assumed during the early first millennium was replaced by an amelioration after about 600 BC. Warmer and drier conditions prevailed until, by about 300 BC, the climate was probably very much like that of today. Upland settlement remained sparse, mostly focused around the fringes and in sheltered valleys, but in lowland areas settlement probably expanded.

In contrast to earlier periods, the archaeology of the later first millennium BC is dominated by its settlements. Most well known are the hillforts, of which over 3000 have been recorded in Britain as a whole. But the term hillfort is used very widely and is often mistakenly applied to any hill-top defended settlement, to the extent that many regional and chronological variations are concealed. In addition to hillforts, several other types of settlement may be recognized: palisaded enclosures of various sorts, unenclosed villages, brochs, duns, raths, crannogs, and many more. So many settlements are known in some areas that an overall increase in the size of the population, and in population density, is suggested. Perhaps most surprising is that even the heavy clay lands of southern Britain, traditionally regarded as densely wooded and unpopulated until medieval times, were under intensive exploitation by the first century BC.

Aggression and warfare continued to be central to social relations in the later first millennium, although the ways of containing and legitimizing them changed over time. In this, settlements themselves were not the main factor, rather they were simply reflections of specific types of social and economic organization—the form of an individual site being largely dictated by its status, economic function, subsistence base, and local environment. Again, taking Britain as a whole it is evident that the large regional groupings of the earlier first millennium started to disintegrate after about 600 BC. This is most clearly visible in the growing regionalization of artefact styles and settlement types, diversification of the subsistence base and greater self-sufficiency among individual communities. Control of the supply of essential resources, among them metal ores, salt and imported luxury items, also became important in some areas. These changes are the key to understanding the differing responses to the problems of the early first millennium. In very general terms, five regions, each pursuing a slightly different course of development, can be identified: southern, central and western England; eastern England; Atlantic Britain; northern and northeastern England; and eastern Scotland. Each area is considered in detail in the following sections.

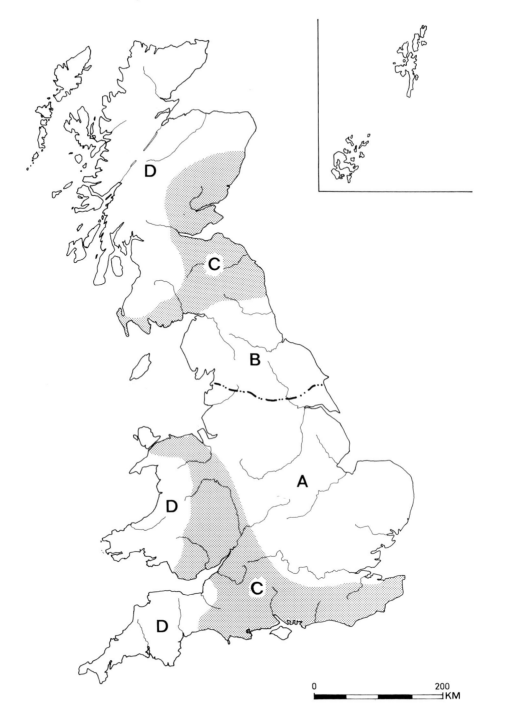

78 Generalized distribution of the main regional settlement types in Britain during the fifth to second centuries BC. (A) = Hamlets and open settlements; (B) = enclosed homesteads; (C) = hillfort dominated zones; (D) = defended homesteads and enclosures. [*Based on Cunliffe 1978 figure 16.2 and Rivet (ed.) 1967 end map*]

Southern, central and western England, and North Wales

This region, occupying a broad crescent sweeping across the country from Kent and Sussex in the south, westward through Hampshire and Dorset, northward through Wiltshire, Gloucestershire, Hereford and Worcester, and then up through the Welsh Marches into North Wales, has been christened the hillfort-dominated zone by Barry Cunliffe. It was in this area that the greatest effects of early first-millennium changes were felt, and here many of the earliest hillforts sprang up.

The early hillforts

In the years following 600 BC a rash of defended sites spread across this area. Broadly speaking they fall into two types—small defended village-like hillfort settlements and large hill-top enclosures.

The defended village-like hillforts followed the tradition of hillfort building which emerged in the eighth or seventh century BC; indeed sites like Breiddin, Powys, and Crickley Hill, Gloucestershire, continued through several phases spanning the middle years of the first millennium. In general

79 Reconstruction drawings of the successive phases of occupation within the hillfort on Crickley Hill, Gloucestershire. (a) Long house period settlement dated to about 600 BC. (b) Round house period settlement dated to about 500 BC. [*After Dixon and Borne 1977 figures 2 and 3*]

these sites were fairly small, between 0.5 and 2.5 hectares ($1\frac{1}{4}$ and 6 acres), and were set in easily defensible positions—hill-tops, promontories and escarpments. All have well-constructed ramparts, often timber revetted, with faced inner and outer walls. A single line of defences was preferred, and gateways, as weak points, received special attention. Many forts had elaborate gate-towers over the entranceways. In southern England outworks and rampart extensions were constructed to create a tunnel-shaped or oblique approach to the gates themselves, and as time went by these elaborations tended to set the gateway further and further back from the portal. In the west an alternative elaboration was common, a pair of guard chambers flanked the entrance just inside the gateway, as for example at Leckhampton, Gloucestershire, and Titterstone Clee, Shropshire.

Inside these forts occupation was usually fairly dense, and many show signs of periodic remodelling. At Crickley Hill, Gloucestershire, two phases can be discerned. The early phase was characterized by rectangular houses together with 4-post structures of a type found widely in Britain and generally interpreted as raised granaries. Later, the rectangular houses were replaced by round houses, post-built and up to 15 metres (49 feet) in diameter. At Moel-y-Gaer, Clwyd, two phases can also be recognized. At first the site was bounded by a timber palisade with post-built round structures, some of which were dwellings in the interior. In the second phase 4-posters clustered immediately behind a

a.

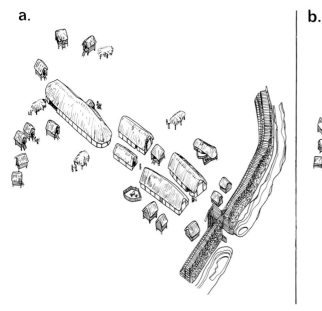

b.

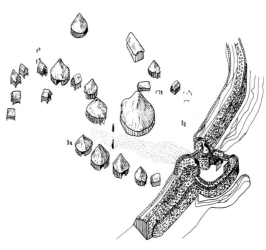

substantial rampart, while further inside the fort, stake walled round structures predominated. Further south, at Danebury, Hampshire, the early phase, radiocarbon dated to about 500 ± 80 BC, also contained many round houses, but instead of 4-posters, which were rather few in number, circular pits or silos were dug into the solid chalk. It was estimated that the total grain capacity of the investigated pits for this early phase was about 1163 cubic metres (1521 cubic yards). Assuming this sample (about one-fifth of the area within the fort) is representative, then the hillfort as a whole may have had the capacity to store up to 6000 cubic metres (7800 cubic yards) of grain. If each pit had a life of about 10 years before being replaced then the annual capacity would be about 621 cubic metres (807 cubic yards), quite enough to feed over 1000 people for a year and still leave sufficient for seed corn.

Within most early hillforts which have been excavated there is evidence for discrete patterning of activities in the layout of the interior, with roadways, living areas, storage areas and so on. To what extent this results from deliberate planning, or simply the commonsense of the inhabitants wanting to minimize the risk of fire spreading through the site and ordering their daily activities, is a matter for debate. It does, however, seem that, once established, patterns of use within the interior of most sites were adhered to for long periods.

Experiments have shown that pits provide an extremely efficient way of storing grain. Research by Peter Reynolds at the Butser Hill Experimental Farm, Hampshire, has demonstrated that, once sealed down, grain-filled pits develop a carbon dioxide rich atmosphere which prevents the germination of all but the outermost layer of grain. Only about 2 per cent of the amount stored is lost. Moreover, the germination rate of seed corn stored in this way is high, and, as a bonus, once the pit is sealed the ground surface above is free for other uses.

The early hillforts certainly saw action. At Crickley Hill, Gloucestershire, the fort was attacked and overrun at the end of the long-house period of occupation. Philip Dixon, the excavator of the site, believes that a new population with contrasting traditions of building took over the fort, remodelled its defences and constructed round houses in the interior. At other sites, burnt ramparts and periods of rebuilding after episodes of destruction attest the active role that many hillforts played in inter-group warfare.

Hill-top enclosures

The second class of sites of this period are the large hill-top enclosures, generally over 16 hectares (40 acres) in area, and defended by one or more lines of ramparts along weak parts of their perimeter, but often defined by natural slopes where these offered suitable protection. Among the most well-known examples are Nottingham Hill and Norbury Camp, Gloucestershire, Bathampton, Avon, Balksbury, Hampshire, and Ogbury, Wiltshire. Excavations at Balksbury revealed a dump rampart with an outer ditch. Very little evidence for occupation was found in the interior, at least in the areas examined. Equally scant traces of occupation were found in the cuttings made through the ramparts at Bathampton Down, Avon, in 1965, although at Norbury, Gloucestershire, excavations in 1977 revealed the presence of 4-posters in the central part of the interior.

The function of these large enclosures is unclear. Their great size and apparent low density of occu-

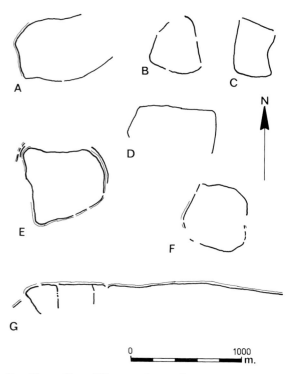

80 Plans of large hill-top enclosures in southern England. (A) Bathampton, Avon; (B) Balksbury, Berkshire; (C) Martinsell, Wiltshire; (D) Norbury Camp, Gloucestershire; (E) Walbury, Berkshire; (F) Bosedown, Berkshire; (G) Bindon Hill, Dorset. [*(A), (C), (E)–(G) After Cunliffe 1984 figure 2.6; (B) after Palmer 1984 figure 6; (D) after RCHM 1976, 89*]

pation suggests that they were stock enclosures and storage places, perhaps with settlement confined to a small area, but verification of this must await more excavation.

Developed hillforts

In the fourth century BC many of the early hillforts like Crickley Hill were abandoned and not reoccupied, while others were elaborated and extended. In a few cases new sites were established. These developed hillforts, as they are called, tend to be larger than the early hillforts. Their defences often follow the natural contours of a suitable hill, and the area enclosed may be as much as 10 hectares (25 acres). Multiple ramparts are usual, but rampart construction began to depart from the timber-laced forms of the seventh to fifth centuries and instead glacis style ramparts with a slightly battered front face forming a more or less continuous profile with the inner edge of the ditch became common. Careful use of existing slopes and natural features to exaggerate the scale of the ramparts at these sites is common, and it must be concluded that in many cases ostentation was as important as defence.

81 Hillfort development in Hampshire. (a) Distribution of hillforts *c.*550–400 BC; (b) distribution of hillforts *c.*300 BC. Open circles indicate sites possibly occupied in each respective phase. [*Based on Cunliffe 1983 figure 28*]

The density of developed hillforts is less than the early hillforts, and where detailed spatial studies have been carried out, such as in central Hampshire, it seems that one site on each naturally defined block of land, perhaps 10 to 20 square kilometres (4 to 8 square miles) in area, emerged as a developed hillfort with the simultaneous loss of surrounding early sites. It is also notable that many developed hillforts lie on the junction of two or more environmental zones suggesting that those living in them depended on the organized control of a wide range of surrounding resources.

Danebury, Hampshire, excavated by Barry Cunliffe, is probably the most intensively studied developed hillfort in Britain. Over one-fifth of the interior has been investigated, and the patterns revealed seem to be matched by evidence from other sites as far afield as Moel-y-Gaer, Clwyd, and Cadbury Castle, Somerset. Modifications to the defences at Danebury soon after about 400 BC involved the construction of a second line of ramparts and the building of outworks at the entrances. The eastern entrance was particularly heavily defended with claw-like hornworks projecting beyond the line of the ramparts creating a curved entrance passage, above which was a strategically placed command post with a clear view over the entire entrance area and ideally suited for slingers. At Danebury, as at many sites of this period, clay sling shot or suitable natural pebbles have been found in considerable quantities emphasizing the importance of this form

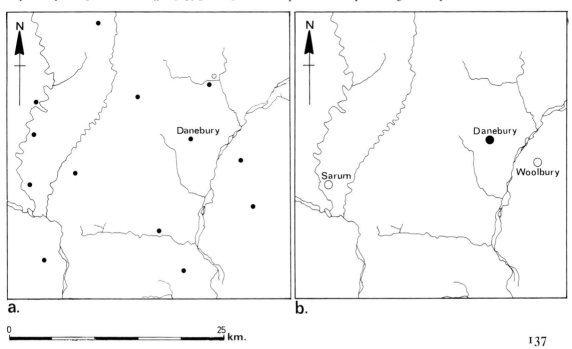

a.　b.

0 ⸻ 25 km.

137

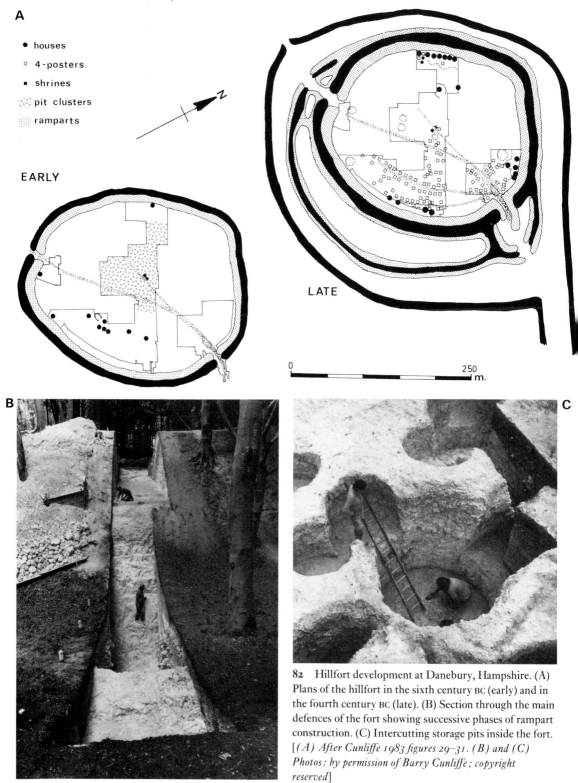

- houses
- 4-posters
- shrines
- pit clusters
- ramparts

EARLY

LATE

0   250
m.

82   Hillfort development at Danebury, Hampshire. (A) Plans of the hillfort in the sixth century BC (early) and in the fourth century BC (late). (B) Section through the main defences of the fort showing successive phases of rampart construction. (C) Intercutting storage pits inside the fort. [*(A) After Cunliffe 1983 figures 29–31. (B) and (C) Photos: by permission of Barry Cunliffe; copyright reserved*]

of warfare. The interior of the site was densely occupied with circular houses set round the inner edge of the rampart, possibly as many as 50 being in use at any one time. Some areas of the interior were given over to storage, either in pits or in 4-posters. Roadways ran through the site and these were maintained throughout the period of occupation. The implications of the evidence recovered from Danebury are that occupation was continuous, intensive and under the control of a strong centralized power.

In North Wales topographic conditions limit the morphology of the hillforts present, and a form of defended hill-top settlement surrounded by a stone wall developed. The evidence from forts in Gwynedd, such as Garn Boduan, Tre'r Ceiri and Conway Mountain, shows that many of them were occupied by sizable communities of perhaps 100 to 400 people, to judge from the number of visible stone houses foundations. Almost nothing is known of the economy or date of these sites, although sheep may have been important.

The absence of a natural water supply on most hillforts is often raised as an objection to their suitability for settlement. There is little doubt that in most cases collected rainfall must have been supplemented by water carried to the site from springs or streams elsewhere. At Breiddin, Powys, a square pond inside the defences may have acted as the main reservoir, while at other sites clay-lined pits have been interpreted as water containers. Collecting and carrying water considerable distances is not considered a problem by many communities living in Africa or Asia today, and presumably the same applied during prehistoric times in Britain.

Determining the economy of the hillforts is not easy. The old idea that they were only occupied in times of trouble finds little support from recent large-scale excavations, but whether the population of the hillforts went out to farm the adjacent land or were in some senses specialists relying on food produced elsewhere and only consumed on the hillfort is far from clear. Although many thousands of animal bones have been recovered from hillfort sites, interpreting the patterns is made no easier. Difficulties of comparing the Wessex sites with those in the Marches are compounded by the fact that acid soils in the west have robbed us of the animal bones. At the risk of over-generalization, the pattern which is now emerging is one of a mixed economy throughout the hillfort-dominated zone, perhaps with slight variations in the relative importance of pasture as against arable between regions. Celtic

fields and various boundaries are associated with individual hillforts as far apart as the Sussex chalklands and Long Mynyd in the central Welsh Marches. Querns, grain storage facilities and evidence of animal herding and processing animal products are universal.

Farmsteads and hamlets

Hillforts were not the only settlements in this southern and western part of England and North Wales. Scattered widely around the hillforts were various open settlements and enclosures which range in size from single farmsteads to hamlets of perhaps five or six households. In Wessex, square, sub-rectangular and rounded enclosures are known, often with one or more large round houses as the principal dwellings and scatters of pits and 4-posters round about. Little Woodbury, Wiltshire, is one such enclosure with an area of about 1.6 hectares (4 acres). Within the excavated portion were the postholes of a single large house, numerous pits, and 4-posters. Other structures probably lie in the unexcavated part of the site, but enough is known to be able to say that the occupants were engaged in mixed farming: cultivation of cereals and herding cattle and sheep. As on the hillforts, most enclosures show that activities were strictly ordered within the boundary earthwork.

One particularly distinctive type of settlement is the 'banjo' enclosure, so called because of their banjo-shaped ground plans—a circular focal enclosure with two parallel projecting antenna-like ditches. It has been suggested that the design of these enclosures was to facilitate livestock management, for example herding cattle to be milked or sheltered in the enclosure. This might be so, but excavations at a number of sites in Wessex show that the occupants were involved in mixed farming rather than specifically pastoral farming. At Owslebury, Hampshire, excavations by John Collis revealed traces of fields round about the banjo enclosure. More work is needed to establish the importance of these enclosures relative to hillforts, for there are hints that some banjos may be high-status settlements.

In North Wales, various circular enclosures, again probably stock enclosures with a central occupation area, lie around the hillforts. Various types have been defined on morphological grounds by Christopher Smith, but accurate dating is lacking, and it is not certain that all belong to this period.

In many areas Celtic fields were founded, or

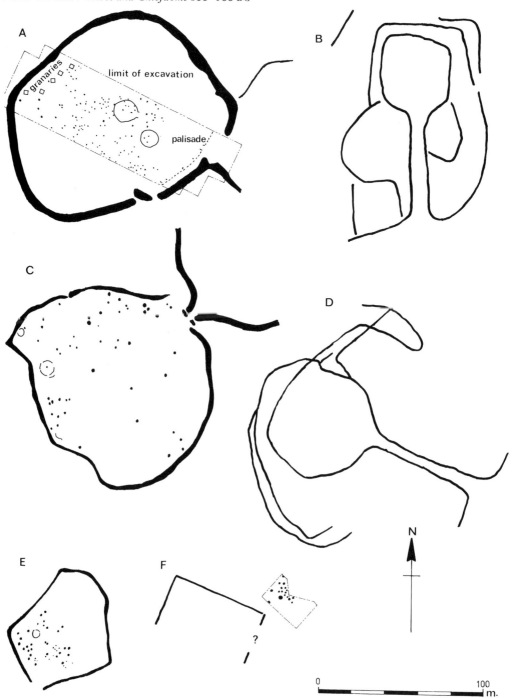

83 Plans of farmsteads and settlements in southern England dating to between the fifth and second centuries BC. Pits, postholes and ditches shown in solid black. (A) Little Woodbury, Wiltshire; (B) Upper Cranborne, Hampshire; (C) Gussage All Saints, Dorset; (D) Preshaw House, Hampshire; (E) Tollard Royal, Wiltshire; (F) Guiting Power, Gloucestershire. [*(A) After Bersu 1940 figure 1 and plate 1 ; (B) and (D) after Cunliffe 1978 figure 11.3 ; (C) after Wainwright and Switsur 1976 figure 3 ; (E) after Wainwright 1968 figure 3 ; (F) after Saville 1979 figures 2 and 12*]

84 Celtic fields at Smacam Down, Cerne Abbas, Dorset. [*Photo: Cambridge University Collection; copyright reserved*]

reused from earlier times. A light ard pulled by oxen was one of the tools used in tillage, and iron shares have been found at Danebury and a number of other sites. As an illustration of the spread of farming at this time mention may be made of the cultivation marks, putatively of later first-millennium BC date, found at Almonsbury, Avon, during the construction of the M5 motorway. The interesting point about them is that they are on heavy clay soil in the lower Severn valley.

The pattern of development within the farmsteads and hamlets of the hillfort zone is far from consistent. In contrast to the sites already mentioned there are some which were not bounded by enclosures until the second century or later, while others start as an enclosure but later become open sites. Winnall Down, Hampshire, is a case of this last-mentioned trend. Occupation during the sixth to third centuries was within to a D-shaped enclosure of about 0.4 hectares (1 acre). There was an elaborate gateway, houses, pits and the ubiquitous 4- and 6-posters. From the third century, however, the enclosure was abandoned and an open settlement occupied about the same area, by this time compris-

ing round houses set within circular gullies, pits, a rectangular structure and 4-posters. Cattle were the main source of animal food, milk and meat, in this later phase, but sheep were common, possibly for their wool. At Guiting Power, Gloucestershire, a cluster of 20 rock-cut pits represents the remains of a small open settlement in the heart of the Cotswolds. Because of heavy ploughing at this site in recent centuries no houses were found. Sheep were the most numerous animal represented by bones from the pits, but cattle were probably more important in the diet of the inhabitants.

In the major lowland areas within the hillfort dominated zone, for example the Severn valley, large multiple enclosures of village-like proportions are known as well as the smaller hamlet and farmstead sized units. At Beckford, Hereford and Worcester, for example, a series of ditched enclosures, each containing round houses, storage pits and smaller enclosures, have been revealed by excavation. Each enclosure defined an area within the overall settlement, which in total covered several hectares. Each enclosure seems to have been individually owned and occupied for a long period.

At some non-hillfort sites there is evidence for specialization of production, or at least a focus on specific resources. Frank Green has found that regional variations in the types of crops grown can be detected in Wessex. At Winnall Down, Hampshire, sheep formed a very important part of the economy while cattle formed the important part of the diet. In the upper Thames valley, Richard Hingley has identified variations in the form and layout of settlements which led him to postulate a mixed arable and pasture based economy with a high density of open settlements along the river valleys; this contrasted with spatially isolated enclosed settlements pursuing a subsistence economy with greater emphasis on pastoralism on the surrounding higher ground. Differences in the social organization of the communities living in these two areas may also be suspected. Many other cases of similar localized variations undoubtedly await discovery through research and excavation. Craft production too may be seen as a part-time occupation of the farmers living on some sites. Weaving is frequently represented by weights and combs, while elsewhere metalworking was carried out. At Gussage All Saints, Dorset, both ironworking and bronzeworking took place on a considerable scale during the second century BC, the latter focusing on the manufacture of horse harness and cart/waggon fittings.

Structure in the landscape

Placing the hillforts and other settlements into a coherent pattern is not easy. It does, however, seem that by the third century or so the landscape was dominated by major hillforts and villages around which were smaller settlement units perhaps somehow dependent on the larger. Hillforts as central places, in the sense spoken of by geographers, have recently been widely debated, but unless it can be shown that non-hillfort settlements were free to attach themselves to any hillfort (for whatever reasons), such models are quite inappropriate. More likely is a pattern where settlements were attached to a central hillfort or village by formal and long-lasting ties of some sort, perhaps kinship, patronage or alliances. Henry Gent has demonstrated that the

85 Simplified models of economic, spatial and social relationships between developed hillforts and surrounding settlements. (a) Economic relationships of a developed hillfort in terms of the materials and goods brought to the site from near and far. (b) Spatial model of developed hillfort and contemporary settlements in the vicinity. (c) Two possible alternative models of social order in developed hillforts and nearby settlements. [*After Cunliffe 1984 figures 10.3, 10.4 and 10.5 with minor changes*]

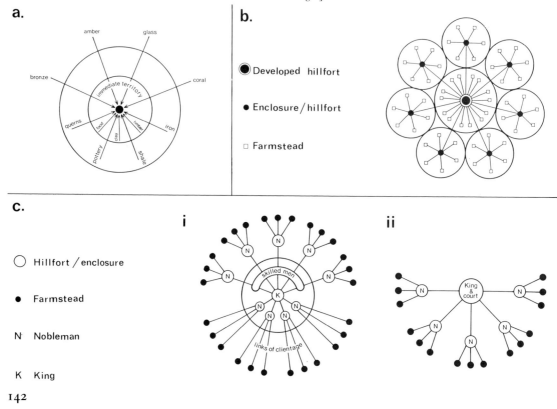

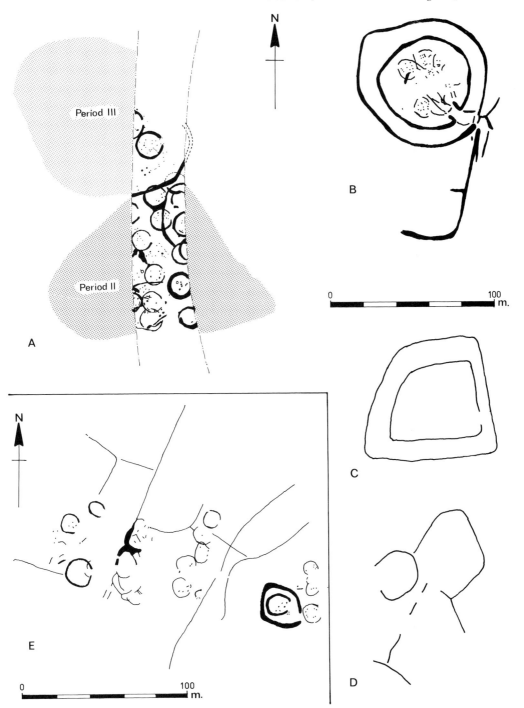

86 Plans of enclosed and unenclosed fourth- to second-century BC settlements in eastern and central England. (A) Little Waltham, Essex; (B) Mingie's Ditch, Oxfordshire; (C) Dun's Tew, Oxfordshire; (D) Enstone, Oxfordshire; (E) Claydon Pike, Gloucestershire. [*(A) After Dury 1978 figure 4; (B)–(E) after Hingley and Miles 1984 figures 4.3, 4.4 and 4.7*]

developed hillforts had a proportionally greater storage capacity than non-hillfort sites, and it does seem that the hillforts acted as centralized storage points. At Danebury, Hampshire, the storage capacity of the pits at any one time greatly exceeded the needs of the likely resident population. Analysis of the carbonized cereal remains from Danebury by Martin Jones has demonstrated that crops were brought to the site from a number of different environments, although exactly whose crops and from where could not of course be determined.

But hillforts were probably more than simply defended food stores. The enormous communal labour required for their construction and their ostentatious form suggests that they were the symbolic if not the actual focus of power for the community. Again, if Danebury is representative then such sites may also have been ritual centres, places for exchange, and possibly redistribution sites for food and goods taken in from smaller settlements round about. These roles will be considered again later in this chapter after a consideration of the evidence for internal trade and ritual.

Eastern England

This area broadly covers East Anglia, the east Midlands, central England north of the Thames, Lincolnshire and Humberside. Of all the regions described here it is probably the most poorly documented. Hillforts are rare. A few notable examples such as Ivinghoe Beacon, Buckinghamshire, Rainsborough Camp, Northamptonshire, and Breedon-on-the-Hill, Leicestershire, lie around the periphery on the higher ground on the Chilterns and the Northamptonshire uplands. These sites are few in number, and on present evidence seem to be mostly of early date. Rainsborough has a fine guard chamber either side of an inturned entrance. By the fourth century BC there were probably few if any hillforts in use in the area.

The settlement pattern of eastern England was dominated by villages, hamlets and farmsteads, some enclosed but most open. The majority are only known through aerial photography as cropmarks, but a few have been excavated. At Little Waltham, near Chelmsford, Essex, the settlement began as an open cluster of houses in the mid third century. Most were surrounded by round drainage gullies, although some had slightly polygonal gullies. Because the site lies on the floodplain of the river Chelmer, 4-posters were preferred to pits for

storage, and as elsewhere were presumably used as granaries. In the later second century BC the site was remodelled slightly with the construction of a defensive palisade enclosure within which there were again round houses. A similar small village-like settlement has been found at Fengate, Cambridgeshire, where over 60 houses were investigated, although not all were in use at any one time and less than half had been used for human habitation; the majority were used for storage and as animal shelters. The site lies on the edge of the fens as they were in late first-millennium BC times, and the mainstay of the subsistence base seems to have been grazing cattle and sheep on the rich fen-edge pastures. Cereals were not produced locally, but may have been imported. Fishing and fowling provided a supplement to the diet. Overall the settlement may have been occupied by perhaps 25 to 30 people.

On the Thames estuary at Mucking, Essex, excavations by Margaret Jones have revealed another extensive spread of over 100 houses represented by circular gullies ranging from 6 metres to over 20 metres (20 to 67 feet) in diameter. These clearly related to a long period of settlement spanning the period fifth century BC to first century AD. Associated with the huts were compounds and pits. The economy of this settlement was probably shepherding. In the Thames valley at Ashville near Abingdon, Oxfordshire, the main period of occupation was represented by 18 house gullies of which perhaps seven were in use at any one time. Mixed farming was practised here, including the cultivation of hulled six-row barley, spelt and lesser amounts of emmer wheat and club wheat. The cultivation cycle provided for the planting of winter wheat, and analysis of the seed remains by Martin Jones suggests that parts of the nearby low-lying damp ground had been brought into cultivation because spike rush (*Eleocharis palustris*) was represented among the cereals.

87 Late first-millennium BC settlements in the Thames valley and eastern England. (A) Aerial view of excavations at Gravelly Guy, Oxfordshire, showing a linear scatter of storage pits, possibly representing the use of narrow strips of land between major boundaries as storage and settlement areas over several centuries. (B) Aerial view of excavations at the Catswater site Fengate, Cambridgeshire, showing round houses and enclosures. [*(A) Photo: George Lambrick for Oxfordshire Archaeological Unit; copyright reserved. (B) Photo: Stephen Upex for Nene Valley Research Committee; copyright reserved*]

Smaller settlements are known across the area too. In the Thames valley at Mount Farm, Berinsfield, Oxfordshire, excavations have revealed a small farm with a group of fields, while nearby at Mingie's Ditch a double circular enclosure with antenna ditches flanking the entrance and round houses and 4-posters in the interior has been investigated. The double enclosure at this site may have provided a stock pen between the ditches. At Farmoor on the Thames flood plain near Stanton Harcourt, Oxfordshire, a seasonal settlement connected with exploitation of the rich riverside pasture was revealed during excavations in 1976. Round houses and stock enclosures were present, but in contrast to the other sites mentioned above there were no traces of cereal production in the vicinity. Many of these small sites include storage facilities in the form of pits and 4-posters, but grain may not always have been stored at settlements. Excavations at Gravelly Guy, Oxfordshire, revealed a dense linear scatter of storage pits which George Lambrick, the excavator of the site, suggests had been dug in a narrow strip

of land between two field-systems, presumably to act as grain stores near to where crops were harvested.

Wild plants and animals do not seem to have provided a significant part of the diet of these farming communities, and even fish bones are rare on riverside sites. One interesting sidelight on the economy of the later first millennium BC is provided by the discovery of the head of a worker bee (*Apis mellifera L.*) preserved in peat dated to about 220 ± 90 BC at Mingie's Ditch, Oxfordshire. It is the earliest known find of a honeybee in Britain so far, but its implications for the availability of beeswax and honey from this period, if not earlier, are considerable.

In the Trent valley of Staffordshire and Nottinghamshire settlement along the river terraces and on the floodplain during the later first millennium BC was just as dense as along the Thames valley. Excavations at Fisherwick beside the Tame in Staffordshire revealed intensive use of this part of the environment. Enclosed homesteads and perhaps unenclosed round houses were relatively evenly scattered along the gravel terraces, each surrounded by a group of hedged and ditched fields. Some of these fields were probably cultivated annually. The settlements, as elsewhere, were connected by ditched and hedged trackways, while similar tracks

88 Settlement and field-systems at Fisherwick, Staffordshire based on evidence recorded during excavations and from aerial photographs. [*After Smith 1979 figure 4*]

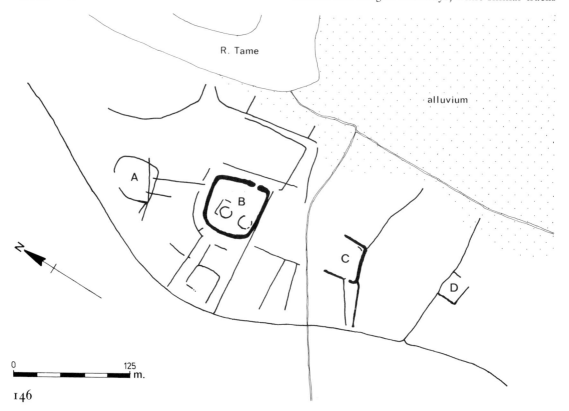

led to areas of open grazing and woodland that lay beyond the enclosed fields. The main emphasis lay on cattle and horse rearing, but arable cultivation was also important both for domestic use and fodder.

The dense scatter of sites already described continues across the east and north Midlands. Research by David Knight has demonstrated that in Northamptonshire and surrounding areas settlement was widespread and dispersed. Typically these sites are interpreted as single family units, farmsteads which variously engaged in craft production and exchange between themselves as well as food production.

Further north, large-scale excavations in advance of gravel quarrying in Humberside at Garton Slack and Wetwang Slack illustrate the high density of settlement in this part of the Yorkshire Wolds. At Wetwang over 80 round houses have been found on the floor of the valley together with 4-posters and pits for grain storage. Nearby was a major cemetery, and tracks and lanes were found linking other nearby sites and providing access to fields. Each hamlet or village may have been occupied by anything from about 35 to 85 individuals. As in other parts of the eastern region, settlements here tended to become more nucleated through time, and the provision of enclosure ditches were also favoured from the second century onwards.

Taken as a whole, the evidence from this area suggests that again some kind of hierarchy of settlement may have existed with villages and major enclosed settlements forming the nodes of a settlement system which also included smaller farmsteads, some with specialized functions, much as with the sites in central and western England.

Atlantic Britain

This area comprises the south-west peninsula, Wales, and all of northern and western Scotland. Surprisingly for such a large area the kinds of settlements, and the pattern of events, are remarkably similar throughout. There are few large forts, except on the eastern edges of the area. All the settlements known are small units, probably family or extended family groups. Many were heavily defended, although as a general rule sites became increasingly well defended as time went by. The visible regional and typological variations probably owe much to specialized economic functions and local traditions.

South-western England

In the south west, a few settlements, such as Foales Arishes and Kestor on Dartmoor, and Bodrifty on Mulfra Hill, near Penzance, Cornwall, which date to the fifth century or so, are comparable to the open-plan settlement of the earlier first millennium BC, with huts scattered among cultivation plots. In general they were replaced after about 400 BC by other forms of settlement. Of these, rounds are possibly the most common type in Cornwall—small circular and sub-circular enclosures usually containing a few houses built against the enclosure wall or bank. They are mostly found in hilly country on good agricultural land, and are usually under 0.8 hectares (2 acres) in area. Few examples have been excavated, but at Trevisker, Cornwall, a round occupied in the second century BC yielded quern-stones and a possible iron sickle which suggests some involvement with agriculture. One of the houses also contained a slab-lined drain which may indicate its use as an animal shelter.

Complementing the rounds, and widely spread over Devon and Cornwall, are the multiple-enclosure forts. Characteristically these are sited on hill-slopes, and comprise an inner enclosure, usually less than 1.5 hectares ($3\frac{3}{4}$ acres) in area, with a single entrance and massive ramparts, around which are concentric ramparts providing stock enclosures integral with the central occupation area. At Milber Down, Devon, antenna ditches like the banjo enclosures of Wessex probably served to funnel animals into the pens or stock yards. The main entranceways to these enclosures are usually sited to give easy access to springs or water sources. Finds include relatively rich ornaments such as shale and glaze beads, and implements of iron and bronze. These sites were clearly pastoral enclosures, and may have been occupied by relatively rich family groups.

The largest settlements in the area are the cliff castles along the coast, usually set on spurs or promontories and defended by a single or multiple rampart across the neck of the projection. Most are less than 2 hectares (5 acres) in area although with precipitous slopes on three sides the area available for settlement was often much less. At The Rumps, St Minver, Cornwall, the three ramparts evolved through several structural phases. Finds of sheep bones and spindle whorls suggest the importance of flocks, while clay ovens and querns attest the use of cereals. Embury Beacon, Hartland, Devon, was found upon excavation to enclose several structures, and from the arrangement of the ramparts it can be

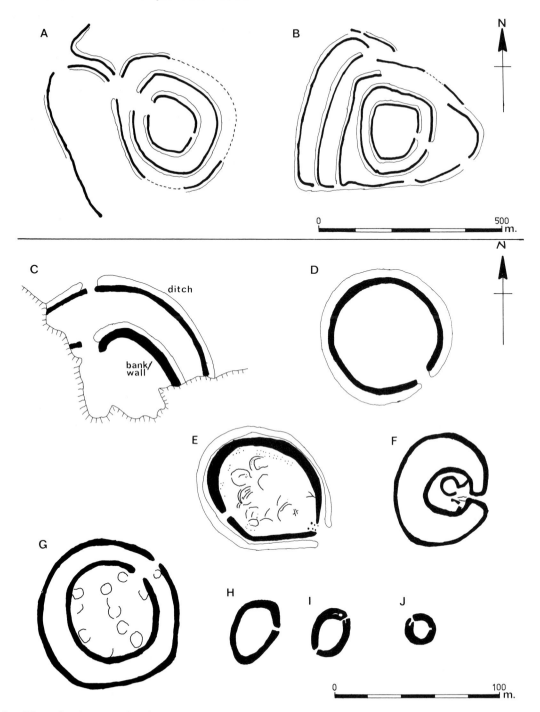

89 Plans of enclosures and settlements in western and Atlantic Britain. (A) Milber Down, Devon; (B) Clovelly Dykes, Devon; (C) The Knave, Rhossili, Glamorgan; (D) Threemilestone Round, Cornwall; (E) Walesland Rath, Dyfed; (F) Llwyn-du-Bach, Gwynedd; (G) Castell Odo, Gwynedd; (H) Ballycastle Dun, Strathclyde; (I) Leccamore Dun, Strathclyde; (J) Dun Lagandh, Highland. [*After Cunliffe 1978 figures 12.5, 12.7, 12.12, 12.14, 12.15 and 12.35*]

suggested that its function was similar to that of the multiple-enclosure forts.

Specialized sites of various sorts also occur in the south west. Coastal sites, either seasonal or permanent, and reliant partly or wholly on the exploitation of marine resources, are relatively common, as at Porth Hallangy Down and Nornour, Scilly. In the Somerset Levels, trackways leading out from the dry islands into the marshes were built, while lake settlements, or at least marsh settlements, are known at Glastonbury and Meare. Great controversy surrounds the interpretation of the evidence recovered by Arthur Bulleid and H. St George Gray during their excavations at these two waterlogged sites in the early years of this century. Differential desiccation of the encapsulating peat caused warping and stratigraphic dislocation which was not properly appreciated at the time, and while it seems clear that occupation took place at these sites, the extent and duration of settlement is uncertain. David Clarke has suggested that at Glastonbury many different types of structure lay within the settlement, including houses, ancillary huts, workshop huts, work floors, storehouses, stables, byres and kennels. These he proposed could be arranged into sectors, each sector being occupied by a single social unit, probably a kinship based unit—an extended family of perhaps 15 to 20 individuals. Overall, Clarke suggested that the population fluctuated between 65 and 100 people. Among the activities undertaken by the inhabitants was the manufacture of glass beads.

Rather similar to Glastonbury is the site at Meare Village West. Here excavations again revealed a number of house sites and evidence for various crafts. The site was probably fairly permanently occupied, and Bryony Orme has suggested that it may have served as a periodic rural market or exchange centre for food and goods. Not all the settlements of this period in the Levels were permanently occupied, and recent investigations at Meare Village East by John Coles and Bryony Orme suggest seasonal occupation here. Exploitation of a relatively restricted range of resources is, however, clear at all these sites, and, as at Fengate, marshland grazing was undoubtedly a mainstay of the subsistence economy.

South and central Wales

In south and central Wales settlements similar to those in Devon and Cornwall are represented; no hillforts on the scale of the English examples are present west of the Marches. Raths, the Welsh equivalent of rounds, are widespread, and total excavation of Walesland Rath near Haverfordwest, Dyfed, by Geoffrey Wainwright in 1967–8 gives a clear insight into the development of one such site. The enclosed area was oval in plan, about 64 by 49 metres (210 by 161 feet), and defined by a bank and ditch with two opposed entranceways. Inside were at least three timber round houses and many postholes suggestive of other buildings both against the rampart and free standing. There was evidence of bronze working, but little trace of subsistence pursuits.

Cliff castles and promontory forts are found along the coast of south-west Dyfed and, to a lesser extent, Glamorgan. The only excavated example is Coygan Camp, Dyfed, where occupation was probably concentrated in the lee of the rampart. Among the objects recorded were a few personal ornaments, hide dressing equipment, fragments of two quernstones and various rubbing stones. Sling stones suggest the need for a constant supply of missiles for defence. Cattle bones were the most numerous animal remains found, suggesting an economy based on stock rearing. Arable cultivation was probably of secondary importance.

Multiple-enclosure settlements comparable to the Cornish examples are also found widely in all four of the counties of South Wales, as at Mynydd Bychan, Glamorgan. In the upper Severn valley broadly similar sites have been recorded through aerial photography, and one at Collfryn, Powys, has been excavated to reveal four roughly concentric lines of enclosure ditches and intensive internal occupation including round houses from the fourth to first century BC. Unlike most enclosures in southern and central England, these sites apparently lack any associated field-systems. Some caves were used for occupation, possibly seasonal, and often connected with the exploitation of coastal resources.

Western and northern Scotland

In western and northern Scotland many of the features now familiar from western areas again appear. Promontory forts along the coast of Highland, Orkney and Shetland are well known, some such as Clickhimin containing block-houses. Open settlements of the seventh to third centuries are known, as for example with the single round house built into the ruined passage grave at Quanterness, Orkney. Finds were few, but sheep, cattle and pig were kept, and marine resources supplemented the diet. At Kilphedir, Highland, excavations revealed a group of five round houses dating to the fifth century BC which were superseded in the second century BC by a more massive building with thick stone walls. Limited cultivation was undertaken in the vicinity. Burnt mounds, which began to be built in the second millennium BC (see p. 116), continued to be built and used throughout the north, and indeed in other western areas.

Lake settlements, or crannogs, are found in south-west Scotland. Usually built at the edge of a loch, these sites consist of an artificial island composed of layers of brushwood and rubble revetted by vertical piles. The island was joined to the shore by a causeway. Occupation was usually confined to a single house. Perhaps the best known example is on Milton Loch, Dumfries and Galloway. Dating to the fourth or fifth century BC, this site had a small jetty and harbour. The house was 12.8 metres (42 feet) in diameter, and was divided internally into several rooms. Another example at Oakbank, Lock Tay, Tayside, was the homestead of a small family of farmers living in the loch and farming the land on the adjacent shore, while also taking advantage of the fish and aquatic resources.

From the second century, or possibly earlier, distinctive settlements known as duns were con-structed widely over western parts of Scotland. These were essentially small dry-stone-walled en-closures mostly less than 0.3 hectares ($\frac{3}{4}$ acre) internally. The walls were high, perhaps 3 metres (10 feet) or so, and generally fairly thick. They seem to be the equivalent of the rounds and raths of southern parts of the Atlantic seaboard—the defen-ded homesteads of small groups farming nearby land. Dennis Harding has recently emphasized the need to distinguish between dun enclosures, which bear many similarities to the raths and rounds of other areas, and dun houses, which are single fortified dwellings, possibly completely roofed over as a single structure.

The overall impression presented by the settle-ments and economic evidence from the Atlantic areas of Britain is one of small-scale groups pursuing a mainly pastoral lifestyle supplemented where possible with cereal production and the use of more specialized wetland resources. Whether transhum-ance was a regular feature of the farming cycle is not clear. Society was probably fragmentary, based on kinship groups with little overall centralized control, possibly the continuation of an earlier tribal system.

Northern and north-eastern England

This area covers Yorkshire, Northumberland and the northern uplands extending across the Pennines into Cumbria. This is not strictly hillfort country, although a few examples are known on the Pennines and upland peripheries of Northumberland, mostly of early date. Enclosed homesteads of various sorts predominated in the area by the second century BC, and as in other areas there is a general tendency for later sites to be defended.

On the Yorkshire Wolds and the east side of the area, palisaded enclosures of the type established in the earlier first millennium BC continued to be used and built. At Staple Howe, North Yorkshire, the enclosure with its oval house built in the sixth century BC, if not earlier, continued with various modifications down to the second century or so. Cattle, sheep and pigs were kept, and wheat was cultivated by the inhabitants. Off the higher ground at Thorpe Thewles, Cleveland, a sub-rectangular enclosure built about 200 BC provides a glimpse of valley settlements in this area. A well-built round house with a drainage gully some 19 metres (62 feet) in diameter lay within the enclosure. The ramparts would have provided defence against wolves and wild animals and the site probably served as a stock corral as well as a settlement. This site provides an exception to the general trend for increasing defence later in the period because in subsequent phases the enclosure ditch was abandoned and a small nu-cleated settlement of several houses developed.

In Northumberland, and northwards into Bor-ders, palisaded enclosures were again the norm. Many examples are known, largely through the surveys and excavations of George Jobey. Most enclosures seem to have been for pastoral uses. At White Hill, Borders, two concentric palisades set between 6 and 15 metres (20 and 49 feet) apart provided a stock corral rather similar to those of the multiple enclosures in Atlantic Britain. The size of these enclosures varies considerably from just one round house to perhaps seven or eight in any one phase of occupation. Colin Burgess has suggested that population levels at these sites varied consider-ably too, ranging from 40 to 100 people per settlement. There is a general tendency, as for example at Fenton Hill and Huckhoe, Northumber-land, for palisaded enclosures to be replaced by stone ramparts, often timber revetted, although this is not a universal pattern. Sites which had ramparts added look very much like small hillforts, but being less than 1 hectare ($2\frac{1}{2}$ acres) they are better described as

90 Central area of the enclosed settlement at Thorpe
Thewles, Cleveland, under excavation. Pits, postholes,
gullies and the foundations of a large round house can be
seen partly cleared. [*Photo: Cleveland County
Archaeology Section; copyright reserved*]

defended homesteads. In the fourth century BC there
is some evidence for expansion into the uplands
again, especially on the North York Moors, where
environmental evidence points to renewed episodes
of clearance, and to a lesser extent on the Cheviots.

On the Pennines and the north-western part of
the area, dating evidence for the known sites is very
poor. Single huts up in the hills are relatively
common and work by Arthur Raistrick in the
Wharfedale area of Yorkshire has shown how they
cluster along the main river valleys leading into the
uplands. Here earthworks, field-systems and enclo-

sures of this period all survive as relict landscapes
among the more modern field patterns. Transhum-
ance may have been a feature of the farming system
of these areas, but at Grassington, North Yorkshire,
and several other sites, nucleated settlements associated with fairly extensive field-systems are present from the second century BC or a little later. Cave
sites are also occupied in these areas, presumably on
a seasonal basis.

Eastern Scotland

In the northern part of the Tyne-Forth province, in
north Northumberland, Borders and Lothian a
pattern of settlement rather similar to that of
southern England and the Welsh Border is represented. Hillforts with timber-laced ramparts were built

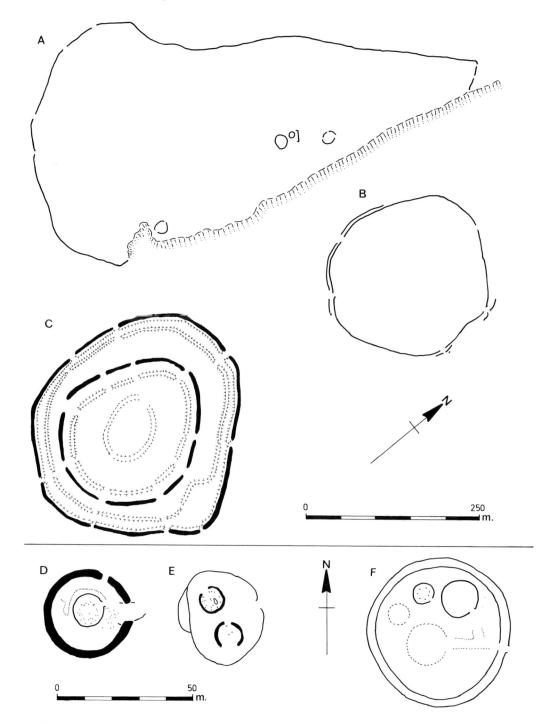

91 Hillforts and palisaded enclosures of sixth- to second-century BC date in Northumberland and eastern Scotland. (A) Traprain Law, Lothian; (B) Eildon Hill, Borders; (C) The Brown Caterthun, Tayside; (D) West Plean, Central; (E) Glenachan Rig, Borders; (F) High Knowles, Northumberland. [*(A)–(C) After Feachem 1966 figures 14, 15 and 10; (D)–(F) after Cunliffe 1978 figure 12.24*]

from the sixth century BC, for example at Finavon and Monifieth, Tayside, and continued in use through much of the later first millennium. Curiously, vertical timber-lacing such as is common in southern England is rare in Scotland; instead horizontal timbers predominate.

A few hillforts in eastern Scotland attained considerable size and were densely occupied. At Eildon Hill North, Borders, it is estimated that there are over 500 houses within the enclosed area of 16.2 hectares (40 acres). Further south at Yeavering Bell, Northumberland there are about 130 houses in the fort of 5.3 hectares (13 acres).

In all there are 1000 or so small hillforts or defended homesteads known in the Tyne-Forth area, but little is known of the economy of these sites – pastoral-based subsistence seems likely. Whether the two-tier hierarchy of small homesteads and large hillforts related to a social organization which operated in anything like the same way as that of southern England is not known.

Crafts, industry and internal exchange

The production and exchange of raw materials and finished goods became increasingly complicated during the later first millennium BC. Many different kinds of objects were used, most requiring relatively specialized craftsmanship. Barry Cunliffe has suggested that two distinct levels can be identified: home-based production, and specialist production for regional distribution. These two spheres can be carried over as the basis for interpreting trade and exchange. As with earlier periods, there is no satisfactory way of knowing how trade was conducted, at what levels within society it took place, or indeed how frequently. It is noteworthy, however, that a collection of weights was found at Danebury, Hampshire, suggesting an interest in equivalence and standardization at this time.

In the west, especially in Atlantic Britain, home production seems to account for almost all of the goods produced and used, while in the east the two levels are more easily visible both in manufacturing terms and in the consumption of different types of goods on different types of site. Some mention has already been made of the possibility that individual sites specialized in certain types of production, both agricultural and industrial, and this will be discussed further below.

Domestic crafts

The most widespread household crafts were undoubtedly those we know least about: woodworking and textile manufacture. With rare exceptions, such as the wooden objects from waterlogged deposits and the stains of decayed structures, only the tools used in these crafts survive. Carpenter's tools known include saws, axes, adzes, chisels and gouges. In addition to the post-built round houses, ramparts and settlement fixtures, boats are known from the River Humber, wooden carts or chariots with iron-rimmed wheels are known from burials at Wetwang Slack, Humberside, and bowls, ladles, dishes, mallets, ladders, spear shafts, handles of various sorts, and sword scabbards are known from the Somerset Lake villages and elsewhere. Hurdle making and basketry is also evidenced at these sites, and trackways were built over wet ground where necessary.

Textile production was widespread, to judge from the importance attached to sheep farming and the distribution of spindle whorls for spinning wool into yarn, bone weaving combs or beaters for packing the weft tight against each other, and triangular clay loom weights for stretching the warp on upright looms. The nature of the cloth produced, whether it was coloured or not with one of the many available natural dyes, for example, is not known. The various pins and brooches of seventh-century and later date suggest widespread use of woollen cloth for garments, although leather working, presumably for making clothes, harness and utensils, continued throughout the first millennium BC.

Regional production

Although ironworking began as early as the seventh century BC, it was not until the fourth or third century that there is widespread evidence for smelting and the forging of iron objects. Most areas of Britain lie relatively near to supplies of iron ore. Exactly how the ore was distributed is not at present clear, but it seems likely that smelting took place near the source and that ready-smelted ingots were transported to consumer blacksmiths. The most likely candidates for such ingots are the so-called currency bars found in two basic shapes: sword-shaped bars and spit-shaped bars. Much has been written about these bars and their possible use as mediums of exchange. They almost all derive from the areas where a settlement hierarchy can be discerned in the south and east, and over one third of all examples known come from hillforts, often in

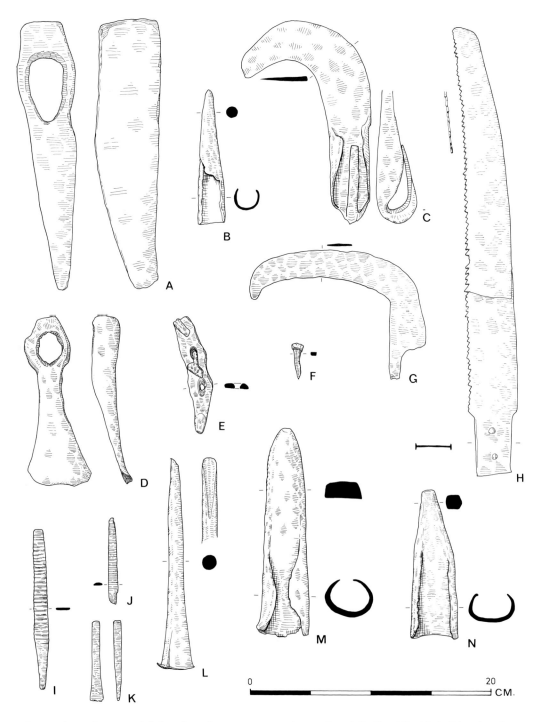

92 Iron tools, equipment and fittings from the Danebury hillfort, Hampshire. (A) Pick/hammer; (B) ferrule; (C) and (G) hook-shaped cutting tools; (D) adze; (E) part of a horseshoe; (F) horseshoe nail; (H) saw; (I) and (J) files; (K) chisel; (L) socketed gouge; (M) and (N) ploughshares. [*After Cunliffe 1984 figures 7.9, 7.11, 7.12 and 7.14*]

hoards. The fact that some have been found sawn up into pieces as if awaiting forging may suggest that they simply relate to the distribution of raw material.

A few blacksmiths' tools such as tongs, punches and hammers are known from sites widely scattered around the country, but the main source of evidence for smithing comes from the presence of iron slags and forging waste. Actual smelting furnaces are known at Kestor, Dartmoor, and West Brandon, Durham, and in both cases comprise small pits about 0.5 metres (20 inches) across with a rest for a pair of bellows. Blacksmiths produced a variety of tools for other crafts and farming, as well as ornaments, pins and brooches.

Gold and silver were not extensively worked between the seventh and the second centuries BC, although in the first century BC/AD there was renewed interest in these metals. Bronze continued to be worked, possibly by part-time metalworkers/farmers. Crucibles and waste casting debris is known from a wide range of sites but perhaps the most fully investigated is the farmstead enclosure at Gussage All Saints, Dorset. Here both ironworking and bronzeworking were carried out in the second century BC, but the bronze worker specialized in the manufacture of horse harness fittings including terret rings, bridle bits, linchpins for securing wheels to fixed axles, strap ends and various other loops and fasteners. These objects were clearly being made for exchange or redistribution of some kind since the quantities involved were far in excess of the needs of the resident community. As an example of the way in which some bronze objects were distributed, mention may be made of the bronze brooches of Wessex type made in imitation of La Tène types fashionable on the Continent, in this case with incised lines and dots on the bow. Some 15 almost identical examples are known, and all were found within a 50 kilometre (31 miles) radius of Salisbury, although the exact place of manufacture is unknown.

Much of the pottery used on sites of the period between 600 and 200 BC was locally made. The large bucket-shaped forms of the earlier first millennium were replaced by a variety of wares including bowls, dishes and jars. Marked regional styles can be identified, reflected in both the form of the vessels and their decoration. Most of these style zones cover irregular-shaped areas about 150 kilometres (93 miles) across. Petrological studies of fourth- to second-century pottery in the west of England by David Peacock has shown that superimposed on local production is a series of regional production

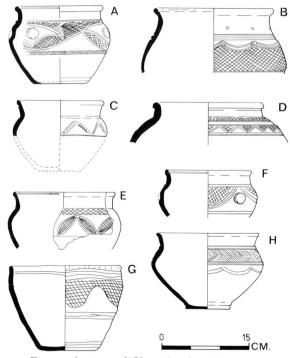

93 Decorated pottery of 'Glastonbury' style from the south west of England, mostly third- to first-century BC in date. [*After Peacock 1969 figure 5*]

centres which disseminated pottery over distances of about 80 to 100 kilometres (50 to 62 miles) from their source. Particularly distinctive are the three areas in the triangle of land between the River Wye and the River Severn in the southern Welsh Marches, which are known for the manufacture of pottery decorated with incised lines and stamped motifs which was distributed in the Marches, middle Severn valley and Cotswolds. Rather similar is the spread of so-called Glastonbury style ware—a dark well-finished pottery heavily ornamented with curvilinear incised decoration—found widely over south-western Britain from Avon down to Cornwall and manufactured at six or more regional centres, each distinctive because of the types of rock included as tempering agents. The rocks include Gabbroic rock from the Lizard, Mendip limestone from Somerset, and Old Red Sandstone from Somerset and Avon.

One of the most important products of the period was salt, and production during the later first millennium expanded greatly. Manufacture was principally in coastal regions, especially in Lincolnshire, Essex, Kent, Sussex, Hampshire, Dorset, Devon, Cornwall, Somerset, Lancashire and Cumbria. The techniques of production followed the methods established several centuries earlier (see p. 129). The brine springs of Droitwich and the south Cheshire area were also used. Investigations by Elaine Morris of the distribution of briquetage shows that salt from these west Midland sources was transported over distances of anything up to 120 kilometres (75 miles) from source.

Smaller personal items such as ornaments were made wherever the availability of materials permitted. On the south coast at Kimmeridge a major shaleworking industry developed and many sites in the area, for example the enclosure at Eldon's Seat, Dorset, yield evidence of shaleworking. In the north of England jet was worked in similar ways. At Glastonbury, glass beads were manufactured, and boneworking to make handles for composite tools was another widespread activity. There is some evidence, especially in western and Atlantic Britain, that flint was still worked on a small scale for making edged tools.

Luxury goods

Luxury goods continued to be made following earlier traditions. Of great importance were weaponry and parade gear. Again Continental influence was strong, especially with the major innovation of decoration on fine objects after the fourth century BC. This ornamentation comprised increasingly complicated curvilinear designs based on the 'Celtic' or La Tène style art. Amongst the earliest recipients of such treatment were the iron daggers which became very popular in the fourth century although they originated a little earlier. These daggers had bronze sheaths, and examples such as the one from the Thames at Richmond, now in the British Museum were covered in decoration. By the third century, when swords came back into fashion, the elaboration of weapons with intricate design work was well established, and by the second century there were numerous schools of local craftsmen in Britain producing finely ornamented cast and beaten metalwork. Among the most spectacular pieces are the Witham shield, from the river Witham in Lincolnshire, and the Torrs pony headgear from Dumfries and Galloway.

Overall, it is clear that no particular classes of site were exclusively the focus of particular crafts or industries, although larger settlements with higher populations naturally provided the setting for a wider overall range of crafts. At Danebury, for example, potting, leatherworking, textileworking, woodworking and metalworking were undertaken.

In southern and eastern England at least it seems that farmer-specialists may have been active, producing a restricted range of products for redistribution over relatively small areas. Barry Cunliffe has suggested that hillforts may have played a vital role in this redistribution, not only providing raw materials such as iron and salt to outlying farms but also taking in specialist produce and either redirecting it to where it was needed or using it in inter-regional exchange. It is indeed possible that the exchange of fine objects was restricted to a high level of society.

Throughout the period foreign influence on the development and innovation of goods was strong, and here again hillforts may have had a role to play.

Foreign trade and foreign relations

From the fifth century down to the end of the third century BC contacts between Britain and other parts of Europe were maintained along much the same lines as during the earlier part of the first millennium. Goods and ideas travelled in both directions, serving to enrich cultures over wide areas and providing a stimulus to innovation. Three main axes of contact can be discerned: cross-Channel trade, trade with northern Europe and trade along the western seaways.

The fifth and early fourth centuries correspond to the period of Hallstatt D on the Continent, and communities in the Thames valley were clearly in close contact with Europe. Among the items imported to Britain are a short iron sword with antenna-shaped hilt from the Thames in the London area and a hemispherical cauldron from the same general provenance. Fibulae brooches were also imported — about 80 are so far known from Britain — and a bronze ribbed pail dug up at Weybridge, Surrey, was probably made by a European metalworker some time in the sixth century BC, although exactly when it arrived in Britain is uncertain.

By 600 BC central European communities were closely connected to the emergent classical civilizations of the Mediterranean world and were fairly large-scale importers of goods from that area, especially drinking and feasting equipment. Some of this may have made its way to Britain too, although everything so far found here of appropriate date is without a secure archaeological context. Among the more likely imports are a fragment of Rhodian type amphora of late seventh- or early sixth-century date from Minster, Kent, an Etruscan bronze oenoche of late sixth- or early fifth-century date from North-ampton, a trefoil-mouthed flagon of early fifth-century date from the river Crouch, Essex, and two bronze jugs of fourth-century date, one from Tew-kesbury, Gloucestershire and one from Bath, Avon. Pottery was also imported—a Greek black figure kylix comes from the Thames Reading, Berkshire, and other finds include vessels from the Thames in London.

Metalwork in the La Tène style, which developed in Europe at the beginning of the fifth century BC, also appears in Britain very soon after. Again the Thames valley was a major contact area and the influence on dagger production and dagger sheaths in the area has already been noted (above p. 157), as has the change to swords in the third century BC. Ornaments of La Tène style, either imports or direct copies, are found widely over central and southern England, but in fairly small numbers.

A second major area in direct contact with the Continent at this time was Humberside. A large number of early La Tène imports and local copies of Continental material concentrate in this area, which also corresponds to the distribution of a distinctive inhumation burial tradition which followed Conti-nental practices. Indeed it has been suggested that this area was colonized by immigrants from the Continent at this time, but, as Timothy Champion has pointed out, the traditions represented cannot be traced to any specific area of the Continent and may therefore be more profitably seen as the result of close trading ties and the local adaptation to wider ideas.

Communities in Scotland maintained contacts with north European groups through the sixth and fifth centuries, exemplified by the distribution of imported or copied objects such as the distinctive sun-flower head swan's-neck type pins, of which eight examples are known in the area.

In western Britain the main axis of contact from the fifth century onwards was between the south-west peninsula and Iberia and the Mediterranean. Tin was the common theme of this contact, Devon and Cornwall being major suppliers of what in European terms is a fairly scarce metal. Two bronze fibulae brooches of Iberian origin were found accompanying burials in an inhumation cemetery at Harlyn Bay, Cornwall, and a third example has been found at Mount Batten overlooking Plymouth Sound, Devon, which was active as a trading port at this time. Greek coins were also possibly introduced from this period as a result of trade along the western seaways with the Mediterranean. A number have

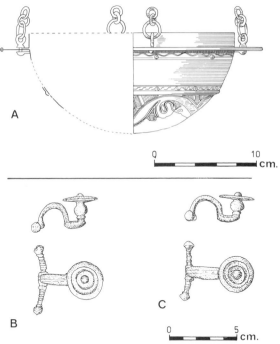

94 Examples of fourth- to second-century BC metalwork imported to western Britain. (A) Bronze decorated hanging bowl found at Cerrig-y-Drudion, Clwyd; (B) and (C) bronze brooches from a cemetery at Harlyn Bay, Cornwall. [*(A) After Smith 1926 figure 2; (B) and (C) after Whimster 1977 figure 30*]

been found in south-western Britain, but only one, issued by Ptolemy V (204–181 BC), from Winches-ter, Hampshire, comes from a secure archaeological context.

The western trade route also allowed contact between western Britain and Gaul, and it may have been through this route that a remarkable bronze hanging bowl, found in a stone cist apparently without any trace of a body at Cerrig-y-Drudion, Clwyd, came to Britain. This vessel is hemispherical in shape with a horizontal flange to which are attached four chains for suspension. The underside is decorated with an elaborate scheme of incised palmettes and acanthus half-palmettes thrown into relief by a cross-hatched background. It was prob-ably made in western France in the fourth century BC.

In the third and second centuries BC contact along all three main axes of trade slowed down and remained at a relatively low level until the beginning of the first century BC when a new episode of intense contact along the western seaways began and new trading ports like Hengistbury Head, Dorset, developed. Interestingly, this hiatus in foreign trade engendered greater local initiative among craftsmen in southern England who continued to develop their products relatively free from Continental influences.

Burial and ritual

Like so many features of society between 600 and 100 BC, evidence for burial and ritual follows closely the patterns prevailing in the earlier first millennium BC. Interest in rivers, lakes and wet places continued, and large amounts of metalwork of the finest quality have been found in such places. The wealth of material from the Thames and the Witham has already been mentioned in this chapter.

Barrow burial lingered on among a few communities, and deposits of later first-millennium BC date are known, for example at Caburn, Sussex, Buntley and Creeting St Mary, Suffolk, and Warborough Hill, Norfolk, where cremations have been found with pottery of sixth-century date. At Handley Down, Dorset, a square barrow loosely dated to this period was excavated in 1969 and was found to contain a cremation deposit. Research by Rowan Whimster has shown that from the fifth century BC onwards a few distinct regional traditions of burial can be identified, although over much of Britain the burial record for the later first millennium is largely absent.

In the Atlantic area inhumation graves and cemeteries of stone-lined cists were common. Burials were usually crouched, and grave goods poor, at best simply a few personal ornaments such as pins, brooches or a bracelet. The largest cemetery so far known is at Harlyn Bay, Cornwall, where some 130 or so burials were found about 1900, mostly preserved beneath a large sand dune. Other cemeteries include Trelan Bahow in Scilly, Trevone, Cornwall, and Mount Batten, Devon. In some parts of western Britain cist burials may have been a lot more common than is often supposed; the lack of grave goods, and, in acid soil areas, the lack of preserved skeletons, makes identification very difficult. The presence of a hanging bowl in a cist at Cerrig-Druy-dion, Clwyd, may indicate the existence of occasional rather richer burials. In Scotland cist burials, both singly and in cemeteries, are widespread.

Some graves in the west lack the elaboration of cists. At Stackpole Warren, Dyfed, the crouched inhumation of an adult, dated to 160 ± 55 BC, was found in a simple grave near a standing stone erected perhaps a millennia earlier.

The Arras tradition

The best-known group of burials dating to between the fourth century and the late second century BC are those in North Yorkshire and Humberside, generally called the Arras tradition after the cemetery of that name excavated at the turn of the century. Many thousands of graves are now known in the area, both individual isolated burials and extensive cemeteries. The Danes Graves cemetery alone contained up to 500 burials. Most graves originally lay under barrows surrounded by rectangular or square ditches. Subsequent agriculture has largely removed the barrows but the ditches can still be seen as cropmarks on aerial photographs. The burials were inhumations and mostly crouched, although some are found extended, and some have wooden coffins. Grave goods include brooches of La Tène types, bracelets, pins and other ornaments. At Barton Fleming, Humberside, excavations by Ian Stead found that burials formed a linear cemetery along the line of an earlier land boundary. Most of the burials were orientated north-south and grave goods included pottery, pig bones and small ornaments. Some burials were, however, aligned east-west and these contained a slightly different range of grave goods including iron knives and swords.

Among the more unusual burials in the Arras tradition are those containing wheeled vehicles. At least ten are known from older excavations, but since 1980 several new examples have come to light at Wetwang, Humberside. These finds have not yet been fully published but preliminary accounts allow the main features to be described. Outwardly the square barrows and central graves were similar to the rest of the burials in the area, but the circumstances of deposition were rather different. Of the three found in 1984 two were male graves, and the other contained a female. All shared a number of features in common. First a large pit had been dug to contain the whole deposit. Next the vehicle, variously described as a cart or chariot, was dismantled. The wheels were placed in the grave first, followed by the body of the deceased. Each interment was accompanied by a range of grave goods: the woman had a side of pork, an iron mirror, a dress pin and a work-box of bronze, the men their swords, spears and shields. Above the body were the remains of the rest of the vehicle including the pole, all the harness fittings for two horses and possibly the wooden chassis of the vehicle on the top.

A

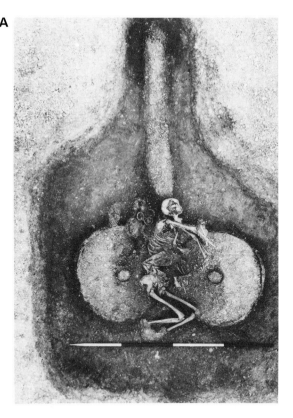

B

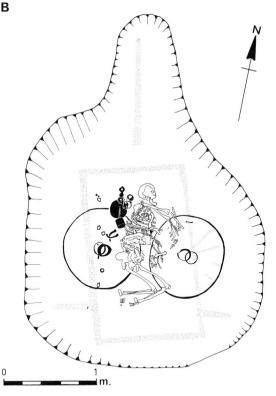

95 Chariot/cart burial number 2 at Wetwang Slack, Humberside. (A) View of the burial under excavation. Scale totals 2 metres. (B) Plan of the burial. The stippled features represent shadow marks indicating decayed wood. [*(A) Photo: Bill Marsden for Humberside County Council Archaeological Unit; copyright reserved. (B) After Dent 1985 figure 3*]

Southern England

In southern England burials have been recorded on settlements and hillforts, often disarticulated skeletons in pits and ditches. At Danebury, Hampshire, for example over 70 individuals were represented among such interments (ten per cent of all pits examined contained some human bones), some possibly deposited as a result of a battle at the site. Similar deposits are known on non-hillfort sites too; at Gussage All Saints, Dorset, seven individuals were represented in pits assigned to the second phase of the settlement, while at Winnall Down, Hampshire, 18 burials including men, women and children were found in quarries contemporary with the fourth phase of occupation at the site dated to the third to first century BC.

Heads, wells and shafts

A preoccupation with human heads can be glimpsed at this period, and is a common theme of Celtic ritual throughout Europe which persisted into the first century BC and later (see p. 180). Decapitated anthropomorphic figurines have been found, for example at Garton Slack, Humberside, but more gruesome is the evidence for the display of human heads found at a number of sites. The best known is Bredon Hill, Hereford and Worcester, where six human skulls were found in a line within the collapsed entranceway of the hillfort and were thought by the excavator Hugh Hencken to represent trophies placed above the gate. At Danebury, Hampshire, eight pits inside the fort contained single human skulls within their backfill, of which six belonged to adult males, one was from an adult female and one belonged to a child. There were also hints that cannibalism may have been practised on a very small scale, perhaps the ritual consumption of an enemy to symbolize subjugation.

Specifically ritual sites of this period are as hard to identify as formal burials. Anne Ross has suggested that a large number of shafts and deep pits in southeastern England were ritual shafts, but their interpretation is problematical, and some may simply be wells. Shrines have been located within some hillforts, for example at Danebury, Hampshire. Here Barry Cunliffe has suggested that four square-shaped buildings in the centre of the fort served such a function, and he cites a comparable example from Cadbury Castle, Somerset. Some Roman temples may have been built on earlier shrines, as perhaps at Maiden Castle, Dorset. On the Cotswolds at West Hill, Uley, Gloucestershire, a large rectangular ritual enclosure some 48 metres long by 25 metres (157 feet by 82 feet) wide and bounded by rock-cut ditches underlay an early Roman temple of classical design.

Classical writers relate that the Druids were a powerful class of religious leaders in the later first millennium BC, and although there is no firm archaeological evidence for them it may be assumed that they serviced the ritual centres at this time. Classical sources also suggest that, in addition to formal ritual shrines, natural places such as groves and springs were used as sacred retreats.

Society and politics

By the second century BC Celtic society in Britain had reached a level of complexity previously unattained. Population estimates are always difficult with incomplete information, but with hillforts and larger settlements housing perhaps 150 to 200 people, and smaller settlements up to 20, an overall population well in excess of one million must be envisaged. Most of the landscape was used in some way, although there were marked regional differences which allow two general patterns of social organization to be glimpsed—chiefdoms and tribes.

In the north and west, settlement patterns suggest specialization in the use of resources with small-scale communities, and little or no centralized control. There is little evidence for formal demarcation of territories or of investment in the landscape by way of fields and boundaries. To judge from the widespread distribution of heavily defended sites, warfare and raiding were prevalent. Evidence for storage at these sites is scant but as livestock probably formed the mainstay of the subsistence economy, food and wealth would effectively have been tied up in the animals and so, as it were, stored on the hoof. Access to high-quality goods was possible, as demonstrated by the incidence of rich deposits in graves and wet places in western regions, but in comparison with the south and east, Atlantic

Britain was generally rather poor. This is not to say, however, that social organization was not complex and political ties not deep rooted. In small-scale dispersed societies arrangements had to be made for the provision of wives and inheritance sufficient to maintain viable productive and reproductive units. Kinship ties probably provided the basis of political structure and a loose-knit tribal network based on descent patterns, inheritance and alliances seems to fit the evidence.

In southern, central and eastern England, and in parts of eastern Scotland, the pattern is rather different since various forms of settlement hierarchy can be identified, either homesteads and hillforts or farmsteads and villages. In either case nucleated settlements provided focal points, nodes in the settlement system which may also have been nodes in the political system. In this respect, the villages of eastern and central England may have performed similar roles to the hillforts of southern and western areas. The considerable number of developed hillforts suggests that if they do represent political centres then territories were relatively small. Warfare remained widespread if not endemic in the hillfort zone, but by the second century forts and weapons had taken on such an ostentatious air to their design, that it is questionable whether massed warfare and raiding continued in the same way as previously. It is possible that more formalized warfare was undertaken by a warrior class or that single combat by champions had taken over. Warriors were certainly present, and it is tempting to identify also a priest class, a class of specialist craftsmen, and a class of part-time specialist craftsmen/farmers.

The precise role of the developed hillforts and their place in the organization of society is not at all clear. They appear to be well spaced and so may have been situated within reasonably well-defined territories, and they were maintained, repaired and periodically remodelled by powerful authorities able to order reserves of manpower. They probably provided for their hinterland such services as religious centres, a nucleated residence for a substantial body of people, some form of storage and redistributive capacity and a workplace for some craftsmen. The coercive power implicit both in the ordered layout of buildings and in the monumentally planned and executed defences, together with the role of redistribution, suggests the centralized power of a chiefdom. Whether the heads of such societies actually lived in the hillforts is quite another matter. It is tempting to suggest that they did simply because of the scale of the sites, and this may be true. Barry Cunliffe has, for example, proposed two possible models for Danebury. In the first the chief or king, the nobility as heads of kinship groups holding the surrounding farms, and some or all of the skilled craftsmen lived in the hillfort. In the second only the chief and his court or entourage lived in the hillfort while the nobility lived in other settlements round about, perhaps with yet another tier of site representing farm units below them. Choosing between these two is quite impossible given present evidence, but other possibilities must also be considered. As John Collis has pointed out, there is in fact very little evidence for the presence of wealthy people in hillforts, and it may be that the occupants were simply administrators of the various activities which took place at the hillforts. Again, until more is known of the status of sites round about hillforts, it is only possible to speculate.

Whatever the reality of the functioning of the various systems visible in different parts of the country, strong political units capable of mobilizing considerable resources are clearly represented throughout Britain. Moreover, the basic unit, the household, is virtually the same; even the dimensions and the construction of round houses are similar over the whole country. In the last episode of prehistory in Britain during the century and a half leading up to the Roman Conquest it is the ability of these political units to combine and work together in different arrangements that largely determined the course of events in different areas.

7 Questions of Balance

Political Societies 100 BC–AD 50

Hands across the water

After perhaps two centuries of relative isolation, the communities of southern England again became closely involved with their neighbours across the English Channel from about 120 BC onwards. The reasons for this are not entirely clear, but a major contributory factor must have been the effects of a westward expansion of Roman power and an extension of trading at this time. The first century BC was a period of major change in Roman politics. The State was rapidly evolving, largely under pressure from ambitious leaders with an efficient military machine at their disposal. By 100 BC Roman provinces had been established along the northern coast of the Mediterranean from Portugal to Asia Minor. North of the Alps the provinces of Cisalpine and Narbonensis Gaul had been founded. Thus in 62 BC, when Pompey returned to Rome triumphant at his conquests in the East, his rival Julius Caesar sought an equivalent chance to bolster his military prestige and to build up his financial resources in the west. Three years later he began his famous campaigns to conquer Gaul. By 57 BC he had taken Gaul and soon after established the frontiers of the Roman world along the coast of northern France and Belgium and eastwards along the Rhine. Britain remained outside direct Roman rule for nearly a century after the conquest of Gaul, but throughout that time languished on the periphery of one of the greatest civilizations in history.

For the archaeologist, Britain's proximity to the Roman world provides an important additional source of information for later prehistory: the writings of classical scholars. A few pre-first-century BC references to Britain are known, largely through being reiterated in later texts, but Greek and Roman geographers, ethnographers, historians, philosophers and poets were using information about Britain in their writings much more often from the first century BC onwards. The account of the Gallic Wars by Caesar himself, and the works of Poseidonius copied by Strabo (c.64 BC–AD 21 +) and Tacitus (AD 56–115 +) are among the most extensive, but in all over 120 classical authors speak of Britain.

Among the information contained in classical texts are the names of people and places—the earliest individuals known in British history—accounts of battles, and descriptions of the country and its people. Caesar (*Gallic Wars* V, 14,3) remarks that the Britons dye their bodies with woad to produce a blue colour and that they wear their hair long and shave the whole of their bodies except the head and the upper lip. Tacitus (*Agricola* II) makes a distinction between the large-limbed red-haired people of the north, who he thought were of Germanic origin, and the swarthy curly-haired people of the west. Elsewhere details of warfare, marital customs, religious beliefs and even glimpses of political and social organization can be found. Because the classics have long been held in high regard by scholars of literature and antiquarians alike these commentaries have profoundly influenced our understanding of later prehistoric times, sometimes at the expense of the archaeological evidence.

In addition to the truly classical sources, mention may also be made of the Irish epic folk-tales such as the *Cattle raid of Cooley*, first written down in the early Middle Ages, but arguably derived from far more ancient oral traditions. Unfortunately the influence of Christianity and classical sources in these texts are so strong that in many cases it is almost impossible to disentangle what has been copied to impress the reader from what might have been derived from local folk-tales. Accordingly these sources are very difficult to use. Indeed all literary references to Britain of early date have to be treated with appropriate caution and due consideration of the sources of information available to the writer: first-hand experience, secondary sources, informers, or simply their imagination. Their reasons for writing must also be examined. In the past much attention was given to squaring comments by classical scholars with archaeological evidence, most of it in vain. Archaeological and literary evidence are better seen as being complementary rather than overlapping, and neither should be forced together to substantiate the claims of the other.

Contemporary with the increase in classical references to Britain comes the earliest evidence for writing in Britain. From the first century BC papyrus was certainly used in Britain during the manufacture of potin coins which are mostly found in south-eastern England. It is unlikely that papyrus was imported simply to cut up into strips to use in making coin moulds and the only reasonable explanation is that it was already here in its usual role as material for writing on. Other types of coin minted in Britain from the first century BC onwards bear the names of individuals written in the Latin alphabet, as on Roman coins. Indeed Roman die-makers may have been involved in the establishment of some mints. A fragment of pottery dated to the early first century AD from the site of Skeleton Green, Braughing, Hertfordshire, has the name CIINATIN cut on its shoulder as a graffito. However, the site was certainly closely involved in trade with the Roman world, so whether the letters were cut by a trader or a native inhabitant is not known. The extent to which Latin was used in Britain at this time is not known either.

International trade and exchange
100–55 BC

Of the known principal routes of trade and exchange between Britain and the Continent (see above pp. 156–8) it was those along the western seaways which

96 Excavations in progress at Hengistbury Head on the west side of Christchurch Harbour, Dorset. This site emerged as one of the most important ports in southern England during the second and early first century BC. [*Photo: by permission of Barry Cunliffe; copyright reserved*]

carried the acceleration of contact between the two during the early first century BC. The West Country, particularly western Hampshire, Dorset, Devon and Cornwall, was closely linked to northern and western France, and also directly with the Mediterranean.

Closely connected with the rise of foreign trade at this time was the development of trading ports where natural harbours provided good places for ships to dock. Among the most extensively excavated is the site of Hengistbury Head, Dorset. Here, ships from the Continent had been anchoring in the spacious harbour since perhaps the second millennium BC, but from 150 BC onwards many more ships came and went, and greater quantities of material passed through this port. The headland was defended by two lines of ramparts, and occupation was widespread. Investigations under the direction of Barry Cunliffe have demonstrated that the range of goods imported included wine in amphorae (Dressel IA types) from Italy, fine black cordoned and graphite-coated pottery from Brittany, glass probably from the Mediterranean, and coins from northern France. These coins, so called Armorican types, are mostly found in the south west of England, and stand at the head of a long series of imported and indigenously produced coins. Hengistbury Head was also the site of manufacturing industries, bronzeworking and ironworking are attested and there are the remains of two hearths for the extraction of silver from argentiferous copper or lead. Other ports have been located, at Mount Batten in Plymouth Sound, Devon and in Poole Harbour, Dorset.

Metal seems to have been the unifying factor in the Atlantic trading of the early first century BC. Tin, copper, iron and lead are available in the south west and were at this time probably the main export. The distribution of imported objects inland from the south coast reinforces this interpretation and allows shale and salt to be added to the list of probable exports. Many different types of site, including hillforts and defended farmsteads, have yielded imports resulting from this trade. At Carn Euny, Cornwall, for example, sherds of Dressel IA amphorae suggest that wine was sometimes served by the head of that community, just as do sherds of similar vessels found within the massive stronghold at Maiden Castle, Dorset. The effects of the trade were relatively restricted to the south west.

On a wider front trading links extended beyond the south-west peninsula, although perhaps on a less intensive scale. Particularly important is the find of a lead anchor stock in shallow water at Porth Felen off the treacherous coast of the Llyn Peninsula, Gwynedd. This stock, which weighs over 70 kilograms (154 lbs), is of Mediterranean origin and was undoubtedly lost from a ship sailing in the area during the late second or early first century BC. The reason for the voyage is unknown, but the metal resources of North Wales may be counted as one obvious attraction.

The Veneti and the Belgae

Caesar (*Gallic Wars* III) suggests that a tribe living in south-western Brittany known as the Veneti was deeply involved in the seaborne trade of the Atlantic province in the early first century BC, and that they had the largest fleet of ships and the greatest experience of navigation in the area. Because of their skills and independence, Caesar destroyed their fleet and subjugated the tribe shortly after the conquest of Gaul. However, it is another of Caesar's comments which has provoked the most interest and debate. When describing Britain (*Gallic Wars* V, 12), Caesar claimed that the maritime part (usually taken to mean south-eastern England) was inhabited by people who had crossed over from Belgium to invade and loot but who had then stayed to till the fields and who were known by the names of the states from which they derived. Evidence for the arrival of these so called 'Belgic' peoples (the Belgae) has frequently been sought in the archaeological remains, especially the distribution of coins derived from northern France (Gallo-Belgic types), the distribution of cremation cemeteries and the distribution of certain types of pottery which are all found in Kent and Essex and which would therefore be appropriately located to have arrived through such an invasion. From this core area various schemes were proposed to account for the spread of the coins and pottery further inland so that by the mid first century BC a Belgic expansion into large areas of southern England was postulated.

Much of the evidence crucial to these arguments can now be questioned, however. Ann Birchell demonstrated that the pottery is too late in date to be connected with the arrival of any immigrants in the first half of the first century BC. The cremation cemeteries are also too late because of associations with the pottery. Moreover, Derek Allen has shown that the earliest coins of the Gallo-Belgic series are too early to be connected with a Belgic invasion. Rather different explanations must now be sought for the various components formerly attributed to

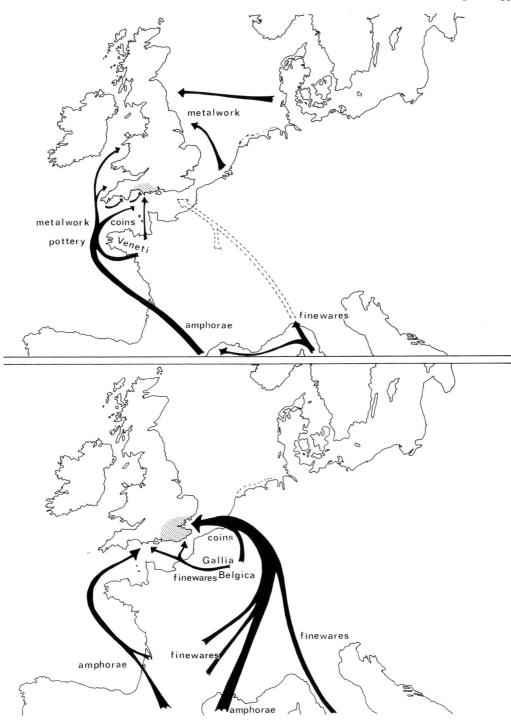

97 Continental sources of goods imported into Britain.
(a) Third to mid first century BC. (b) Mid first century BC
to first century AD.

the Belgic invasion, and while a few scholars persist in searching for traces of these groups in south-eastern England among later coin distributions, the whole question of the Belgae in Britain perfectly illustrates the impracticality of overlaying archaeological and literary evidence.

That some Gauls sought refuge in Britain at the time of the Roman conquest of their own country can hardly be doubted in view of the close contact that evidently existed between the two countries during the preceding centuries, but finding such people archaeologically is probably a fruitless pursuit. Moreover, Barry Cunliffe has pointed out that if Caesar's words are followed closely, and the people who settled in Britain continued to be called by their tribal name as Caesar says, then the area round the Solent should be regarded as the most likely area of settlement since it is here that the Roman city of Winchester was called *Venta Belgarum*, the capital of the Belgae.

Caesar's expeditions to Britain

The movements of goods and people across the Channel changed after the Roman conquest of Gaul. The destruction of the Veneti fleet must have caused considerable disruption, and certainly the western seaways declined in importance as the opportunities for trade with Continental communities decreased. At about this time, in 55 and 54 BC, Caesar led two separate expeditions into Britain. Neither resulted in Britain being annexed to the Roman world but one of the purposes of the missions was probably to establish formal trading links between Rome and those groups in Britain prepared to enter into alliances and partnerships. Thus in a sense Caesar was paving the way for Roman traders and merchants to establish themselves here, and perhaps at the same time trying to conciliate the Britons in order to make conquest at some later date rather easier.

No archaeological evidence of Caesar's campaigns in Britain is known for certain, despite the fact that heavy casualties were apparently inflicted on the Roman army which must have occasioned burial grounds and, if usual army practice was followed, fortresses and camps too should have left some trace. All knowledge of the campaigns therefore derives from Caesar's accounts of the Gallic Wars (Chapter V), and are a familiar story. News of a proposed invasion in 55 BC reached the leaders of groups in southern England, and they sent envoys to submit to Rome. These were sent back home with generous promises if they kept their resolve, but it seems that when the invasion force, comprising two legions of the Roman army, arrived in Britain they were met with hostilities. After various agreements and further resistance the army found it was making little headway and withdrew to Gaul.

The following year, 54 BC, Caesar returned to Britain with a stronger army. By this time the British chieftains of southern England united against the common foe under a leader named Cassivellaunus who it seems lived north of the Thames, perhaps with his capital at Verulamium near present-day St Albans, Hertfordshire. Despite many set-backs Caesar advanced beyond the Thames into the territory controlled by Cassivellaunus. By this time it was late summer and, after several successful battles against the British, Caesar accepted the surrender of a number of leaders on condition that they paid an annual tribute to the Roman government. After this he returned to Gaul where in the following years other matters occupied him so that no further sorties into Britain were undertaken.

The effects of Caesar's visits to Britain and their aftermath can perhaps be best judged by the number of changes that can be glimpsed in the economy and political organization of the communities throughout the country over the following few decades. In the south east the traditional settlement pattern altered rather markedly and there were also changes in burial rites and the use and circulation of fine objects. Elsewhere changes were less dramatic but nonetheless perceptible. In all, three distinct zones can be recognized from about 50 BC onwards and these have been characterized as a core zone, a periphery zone and an outer zone by Colin Haselgrove in his study of the effects of foreign trade on the development of society in the later first century BC. Each of these zones may be considered in turn.

The core zone

This area lies around the lower Thames valley, including Kent, Surrey, Sussex, London, Essex, Hertfordshire, and parts of Buckinghamshire and north Hampshire. Prior to the arrival of Caesar, this area was closely in touch with the Continent, not so much through trade but through providing help to the Gauls in their fight against Rome. It was through these encounters, as well as through trade, that the earlier Gallo-Belgic series coins found their way to Britain.

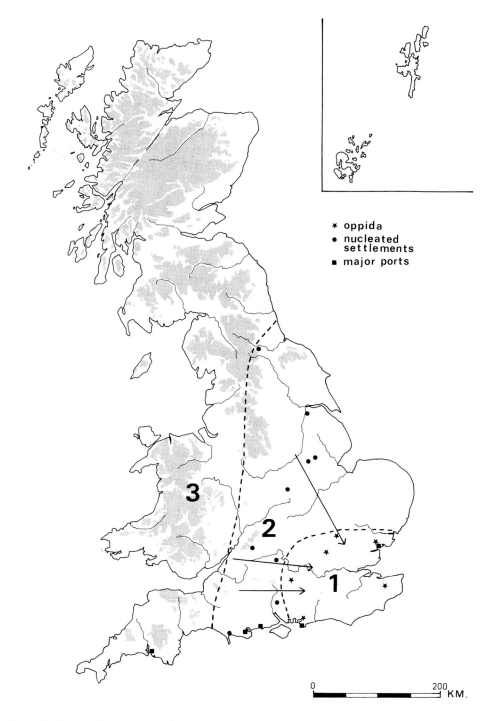

98   Britain in the early first century AD showing the
three main regions and the location of the main *oppida*,
ports and principal known settlements in Areas 1 and 2.

1 = Core zone; 2 = periphery zone; 3 = outer zone.
[*Based on Haselgrove 1982 figure 10.6*]

167

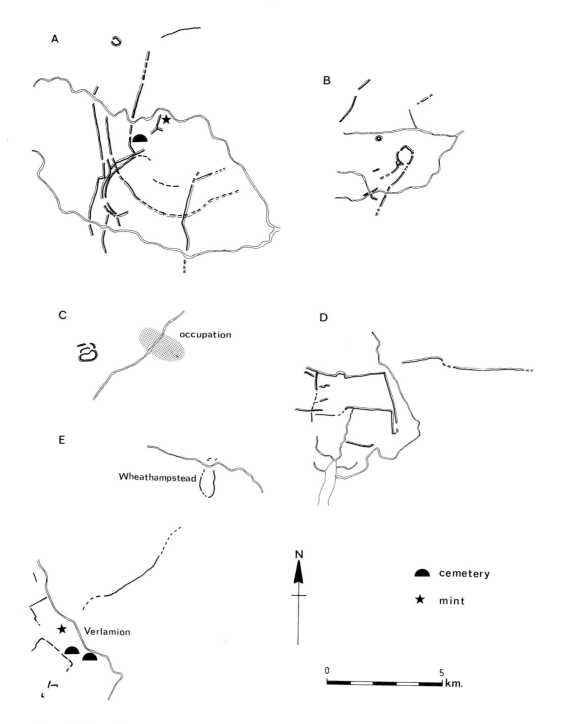

99 Plans of main *oppida* sites of the late first century BC and first century AD in south-eastern England. (A) Colchester (Camulodunum), Essex; (B) Silchester, Hampshire; (C) Canterbury, Kent; (D) Chichester, Sussex; (E) St Albans (Verulamium), Hertfordshire. [*(A)–(C) After Megaw and Simpson 1979 figures 7.16 and 7.17; (D) after Cunliffe 1978 figure 6.6; (E) after Saunders and Havercroft 1982 figure 14*]

Coins and trade

From the Gallo-Belgic coins local copies developed, at first as high-denomination issues in gold, but later lower denominations in silver. Exactly how these were used is not clear, but John Collis has suggested that two levels of coin usage can be seen. Firstly, a high-value series used for high-level transactions, storage of wealth such as might be imagined with the payment of mercenaries, and payments such as bride wealth or tribute. Secondly, at an altogether different level, a low-value coinage probably for everyday transactions. Colin Haselgrove goes further in suggesting that coins may have been used for the movement of goods or services across the established boundaries of existing exchange practices, especially between different spheres of exchange, so that goods and produce could be liberated for use in trade with Rome. At present no firm answers can be provided, but much research into coins of this period is now in progress and should eventually allow their use and development to be more completely understood.

After Caesar, this core area was closely linked to the Continent through trade which increased in volume towards the period of the conquest. Middlemen may have been responsible for carrying out the transactions and transporting goods from the classical world to Britain and vice versa. By this time trade, in the sense that is implied by the use of the word today, probably prevailed. Ports were established and became the focus of transactions. Colchester, Essex, was certainly an important centre for trade, although little is known of the waterfront arrangements. Selsey Bill, Sussex, might have been another such place, but little investigation has been undertaken here.

Settlement

Settlements continued to develop along the lines established in the fifth to first centuries BC. Farmsteads and villages were the main centres of occupation, some enclosed and some not. However, a few settlements stand out as being rather different from the others. They are generally much larger, and tend to be situated in river valleys. They are richer in terms of traded artefacts than contemporary small sites, suggesting that the occupants had greater involvement in foreign trade. Five such sites can be recognized, Skeleton Green (Braughing) and Verulamium, Hertfordshire, Camulodunum (Colchester) Essex, Canterbury, Kent and Silchester, Hampshire. These sites are generally called *oppida* in deference to a term used by Caesar in his commen-

taries, although whether he was actually referring to such settlements at the time is debatable.

The main features of these *oppida* sites are clear enough. They are generally large, Skeleton Green for example covered over 100 hectares (247 acres) at its height, and most are seemingly post-Caesarian foundations. Dykeworks of various sorts define areas within them, and radiate from them, although the dating of these is often far from certain. They are not single occupation sites, but more often clusters of separate components, some of which can be distinguished from each other according to the kinds of activities undertaken within them. Most have an accompanying small hill-top or hill-slope enclosure nearby. A great variety of different activities were undertaken at these sites. At Camulodunum metalworking, coin-making, potting and various other industries were distributed around the occupation area. Rich burials and extensive cemeteries are frequently found nearby. As yet, few large areas within these *oppida* sites have been examined in detail, the single most extensive area probably being at Silchester where excavations directed by Michael Fulford have examined over 600 square metres (717 square yards) of the central area of the settlement. At most *oppida* there is some evidence for rectangular buildings, perhaps in imitation of houses fashionable in the Mediterranean or in Gaul after the conquest, and there is also evidence for a certain amount of planning in the layout of these sites with consistent alignment of plots and buildings. To what extent this could be construed as urbanization is debatable, but it is notable that all the *oppida* became Roman towns of various sorts after the conquest, presumably in recognition of their nodal position in the economic and political organization of the area.

Crafts and industries focused on *oppida*, although were not exclusively undertaken at such sites. Very fine objects were produced, and renewed inspiration from Europe allows the identification of heavy La Tène stage III influences on the design and decoration of objects. Technical innovations were also adopted in the core area, particularly the use of the high-speed potter's wheel for the production of a wide range of new vessel forms including pedestalled jars, beakers, carinated bowls and many cups and bowl forms. Copies of imported pots were also made. Coin production was widespread at *oppidum* sites, and clay flan-moulds for producing standardized metal blanks are a common find. In Kent, potin coins (silver-bronze alloy) were made in strips by forming a two-piece clay mould over papyrus blanks then etching the design in the clay before casting.

169

Evidence that the *oppida* were heavily involved in trade and commerce may be found in the fact that small-denomination coins are more common at such sites than the larger denomination issues which John Collis has shown cluster on the rural settlements round about. Some *oppida* may even have been located on the edge rather than at the centre of their hinterlands to facilitate trade.

Luxury imports

The range of imports brought into the core zone is far greater than at any previous time in prehistory, and seems to reflect the imitation of certain Roman ways of life. Of the objects which survive archaeologically, the greatest proportion relate to eating and drinking activities. Wine, imported in amphorae (Dressel IA and IB forms), from Italy was brought alongside fish products and olive oil, also in amphorae (Dressel forms 6-11 and 20), from Spain. Fine pottery of Gallo-Belgic types in *terra nigra* and *terra rubra*, especially platters, cups and beakers, came from north-east France. Fine red glossy Arretine pottery came from Italy and central Gaul, and central Gaulish micaceous wares travelled to Britain too. In the years immediately preceding the conquest glossy red samian ware, so familiar from Roman sites, began to appear in this country. Metal vessels, including silver cups, bronze flagons, bronze bowls and strainers, probably of Gaulish or Italian manufacture, are also known. In addition to this food, wine and table ware, other luxury goods which have so far come to light include a set of glass gaming-pieces, a medallion of Emperor Augustus made from a cut-down *denarius* mounted in a frame, and even a bronze table.

Access to imported luxuries appears to have been restricted mostly to a high level within society, with only some of the pottery, amphorae and personal

100 Imported luxury goods of early–mid first-century AD date from eastern England. (1)–(3), (6) and (8) = central Gaulish wares; (2), (4) and (5) = *terra rubra*; (7) = *terra nigra*; (9) = Dressel I amphora; (10) = Dressel 2–4 amphora. (1), (6) and (8) from Welwyn Garden City burial, Hertfordshire; (3), (4), (5) and (7) from Skeleton Green, Hertfordshire; (2) from Gatesbury, Hertfordshire; (9) and (10) forms as found in Britain based on Camulodunum, Essex. [(2)–(5) and (7) After Partridge 1981 figures 77 and 78; (1), (6) and (8) after Stead 1967 figure 8; (9) and (10) after Hawkes and Hull 1947 plates 69 and 70]

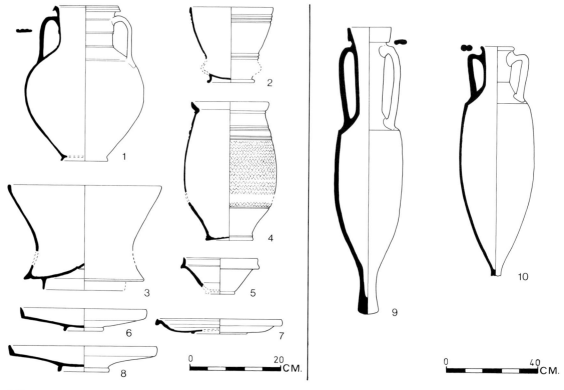

ornaments like brooches commonly finding their way onto lower order sites. Most imported objects may be regarded as presitige items, and it is notable that feasting and drinking rituals again appear so clearly at this time following much the same pattern as they had during the earlier first millennium BC (see above p. 132). Clearly, such rites were still considered important in maintaining and reinforcing the social order. Classical writers record that strong drink, principally wine and beer, was consumed during feasting sessions which could last for days on end, and that brave warriors were honoured with the finest portions of meat at these ceremonies.

Archaeological evidence for the goods exported from Britain is less easy to identify than the luxury goods which were imported. However, the writer Strabo (64 BC–AD 21 +) provides a list of mostly raw materials and resources which would have been in short supply at the heart of the Roman Empire: corn, cattle, gold, silver, hides, slaves and hunting dogs. Most of these could not have been found within south-eastern England, and must therefore have been brought in or acquired from further afield.

Burials

Burials become a prominent feature of the archaeological record in the core area from about 40 BC and reflect changing burial practices. Many of the most richly furnished are found near *oppida*, and it is characteristic of the rich burials in this area that imported luxury goods accompany the deceased. Cremation was the preferred rite.

North of the River Thames is a series of especially rich burials, known as Welwyn type graves after excavated examples at Welwyn Garden City and Welwyn, Hertfordshire. Characteristically these comprise a deep grave-pit in which the cremated remains of the deceased were heaped or scattered on the floor together with supplies of food and wine and the accessories required for its consumption. At Welwyn Garden City, one of the richest graves of the group contained a silver vessel, two bronze vessels, four wooden vessels with metal fittings, five wine amphorae, a Roman Central Gaulish flagon, two imported Central Gaulish platters, 33 other pots, 24 glass gaming-pieces, six bead/bracelet fragments, a bronze strainer, a bronze nail-cleaner, 46 bronze-headed studs, an iron knife, a wooden board and other objects with iron fittings, and a straw mat. Not represented in this grave, but well known from others, are iron fire dogs, often lavishly ornamented with animal heads, and probably one

part of the hearth furnishings in the house of the deceased.

A second burial tradition, concentrated south of the Thames, but occasionally found on the north side, is the cremation cemetery tradition. Best represented at the two large cemeteries at Aylesford and Swarling, both in Kent, the ashes of the deceased are usually buried in, or with, a wheel-turned ceramic urn or other container. A wealth/social differential is evident in the nature of the goods buried with the ashes. Simple graves contain nothing but the ashes and a vessel of some kind, but many were provided with personal ornaments and tinkets. In the richest graves the ashes were buried in or with wooden buckets covered in decorated bronze plates with other bronze vessels, strainers, ladles and jugs set round about. These items were all connected with wine drinking and may imply some symbolic link between red wine and blood as being an essential part of life.

None of the burials mentioned so far was covered by a barrow, but at Lexden, adjacent to the *oppidum* at Camulodunum, Essex, a large barrow over 22 metres (72 feet) in diameter was found to contain an enormous burial pit some 8 metres (26 feet) long in which was a cremation burial, wine amphorae and other vessels, a bronze table, a pedestal for a statuette, a series of bronze figures, bronze embossed plates, studs, hinges and other fittings, silver decorative attachments, bronze mail with silver studs, the silver medallion of the Emperor Augustus mentioned above and the handle from a large crater or wine-serving vessel. Significantly, many of the objects at Lexden appear to have been deliberately broken before deposition, which is rarely the case with other graves known from this time.

Rivers and wet places

Ritual use of rivers and wet places continued. Much La Tène III metalwork has been dredged from the Thames, but the influence of the water cults may have been waning because in keeping with the increased interest in Roman traditions temples are more numerous from the later first century BC, and appear to have provided an alternative context for the deposition of fine and valuable objects, particularly coins and personal ornaments like brooches. Circular temples have been explored at Kelvedon, Essex, and Hayling Island, Sussex. A square temple with a central *cella* is known at Heathrow, London, although its exact date is unclear. Among the objects found at the Hayling Island temple were over 90 coins, of which 22 were Gaulish imports, bronze horse harness, imported pottery, brooches and fragments of four speculum hand-mirrors manufactured in Italy in the early first century AD.

The periphery zone

Westwards and north-westwards of the core zone is a wide peripheral area stretching from the south coast in Hampshire and Dorset northwards to Yorkshire. Communities in this broad band of land were relatively unaffected by Caesar's visits to Britain, except that they may have rallied round their south-eastern neighbours against the Romans and some of the leaders may even have been involved in the pact of allegiance with Rome. Whatever the case, from the mid first century onwards this area appears to have been indirectly involved in trade with the Continent through south-eastern Britain, probably acting as suppliers and producers of goods and materials, for which they were paid in coinage, and in a few of the luxury items such as fine pottery and

wine which were more widely available in the core zone. This disparity in the availability of imported luxury goods between the two zones is more than might be expected if distance from the trading ports was solely to blame. In fact the character of the goods present in the two zones is quite different, with only the most commonly available forms being represented in the periphery zone; the kinds of contexts in which goods were deposited are also different.

Settlements

Settlements in the periphery zone continued to develop in much the same way as they had done for the previous few centuries. At some sites the focus of settlement shifted a little as remodelling and refurbishment were necessary. Among lower order settlements there was a slight tendency for increased nucleation and for the addition of enclosure works to otherwise unenclosed sites, but this was not universal. One explanation for this may be that when goods for export could not be acquired by peaceful means raids were organized to secure supplies. Barry Cunliffe has noted that in Wessex and the upper Thames valley many farmsteads which until the first century BC were undifferentiated in their internal structure often comprised a cluster of separate

101 Aerial view of the massive multiperiod hillfort at Maiden Castle, Dorset. [*Photo: West Air Photography, Weston-super-Mare; copyright reserved*]

compounds forming a cohesive unit after the first century BC.

In the zone dominated by hillforts many of the larger centres continued to be occupied; some, like Maiden Castle, Dorset, were refortified and strengthened, firstly perhaps in response to the need for defence against raids by people living in the core zone for food, and of course people for export as slaves, and secondly in response to the threat of the Roman invasion. The dating of the final phases at most hillforts is complicated by the fact that in the periphery zone pottery styles during the later first century BC and early first century AD are not very different from second- or third-century BC forms, and with very few imports at this time chronological resolution is low. At Danebury, Hampshire, relatively slight occupation in the first century BC is claimed by the excavator in comparison with earlier phases at the site and it is possible that this particular

hillfort simply became a refuge at times of danger, or a site of religious importance only. Elsewhere continued use of sites is attested, although those enclosures situated in close proximity to good communication routes seem to be the most intensively used, for example Maiden Castle, Dorset, overlooking the routeways leading from the important sea ports at Hengistbury Head and Poole Harbour, Dorset, and Salmonsbury, Gloucestershire, beside one of the main north bank tributaries of the upper Thames leading into the agriculturally rich Cotswold uplands.

Where no valley-side enclosures, or sites located at the intersection of communication routes, existed, new ones were created, as at Winchester, Hampshire, Leicester, and Bagendon, Gloucestershire. Morphologically these sites represent the ultimate development in the hillfort/large enclosure tradition. The inhabitants of these sites were certainly closely involved in trade with south-eastern England, for quantities of imported pottery and amphorae are found, although in appreciably smaller quantities than in the core zone.

In eastern England many village-like settlements continued in occupation, and, as with the hillforts and enclosures in the south, became involved in trade with the core zone. Dragonby, Lincolnshire,

102 Plans of high-status large enclosed settlements occupied during the first century BC and first century AD in central and southern England. (A) Dyke Hills, Oxfordshire; (B) Salmonsbury, Gloucestershire; (C) Winchester, Hampshire; (D) Bagendon, Gloucestershire. [(A) and (C) After Megaw and Simpson 1979 figure 7.19; (B) and (D) after RCHM 1976 op. page 19 and op. page 7]

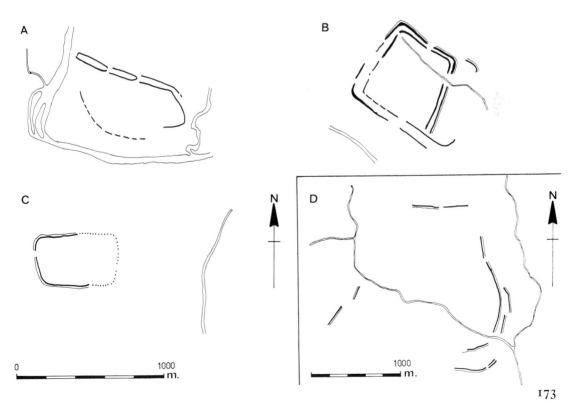

103 Brigantian multiphase settlement at Stanwick, North Yorkshire. (A) Enclosure earthworks on the north-eastern side. (B) Excavations in 1985 in The Tofts near the centre of the site showing drainage gullies of two round houses, the one on the right may have been connected with metalworking. [*(A) Photo: author; copyright reserved. (B) Photo: Colin Haselgrove; copyright reserved*]

174

for example, beside the Jurassic Way and in close proximity to good iron ore reserves, began in the third or second century BC but expanded rapidly in the first century BC, ultimately to cover about 8 hectares (20 acres) when pottery similar to that circulating in the core zone was imported to the site.

No *oppida* of the type known in the core zone can be identified in the periphery zone, although sites such as Bagendon, Gloucestershire, and Grim's Ditch, Oxfordshire, have at various times been credited with such status, and even more unlikely sites have also quite erroneously been drawn into the *oppida* tradition too. In all cases these sites lack the quantity and variety of imported goods, the proximity of rich burials exploiting imported status objects as grave goods, and the evidence for widespread intensive occupation with a semblance of planning and interest in Roman customs. Other contrasts which might be cited include the fact that many of the so-called *oppida* outside the core zone either have a very long history of occupation or were established on the eve of the Roman Conquest.

The old port at Hengistbury, Hampshire, and other south-coast harbours were not totally eclipsed by the shift in trade to the south east; they continued to be active through the first century BC and early first century AD, and to their number may be added another site at Ferriby in the Humber estuary, Humberside, which must also have been providing direct access to European markets for inhabitants of the periphery zone.

Production and exchange

Coins, both large-denomination gold and silver issues and small-denomination bronze issues, were produced by communities living over much of the peripheral zone from Dorset to Yorkshire. The prototypes included both Gallo-Belgic and Armorican issues, and they circulated over wide areas, although mostly within the periphery zone itself. Minting was undertaken at a variety of sites, but mostly the larger hillforts, enclosures and village settlements. Coin output was probably rather less than in the core zone at least until the later part of the first half of the first century AD when output seems to have increased and perhaps spread to parts of the periphery zone which did not previously use coins.

The production of fine metalwork in well-established Celtic traditions reached a peak in the first centuries BC/AD in the periphery zone. Elaborate bronze horse fittings, weapons, ornaments, brooches and mirrors were among the goods produced, often embellished with intricate curvilinear designs. At Stanwick, North Yorkshire, an enclosed settlement of high status, a very well-preserved iron sword in a delicately carved ash wood scabbard was found in a waterlogged section of ditch. This find illustrates something which must have been rather more commonplace than the archaeological record suggests but which is now largely lost to us. Use of gold and silver became more common at this time, and perhaps the height of craftsmanship in these metals are the torcs found almost exclusively in the periphery zone, especially in East Anglia, and the twisted neck-rings from other areas. One of the most famous examples, from Snettisham, Norfolk, is made of several strands of electrum wire twisted together, the ends of which were inserted into large hollow ring terminals splendidly decorated in the La Tène art style.

Burials

In contrast to the core zone, fine indigenously produced objects were used as grave goods in the periphery zone rather than imported objects which seem mostly confined to high status settlements. Three main burial traditions can be identified, again representing developments of earlier traditions. The first is the warrior grave tradition. In this the burial rite was inhumation, and involved only adult males accompanied by weapons, usually a sword, spears, a shield and a knife. At Owslebury, Hampshire, the warrior was estimated to have been aged about 40–50 years at death, and in addition to the usual range of grave goods already listed he had a tinned or silvered bronze belt hook dated to about 25–1 BC. At least 17 other warrior burials are known, spread widely from Dorset to Lincolnshire.

The second class of burial is the wealthy female graves, which are spread over roughly the same area as the male warrior graves, but are distinctive in containing personal ornaments, and usually a mirror. Inhumation was again the rule, sometimes in small cemeteries. Perhaps the most famous such burial is in a cemetery of unknown size at Birdlip overlooking the Severn Valley above Cheltenham, Gloucestershire. The grave goods with this lady comprised a bronze mirror, a silver brooch, a bronze expanding bangle, a bronze animal-head pattern knife handle with an iron blade, a small bronze bowl, a drop handle, a finial loop, tweezers, bronze rings and a collection of beads. A large bronze bowl had been placed over the lady's face in the grave. The other persons in the cemetery here were not accom-

104 Grave goods from the rich early–mid first-century AD graves in the Birdlip cemetery, Gloucestershire. The two semi-circular bronze bucket mounts (bottom right) probably derive from a male grave; the remaining objects were found with an adult female during quarrying in 1879. [*Photo: Gloucester City Museum; copyright reserved*]

panied by grave goods, except one individual who may have had a wooden bucket with bronze fittings.

A third tradition can be recognized in Dorset where the burial rite comprised crouched inhumations in small cemeteries of simple earth graves. Grave goods are generally poor, comprising one or more locally made pots, personal ornaments such as brooches or shale bracelets, and, more often than not, joints of meat.

By the eve of the Roman invasion the practice of cremation burial so common in the core zone was being adopted by some groups further west, but mostly only by those in close contact with groups in the south east.

The outer zone

The Atlantic area forms the third zone of Britain distinguishable in the first centuries BC/AD on the basis of the extent of contact with the classical world through south-eastern England. In fact this area had remarkably little contact, and is notable for its continuity from earlier times rather than any marked changes.

Settlement

From the first century BC settlements in the west of Britain tended to be enclosed and rather better defended than in previous centuries, again perhaps in response to the threat of raids on stock and people from groups living to the east. In the south west, rounds, multiple enclosures and cliff castles remained in use, and new examples were built. One such case is The Rumps, Cornwall, probably built about 100 BC and integral to a pastoral economy in the area. A new class of site which emerged during the later second century BC in the extreme south west was the courtyard house. This comprises a paved central courtyard surrounded by rooms and byres, the whole complex being enclosed by a stout stone

105 Aerial view of the courtyard houses forming a small nucleated settlement/village at Chysauster, Cornwall. [*Photo: West Air Photography, Weston-super-Mare; copyright reserved*]

wall. Houses of this type are normally provided with garden plots or fields nearby, and may form clusters or villages, as at Chysauster and Carn Euny, Cornwall. Closely associated with the occupation of both these sites, and characteristic of most Atlantic areas of Britain from the first century BC onwards, are souterrains or 'fogu', which are underground passages, usually with one or more rooms leading off them. Their function is uncertain; likely suggestions include storage places for dairy produce, animal shelters and places of refuge or hiding during times of trouble.

In Wales, the familiar enclosures and occupation sites continued to be used and built though the centuries leading up to the Roman Conquest and after. In a series of excavations in south-west Wales by the Dyfed Archaeological Trust, something of the density of settlement at this time may be glimpsed. Around Llawhaden, Dyfed, in an area of only 5 square kilometres (2 square miles), some 11 enclosures are still visible as surface earthworks, and

several of them have been excavated. Two, at Dan-y-Coed and Woodside, lie within 300 metres (984 feet) of one another, and were probably established soon after 100 BC. Both are heavily defended and would have been the residence of small family groups of mixed farmers. The reason for two sites so close together may be that inheritance rules allowed property and land rights to be divided equally rather than passed on as a complete unit (so called partible inheritance—Welsh *cyfran*).

In the far north the settlement pattern of hillforts, palisaded enclosures, duns and fortified homesteads continued. The only new addition to the range of settlements at this time were the large brochs which are found widely over the island of Orkney, Shetland, the Western Isles and the Scottish mainland in Highland. These very distinctive settlements comprise dry-stone-built towers 10 metres (33 feet) or more high and perhaps 25 metres (82 feet) or so in diameter. The walls are thick at the bottom, tapering inwards towards the top, and they are usually built with a double skin so that stairways and chambers could be included in the core of the wall. Much debate surrounds their origins, which some see among the duns or wheelhouses of earlier centuries while others argue that brochs themselves can be

106 Late first-century BC and first-century AD settlements in south-west Wales. (A) Woodside Camp, Llawhaden, Dyfed. Two round houses have been revealed in the centre of the excavated area beyond which are the remains of the enclosing bank. Scales each total 2 metres. (B) Reconstructed round house at Castell Henllys, Meline, Dyfed, based on evidence recovered during the excavation of the site. [*(A) Photo: Ken Murphy for Dyfed Archaeological Trust; copyright reserved. (B) Photo: Harold Mytum; copyright reserved*]

107 Aerial view of the Broch of Gurness, Orkney.
[*Photo: Bob Bewley; copyright reserved*]

traced back to the mid first millennium BC as less elaborate versions of the classic broch form. Whichever is the case, by the first century AD regional variations in form can be recognized; with those of Orkney and Sutherland being the more sophisticated. It is likely that brochs originally had several internal wooden floors and were roofed over as a tower house. Had they remained open at the top a fire inside would turn them into a blast furnace with a large flue. The inhabitants of brochs were probably engaged in essentially pastoral farming, although since many are situated on or very near the coast, use of marine resources is also likely. Agriculture was certainly practised in the north, however, and the beam of an ard-plough radiocarbon dated to 80 ± 100 BC has been found at Lockmaben, Dumfries and Galloway.

Trade and ritual

Trading links between the outer zone and areas to the south east are poorly represented archaeologically. A few coins reach border areas, but do not penetrate into the outer zone proper. A few fine objects, such as the iron fire dog from Capel Garmon, Gwynedd, in North Wales and the gold torc from Netherurd, Borders, may represent traded commodities, but craftsmanship in the west was the equal of other areas. Products from workshops in western areas include tankards, weapons, horse-gear and many of the other objects familiar from other areas. One explanation for the wealth of products is that metalworkers fleeing the Roman expansion settled in western areas beyond the reach of Roman arms.

Some cist graves are known, but the burial record continues very much along the lines of previous centuries, and is generally poor. Rivers, lakes, bogs, springs and wet places remained the principal focus of ritual activity in the west throughout the first centuries BC/AD and indeed on into the early Roman period. At Llyn Cerrig Bach, Anglesey, a massive collection of objects including swords, spearheads, horse-gear and chariot fittings, parts of bronze shields, a cauldron, nave hoops, tongs, part of a bronze trumpet and various other fitments of uncertain function was found in a peat-filled lake in 1942–3. Another similar hoard, although more modest in size, has been found at Tal-y-llyn, Gwynedd. As with earlier material there is a high probability that some burials were deposited in the water with these objects, and they probably accumulated over a period of perhaps 100 to 200 years.

A find made in 1984 in Lindow Moss, Cheshire, adds a new dimension to the picture of interest in wet places. Workmen watching a peat cutting machine found parts of a human body preserved in the waterlogged peat about 0.7 metres ($2\frac{1}{4}$ feet) below the present surface. Excavations under the direction of Richard Turner took place and revealed that the body, which was that of a man, had been garrotted and then dumped on the surface of the bog in a shallow pool. Specialist investigations of the body are still continuing, but it seems that other wounds, including blows to the head, may have contributed to his death, which might have been purely ritual or perhaps a punishment for some crime. Details of the stratigraphy in which the body was found, and preliminary radiocarbon dates, suggest that Lindow Man, or Pete Marsh as he is affectionately known to those who found him, was executed some time towards the end of the first millennium BC or early in the first millennium AD.

Political manoeuvrings

In the 97 years between Caesar's visits to Britain and the Claudian invasion of AD 43 there were profound political changes in Britain and in the Roman world which can be glimpsed from documentary and archaeological evidence. In Rome, the Republic finally came to an end in 31 BC with the deaths of Anthony and Cleopatra after years of civil war and power stuggles. Octavius was the only remaining man in power and from 27 BC onwards created the basis for the Roman Empire and was soon recognized as its first Emperor, Augustus. Thereafter control of the Empire was vested in the ruling family regulated through descent as successive Emperors came to power—Tiberius, Gaius (Caligula) and Claudius.

In Britain the treaties established between Rome and the chiefs from the core zone were variously upheld, at least during the life of Julius Caesar. Hostages had been taken by Caesar, and there are at least some suggestions that, when in trouble, afflicted chiefs called on Rome to help them. Taking the distributions of coins minted by groups in the core zone and the periphery, together with documentary references and some backward projection of the names given to specific areas after the Roman Conquest, a crude political map of the name and territory of the main tribes and chiefdoms can be built up. In fact such a map is much more than a political map for it must relate to social, kinship, and alliance groupings in a way that will never be fully understood.

Attempts have been made to devise a dynastic history of the main social units in this twilight period of prehistory, mostly from scant documentary sources. This has largely been grounded in a fundamentally imperialistic ideology narrating events from the Roman viewpoint, rather than from the perspective of the communities in Britain. Such histories are therefore highly contentious in their detail, although two general points of interest can be glimpsed.

Firstly, the known political geography of the immediately pre-roman period broadly reflects the three archaeologically discernible zones in Britain, and the social structures proposed for each. In the core zone there are four or five named groups occupying relatively small areas and, according to the documentary sources, closely related and in active competition. Beyond this in the periphery are perhaps another four or five groups each occupying a very much larger area. In the outer zone a large number of much smaller groups are defined, probably truly tribal units with individual kinship-based segments within them.

Secondly, it is clear from Caesar's accounts that the social groups in the core zone were fragmentary when he encountered them. Each acted relatively independently of the others and, while Cassivellaunus emerged as the leader (?king) of the Britons, his elevation to this position may have been because of his previous prowess in battle rather than anything more formal. The social units which can be mapped, had clearly emerged out of the smaller units of a century earlier. Through various processes of conquest and alliance the Catuvellauni and the Trinovantes were at times united as a single unit, possibly by dynastic marriage and undoubtedly with considerable influence over the surrounding areas. Beyond the core zone a similar pattern of social development seems to have taken place too, and on the basis of the coins from East Anglia, for example, Derek Allen has suggested that the Iceni came together by the mid first century AD from at least three smaller units.

How power was handed down before the first century BC is not known; it may have been competed for or it may have been inherited. By the time that coins were in use, inheritance was practised in some areas. Tincommius, for example, claimed to be the son of Commius when he became leader of the Atrebates about 20 BC, and similar claims are made on the coinage of others. The titles of the leaders at this time also changed, perhaps in line with Roman nomenclature. Tasciovanus, leader of the Catuvellauni, for example, used the term RIGONUS on his coins, which is probably the Celtic version of the latin REX—king.

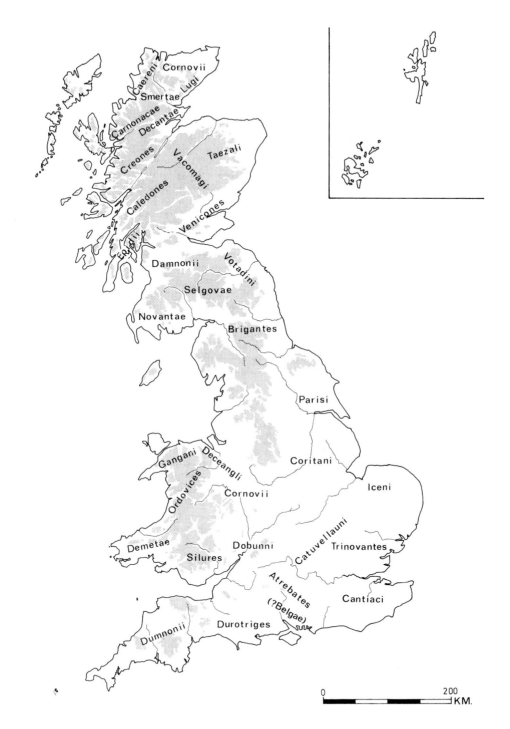

108 Generalized map of the main known tribal
groupings in Britain in the first century AD. [*After
Cunliffe 1978 figures 7.10 and 8.3*]

What seems to have emerged in the core zone by AD 43 is a series of proto-states or kingdoms, heavily involved in foreign trade and with various formal and informal ties to the Roman Empire. Why these changes should have come about is less clear. At a general level Morton Fried has noted that the proximity of an empire state to a rather less complex society causes the latter to react by federating groups into larger political units, and this seems to have been what happened in Britain. With reference to south-eastern England in particular, Richard Bradley and Ian Hodder have suggested that tensions between communities were reduced by increasing the social and political hierarchy, so that reliance on neighbours was replaced by a reliance on the social, economic and political centre. The emergence of *oppida*, and the expression of group identity with coins, were part of these changes in the hierarchy. At the top of the pyramid it was the control of foreign trade and relations with the Roman world—who were, incidentally, the biggest threat to the continued well-being of these groups—which bestowed power and prestige on the leaders. Children may even have been sent to Rome to be educated. The emphasis on imported objects as grave goods would be a natural consequence of this. In contrast, in western areas control over production and redistribution, together perhaps with the old virtues of the warrior defending the community, remained the most important factor in maintaining the social hierarchy, and here grave goods focus on local products and weaponry.

The coming of Rome

The Roman invasion of Britain began in AD 43, but was probably not unexpected despite the fact that its exact timing was unknown. Indeed, if the accounts of the invasion by Cassius Dio Cocceianus written down some 150 years later are to be believed, the Britons were waiting for the arrival of the Romans, but left their posts when news reached them that there was to be a delay in the departure of the invasion fleet.

There were probably many reasons for the invasion of Britain at this time, some of which we shall never know. Political expediency by Claudius in adding to the Empire with a view to improving his popularity with the army, confounding his critics and providing much needed revenue was one factor, but the death of Cunobelin about AD 40 and the accession of his more aggressive sons Togodumnus

and Caratacus, who were far from happy about earlier alliances with Rome, made it timely to take Britain before anti-Roman feeling became too strong. Another factor may have been the attraction of trading with Britain as a part of the Empire free from the tariffs imposed on trading with countries beyond the frontier.

The invasion itself was led by the commander Aulus Plautius and four legions of the Roman army; about 40,000 men including legionaries and auxiliary troops took part, with a fifth legion held in reserve in Gaul. The legions involved were the II *Augusta*, XIV *Gemina*, and XXth which had been drafted in from the Rhineland, and the IX *Hispana* which had come from the province of Pannonia, Yugoslavia, with Aulus Plautius.

The increased production of coins in Britain in the years before the Conquest may be related to paying warriors for participation in the defence of Britain, and it seems certain that some of the dykes and ramparts established round the *oppida* in south-eastern England were thrown up at this time as defensive works. Many are little more than dumps of soil (so-called Fécamp style ramparts). Even the massive hillforts of Maiden Castle, and Hod Hill, Dorset, apparently underwent last minute refortifications of their entranceways in readiness.

The invasion fleet landed at Richborough, and succeeded in taking south-eastern England fairly quickly. The Emperor Claudius himself arrived to lead his army to Camulodunum in the summer of AD 43, and at this time he received the surrender of twelve kings.

Campaigns in the west and north

The Conquest was far from over, however, when Claudius left. By about AD 47 a frontier zone running south-west to north-east from Exeter to the Humber had been established. Once outside the core zone of the south-east, taking the area had been hard. The historian Suetonius relates that Vespasian, the leader of II *Augusta* and responsible for taking the Durotrigian area in Dorset and Somerset, had to take the main hillforts one at a time. The people were prepared. At Hod Hill, Dorset, for example, an extra ditch was being excavated and cupboards had been built into the walls of the huts, perhaps to conceal weapons ready for immediate use by the inhabitants. The superior fighting strength and military equipment of the Roman army prevailed, and all these forts and many more were taken. At Maiden Castle, Dorset, excavations by Sir Mortimer Wheeler revealed what he interpreted as the results of the attack and sacking of the fort. A war cemetery was found in the east entrance where the traditional burial rites had been followed for the fallen. Not all the hillforts in the south west were, it seems, taken by force at this time. At Cadbury Castle, Somerset, for example, the fort was not taken by assault until about AD60 and it may be that the events which occasioned this purge of native forts were bound up in the British revolts between AD 60 and 65, of which the most well known are those led by Boudica of the Iceni in East Anglia.

Forts, fortresses, supply bases, new roads and bridges, and all the usual paraphernalia of a military invasion spread across the countryside as the army consolidated its gains. Pockets of resistance undoubtedly existed and attacks on convoys and camps must have taken place, the plunder from such raids supplementing earlier traded supplies of luxury goods. Research by Malcolm Todd has suggested that in the south west at least some hillforts were used by the Roman Army as camps, thus securing key points. At Hembury, Devon, for example, the military occupation seems to have included the construction of timber buildings, including workshops.

After AD 47 the Roman army pushed westward and northward into Wales, and parts of the south-west peninsula. Excavations by Stanley Stanford at The Wrekin, Shropshire, suggest that the hillfort on this prominent hill was probably destroyed about AD 48–50 when the gate and internal buildings were burnt and never rebuilt. Other hillforts in the Marches had been abandoned earlier, as in southern England, and it is not at present clear how many hillforts were occupied at the time of the Roman Conquest.

The northern frontier was always a problem for the Roman army. The Brigantes who occupied a very large tract of Yorkshire and northern England had probably been one of the twelve tribes to surrender to Claudius in AD43; certainly they were supporters of Rome during the early years of the Conquest. This seems to have changed in AD 69 when Queen Cartimandua lost control of the tribe to Ventius, who had turned against Rome. In AD 71–4 a series of campaigns effectively returned control of the area to Rome. One of the main settlements in the territory of the Brigantes was Stanwick, North Yorkshire, a nucleated settlement of considerable size which in its final phase was refortified against the Romans with additional dyke systems, presumably to protect the occupants, and their stock. The total area enclosed was about 240 hectares (593 acres).

According to Roman Imperial policy the far north was never fully taken, although campaigns were launched into Scotland. For all practical purposes the frontier lay in the Tyne-Forth province. These western and northern areas naturally provided refuges for anti-Roman agitators and probably always provided a source of trouble and constant worry to the Roman authorities.

The classical writers present a rather glossy picture of a well co-ordinated invasion and subjugation of Britain accompanied by some, but not insurmountable, resistance. This is what might be expected from such writers, but the reality may have been rather different. The fact that such large areas were never fully taken and that a strong military presence was maintained throughout the Roman period hints that things may have been more difficult than commonly portrayed. For those living in the core zone the coming of Rome was probably the culmination of a series of processes stretching back a century or more, and for those in appropriate positions in society all the benefits of the Roman world were suddenly available. In the periphery zone and the outer zone, where direct contact with the Roman world had been slight, the invasion may have been seen quite differently.

In contrast to the Norman Conquest of 1066, the Roman invasion was a long drawn out affair. Differences in social organization between the two periods is partly to blame, but sustained resistance must also have had a part to play. If we look for a modern analogy to the conquest of Britain the Russian take-over of Afghanistan might provide a useful model. Here too may be glimpsed certain sectors of society sympathetic to the invasion but fierce resistance in other quarters, particularly in the upland and marginal lands away from the main centres of population.

After the Conquest

The initial impact of the Conquest varied from one region to the next. As already emphasized, the military take-over was neither rapid nor complete. Those who survived the Conquest learned to live under their changed circumstances within a generation or so.

In the north and west there was widespread continuity among small-scale homestead-based communities, and the familiar pattern of raths, rounds, multiple enclosures, duns, brochs, and crannogs which had served successive generations for many centuries continued to be inhabited and new examples built. The uplands were used by the Romans as a source of raw materials, especially minerals, and also a training ground for the army. Some sectors of the north and west became military zones, and the army was seemingly in control of the exploitation of many of the natural resources. Local resistance to the Romans was strong, however, and the writer Tacitus (*Agricola* 18) records that in about AD 77 the Ordovices, living at this time in mid Wales, wiped out an entire squadron of cavalry stationed in their territory.

In southern and eastern England the impact of the invasion was greatest. The high-order settlements of the core zone were mostly used as regional capitals, the focus of trade, commerce and government, perhaps as they had been before the invasion. In the periphery zone regional capitals were often established near to previous high-order settlements, as with Cirencester and Bagendon, Gloucestershire, and Dorchester and Maiden Castle, Dorset, or occasionally directly over the site, as at Winchester and Leicester. In both areas the lower-order settlements fared much the same, and three distinct patterns can be seen. Some carried on very much as before as farmsteads or hamlets among their fields and enclosures. Some were completely changed, possibly through military intervention, and became the centres of estates or small towns of various sorts.

One such site recently examined by the Oxfordshire Archaeological Unit is Claydon Pike, Gloucestershire. Only interim accounts are at present available, but it appears that here a small traditional hamlet continued in occupation until about AD 70 when suddenly everything was changed and both the settlement and the surrounding landscape was reorganized with regular roads and enclosures. The third course of events is for a site to become Romanized. At Park Street, St Albans, and Lockleys, both in Hertfordshire, farmsteads were rapidly converted to Roman villas in classical style, usually relatively simple rectangular structures at first but becoming increasingly sophisticated later through additions and modifications. Whether these were the homes of Roman immigrants who accompanied the invasion or of important Britons given special status is not clear. Many existing shrines continued to be used after the Conquest, some being rebuilt in more classical style. The Druids were not allowed to flourish in Roman Britain, and new formal temples were built in most towns and villages. Roman gods were assimilated with their Celtic counterparts.

By the end of the first century AD much of the south of Britain was caught up in a society altogether different from that of prehistoric times. Different patterns of trade and commerce, a market economy, new ritual arrangements, and a new system of government set the scene for a new era in the history of Britain.

8 All Things Must Pass

Patterns of Society and Change

The inevitability of change

In prehistoric times, as today, nothing lasts for ever. All things change through time, and human societies in particular continually adopt new forms and new patterns of organization. Reconstructing prehistory, and indeed past societies generally, is often likened to piecing together a jigsaw puzzle. But a jigsaw puzzle represents altogether too static a view of prehistory. Communities came and went, the focus of action shifted from area to area, and success was periodically tempered by failure and tragedy. A more apt analogy would be piecing together lengths of a movie-film with various portions missing and many poorly-focused frames.

But if change was inevitable its rate was not constant throughout the 450,000 years or so of man's early presence in Britain. Long periods of very gradual change can be detected, in some cases so slow that the societies in question might almost be described as stagnant. The most clear-cut example is the hunter-gatherer groups living in Britain during the later part of the Pleistocene period. For over 400,000 years their material culture—their tools, ornaments and possessions—underwent the most minimal modification. Looking back it is hard to believe that the hand-axe was the principal stone tool known to man for well over a quarter of a million years. Closer to ourselves in time are the Atlantic seaboard communities of the first and early second millennia BC. These groups again changed relatively little compared with communities elsewhere in Britain, maintaining for several thousand years small homestead settlements.

In contrast, there were also episodes of rapid change. The earliest easily recognizable such period is about 3000 BC, shortly after the development of farming in Britain when new burial rites, settlement patterns and economic organization were adopted within a matter of only a few centuries. Thereafter several other periods of rapid change can be identified, first about 2500 BC, again about 1800 BC, and then again, in some areas at least, immediately prior to the Roman invasion. There can be little doubt that for those living during these periods, life was especially traumatic.

Against this background of differing rates of social change there is also the question of direction of change. Looking back from our own standpoint within a complex twentieth-century AD western society the last 450,000 years of human endeavour may look like a long uphill struggle towards what we might now regard as civilization. Closer scrutiny of the course, or trajectory, of that development, however, suggests that it was far from continually uphill. The definition of 'development' is, of course, fraught with difficulties, but if we take it to mean an increase in technological, economic and social sophistication, it is clear that, while periods of advance can certainly be identified, there were also periods of retreat or decline. Early examples include the gaps in settlement during the Pleistocene period, but even after 10,000 BC, set-backs can be identified and they seem to form a roughly cyclical pattern of advance and retreat. The apparent abandonment of traditional monuments, the regeneration of forest clearances, and a decline of crafts such as potting and flintworking about 2400 BC was, in some areas, the first major set-back. Rather later, about 1000 BC or a little after, the abandonment of the uplands which had previously been extensively, and locally intensively, settled must also have represented a set-back. This last example illustrates a further important feature of prehistoric social change: it is markedly

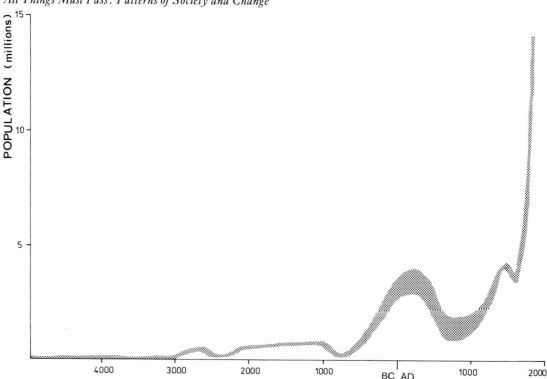

109 A possible population curve for Britain 5000 BC to AD 1801. A 'band of possibility' is used to suggest maximum and minimum likely levels on the basis of the evidence recorded to date. [*Based on Fowler 1978 figure 1 with various modifications*]

regional or localized in its effect. Prehistoric societies were not so much 'primitive' in the sense of being backward and uncultured, but simply small-scale in their organization and operation. Because of this, patterns of change need to be analysed at an appropriate scale.

The causes of the various changes visible at different times in prehistory have been touched upon in Chapters 2–7 above, at least as far as present archaeological evidence allows. No single factor or prime mover, for example invasions, migrations, or population increases, can be, or indeed should be, invoked as a universal explanation for change. Detailed studies of prehistoric societies have time and time again emphasized the fact that a great many factors contribute to social change, and each period needs to be examined closely before hypotheses are presented. Three general points can, however, be made. First, most social change results from a combination of both internal and external factors or influences. Which triggers the other off in any given case is a matter for research. Secondly, it is notable

that change is slowest where opportunities for the combination of internal and external influences are minimized. This might rather flippantly be termed plain old conservatism, but it remains a fact that isolation and autonomy promotes stability. In the case of hunter-gatherers low-population densities dictated social isolation, while the Atlantic seaboard communities throughout later prehistory were isolated because of the geography of the area in which they lived. Thirdly, looking at the whole continuum of prehistory, the intervals between phases of decline have become shorter, and the periods of growth and expansion more rapid. This appears to be something which has continued into historic and indeed recent times.

Whatever the causes of observable changes among prehistoric societies, the consequences always have a knock-on effect for succeeding generations – a social, economic and environmental legacy for both immediate successors and distant descendants to cope with.

Prehistoric inheritance

Contributory to the form of any society is the natural environment in which it finds itself, and its inheritance from earlier generations—in other words, its setting and history. These are most marked among small-scale societies, although still important for more complex societies too.

Among the most influential features to be inherited are the man-made environment, the vegetation cover, soil conditions, animal population, and land use patterns determined by earlier generations. Examples from prehistory which illustrate the effects of this legacy are numerous. For example, the clearings in the post-glacial climax forest cover made by sixth- and fifth-millennium BC hunter-gatherers probably provided the setting in which early farming groups were first able to cultivate land. Later, areas of cleared land allowed large monuments and enclosures to be built. In the uplands, landscape clearance in the early second millennium allowed a major episode of land apportionment about 1400 BC. Over-exploitation of agricultural land in the second millennium had its consequences later as the potential for settlement expansion was restricted by the distribution of productive soils.

Other major inherited determinants of social development include social structure, technology and ritual. Less archaeologically visible features will include language, ideology and political organization. Alongside inherited factors must be set the natural environment because this has always played a part in shaping the development of human societies. In the Pleistocene period the effects of glacial advances and retreats on settlement and hunting patterns is clear enough. Later, climate influenced the distribution of farming, apparently allowing cultivation at higher altitudes in the warmer drier periods of the second millennium BC, for example, and later being at least partly responsible for the abandonment of many upland areas.

The key to man's survival through changing inherited conditions and fluctuating environmental circumstances, and the underlying root cause of much visible change through the prehistoric period, was his ability to adapt to what went on around him.

Remote as prehistoric times may seem, the legacy of our prehistoric ancestors still influences our everyday lives, and we are still adapting to circumstances created several millennia ago. Naturally it is sometimes difficult to trace things back into the remote past; appropriate records simply do not exist. But there are some features of the twentieth century AD which can be traced to very ancient roots.

Landscape and environment

The appearance of the landscape, and the man-made environment, of Britain owes much to prehistoric man, especially in the more remote areas less damaged by modern development. As emphasized in Chapter 1, and illustrated in Chapters 2–7, visible traces of prehistory abound in Britain as barrows, camps, forts, standing stones, stone circles and so on. For every site visible on the surface there are perhaps a score hidden or lost from view. All in some way influence, or once influenced, local topography and landscape. It is salutary to remember that no matter how remote a piece of landscape appears today many people have probably passed that way before, and indeed some of our most remote areas, such as Dartmoor or the Lake District, were once the focus of intensive occupation and exploitation.

Present-day land-use is also affected by our inheritance from prehistoric communities. Much of Britain's open aspect results from clearances wrought by prehistoric farmers. More influential still is the prehistoric over-exploitation of some areas causing soil exhaustion and acidification. Research by Geoffrey Dimbleby has shown that many of today's lowland heaths were usable agricultural lands in the early second millennium BC, but that cultivation and grazing between about 1800 and 800 BC turned them into relatively infertile areas which were further despoiled by the effects of weather. The same applies to much of the uplands, for far from being natural wildernesses untouched by man they are largely areas decimated by second-millennium BC farmers which have had the worst scars healed and smoothed over by the effects of nature during the past two or three millennia.

In a few areas the actual layout of the present-day landscape owes something to our prehistoric forebears. This is particularly well illustrated in West Penwith, Cornwall. Here, the attractive farming landscape is not a modern development but the direct result of prehistoric land division. From about 600 BC the clearance of stones from the fields and intensive cultivation produced the characteristically large dry-stone walls and terraced fields that dominate the modern landscape. Field survey by Nicholas Johnson in the parish of Zennor has shown that perhaps 80 per cent of existing field boundaries originated in prehistoric times, and the same undoubtedly applies to many other parts of the area too. Similar patterns may be seen elsewhere, for example on Dartmoor and the Pennines, often most clearly demonstrated where modern farmland meets unenclosed land and the modern boundaries can be

110 Ancient crafts still practised today. (A) Wooden hurdles made of coppiced hazel and dating to about 2300 BC from Walton Heath, Somerset. (B) Dry-stone-walling in Cotswold limestone revealed in the forecourt area of the chambered tomb at Hazleton, Gloucestershire, probably built about 2800 BC. Behind the wall is the rubble of the cairn which was constructed in a series of bays arranged parallel to a central spine/axis which can be seen as a ridge of pitched stone. Horizontal scale totals 2 metres. [*(A) Photo: Somerset Levels Project; copyright reserved. (B) Photo: Alan Saville; copyright reserved*]

seen continuing into the heathland or moor as prehistoric field walls.

Crafts

Some crafts and technologies still common today have a direct and unbroken line of descent from the prehistoric period. The art of building dry-stone walls carries on today using identical techniques to those used 5000 years ago. Likewise, basket-making, weaving, and hurdle-making have changed little since at least the third millennium BC. Even the splitting and cleaving of timber, the cutting of mortise and tenon joints and the hafting of tools has a history stretching back into prehistoric times. In metalworking too there are very few techniques in use today that were not developed and innovated during prehistory. The list could go on—archery, fishing, boat building, woodland management and so on. The point is that basic crafts and skills such as these originated in prehistoric times, and while their contribution to the economy may have decreased recently they still form a link with the past which represents a valuable heritage of skills, knowledge and experience.

Language and place names

Prehistoric communities influenced today's language and place names. Little is known about the languages spoken in prehistory since there was a total absence of literacy. Nevertheless it seems certain that a form of the Indo-European family of languages overlain by Celtic was spoken in Britain when the Romans arrived. This is known to linguists as British. It was spoken throughout England and Wales, and over most of Scotland. Today it survives through its descendants, Cornish and Welsh. Gaelic was introduced into Scotland from Ireland in the fifth century AD and so does not qualify as a prehistoric language in Britain. It is generally believed that British was adopted in Britain during the first millennium BC, although exactly when, and by what processes, is not known. Before this some form of non-Indo-European language was probably used, and it is just conceivable that Pictish, spoken in Scotland down to the eighth century or so AD, was a descendant of this ancient tongue.

About 350–400 place names relating to Britain are recorded by classical writers before about AD 400. Of these less than 5 per cent are Latin names assigned by the Romans; the rest are Celtic names, and are therefore likely to be prehistoric in origin. Most prominent are the topographic names that are resilient to change, among them river names like the Avon (*Afon* in Welsh, and relating to the British word *Abona* = river) and the Thames (from the British word *Tamessa* based on the root *ta* = to flow). Naturally the spelling and phonetics of these names has changed a little through the later development of the English language, but the roots are still visible. Moreover, Margaret Gelling has suggested that some place names, such as Alne or *Alauna* (as in River Alne, Northumberland) and *Londinium* (modern London) might derive from the pre-British, non-Indo-European language; but of course this cannot be proven.

Customs and traditions

Some customs and traditions still upheld in Britain also have prehistoric ancestry. The calendar of 12 months used today was, of course, a Roman invention, and probably bears little or no relation to calendars used during prehistoric times. However, Alexander Thom, working from regularly occurring alignments in stone circles matched against the declination of the sun at different times of the year, has proposed that prehistoric people divided their year into 16 equal periods. Aubrey Burl suggests that this quite brilliant piece of deduction by Thom might be a slight over-refinement of a simple calendar, and that, if instead alternate months are used, the declinations correspond very closely to those of the four known Celtic festivals together with the solstices and the equinoxes. The important point here is that, whatever the basis for these eight festivals, most of them seem to have become transliterated into the modern calendar through being adopted as Christian festivals when the early Church leaders appropriated pagan customs. In some cases the themes of these pagan, and putatively prehistoric, festivals are perpetuated in their modern counterparts—All Souls' Day, for example, is celebrated at the same time as the Celtic festival of the dead, Samain. Indeed it is also tempting to speculate that rituals such as the horn dance, still carried on at Abbots Bromley, Staffordshire, and known to have been part of mid-winter celebrations before the Civil War, may have roots in prehistoric festivities.

Peripheral to modern life as these various carry-overs from prehistory may seem, their very persistence emphasizes the debt every society owes to its forebears. Natural human curiosity to know more about the past may provide the rationale for further

Festival	Festivities	Approximate date (modern calendar)	Modern equivalent
BELTANE	Festival of optimism symbolized by the lighting of fires through which animals were driven as a purification rite.	about 8th May	?Whitsun
MIDSUMMER SOLSTICE		21st June	Midsummer
LUGHNASA	Festival of the god Lugh, with emphasis on stock rearing and the harvesting of crops.	1–9th August	Lammas/ Harvest festival
AUTUMN EQUINOX		23rd September	
SAMAIN*	Festival of the dead when people from the spirit world become visible to people on earth.	1–6th November	All Souls'/ All Saints'/ Martinmas
MIDWINTER SOLSTICE		21st December	Christmas
IMBOLC	Fertility rituals traditionally associated with the lactation of ewes.	5th February	St Brigid's/ Candlemas
VERNAL EQUINOX		23rd March	?Easter

*Beginning of the Celtic year at which time any barriers between man and the supernatural were lowered.

[*Source: Burl 1983, 34 with additions*]

Table 5   Traditional festivals and their modern counterparts

investigations of prehistory, possibly as part of the current trend to find out more about everything and anything. But prehistoric archaeology is more than simply a forensic discipline—it also has a contribution to make towards the science of society in general.

Prehistory for today

The value of prehistoric studies in the social sciences has long been recognized, and indeed often exploited, as in the writings of the archaeologist Gordon Childe, the sociologist Talcott Parsons and the economist Karl Marx, to name but three. In most cases, however, the prehistoric past has been used to provide a prelude to general discussions of the development of complex societies, or as a historical introduction to the analysis of some contemporary phenomenon. Until recently, prehistoric studies as a section of the social sciences proper have not received the attention they deserve, despite the fact that for over 200 years prehistorians have been collecting and synthesizing information about the development of human societies. Before launching into a discussion of what has been, and what might be, achieved as a contribution to the science of society, it may be helpful to recap briefly the main characteristics of prehistory relevant to such studies of society.

Prehistory as sociology

The greatest strength of prehistory as a social science is the tremendous time-depth offered. In Britain alone evidence is available for over 10,000 years of continuous social development. Within this period there is such great diversity of social complexity and environmental circumstance that no planned sociological study could ever hope to replicate it.

The price that has to be paid for such a rich perspective is that the evidence available is of a type unfamiliar to most social scientists working with contemporary cultures, and not susceptible to their usual methods of analysis. Archaeological evidence basically comprises objects (artefacts, bones, structures and so on) and their relationships to each other in time and space. By inference, relationships between the objects and human behavioural and psychological process can be suggested. In the 1950s and early 1960s the obvious limitations of this for understanding the full range of human activities led to the development of a rather despondent attitude towards the potential of archaeological evidence—a view which sadly is still reflected in the majority of museum displays. More recently, however, and prompted in this country largely by the work of David Clarke, Colin Renfrew, Ian Hodder and others, it has become clear that such a view is ill-founded, and that objects do after all have much to tell about societies as working entities in prehistory.

Three distinct but interrelated levels of inference may be derived from the analysis of prehistoric objects. At the most basic there are functional considerations—the fact that axes can be linked with woodworking, pottery with cooking, specific buildings with habitations, ramparts with defence, and so on—according to traces of wear, use and association. Secondly, something may be said about the way objects were used as an extension of language to project and communicate information and ideas. The scale of the object will largely determine the level of communication, for example a finger ring may communicate status but only to those close enough to see it, while the defences of a hillforts may similarly communicate individual or group status but to a potentially much wider audience. The design and ornamentation of objects may communicate group identity, and the distribution of such pieces may define the territory of that group if that was how the symbols were used. Thirdly, the context of objects and their associations are important because they were selected by their owners/users as being somehow meaningful and significant, to the extent that sets of objects in certain arrangements or deposited in certain ways may reflect particular mental processes, associations of ideas and indeed ideological statements about the user or perpetrator. To take an example from present-day culture, black leather jackets adorned with studs and chains imply affinity not only with a particular group of people who ride motor bikes and listen to distinctive kinds of music, but also with particular attitudes towards violence, hygiene, wealth and property. The presence of weapons in male graves in the early second millennium BC, and also in the later first millennium BC, may similarly be linked not just to the function of the weapons themselves, but often also to associations with a particular class of person with specific ideologies and attitudes which might not necessarily have been characteristic of the society as a whole.

In developing the sociological aspects of Britain's prehistoric past, three distinct spheres of interest can be identified: the human condition, our own society, and other societies.

The human condition

Some consideration of the human condition as exemplified through the long time perspective of prehistory has already been touched upon in this and previous chapters. At the functional level much has been made of the capacity of prehistoric societies to adapt and readapt to changing circumstances. Survival and continuity is clearly illustrated in Britain's past, and it is consoling to see that despite the fact that throughout prehistory communities had the capacity to destroy themselves, and each other, there are apparently no times when total extinction resulted. At another level the ways that communities communicated ideas and expressed affinity is of interest. It must not be assumed that human societies always use the same devices to communicate identity and social order. Richard Bradley has recently shown that in prehistoric times ostentatious behaviour focused on the development of complexity in only one sector of everyday life at a time, and that different sectors were used through time. Among the early farming communities settlements are elaborate and variable but burials follow set patterns and are ostensibly communal. Later, in the early second millennium BC, the reverse is true: burials show great variety and elaboration whereas settlements are very simple in form. The pattern is almost cyclical.

Society today

These general considerations lead towards an understanding of our own society. At the most fundamental level, studies of prehistory contribute towards explaining the unknown and the mysterious. Providing a perspective for the appreciation of unfamiliar features of our landscape is as important as being able to say exactly how they were used. Naturally this promotes a sense of belonging and a greater sense of history which in turn contributes to the development of social attitudes ranging from local pride to national consciousness. Recent work by Ian Hodder has begun to take general lessons from prehistory still further through developing the implications of individual and group identity, and the structural significance of the use of material objects. One case study he develops derives from the observation that, at times of increasing stress, the identity and affinities of self-defined groups are projected more forcefully through imbuing material symbols with special meanings. It can be seen clearly enough in the proliferation of decorated pottery about 2400 BC, when traditional farming society was under stress, and later perhaps when hillforts and enclosures sprang up across western England and a warrior class emerged. Why then, Hodder asks, were the clear warnings of stress displayed in the music, self-decoration and material symbols of violence among youth sub-cultures at the focus of urban violence over the last few years largely ignored?

Looking at others

Finally, it should be clear by now that looking into our own past is like looking into the future of other societies. After all, many different forms of social complexity can be matched in our own past. At the functional level, work such as that undertaken by Peter Reynolds at the Butser Hill Experimental Farm, Hampshire, provides valuable scientific information about the potentials and practicalities of the technology and subsistence practices of later prehistoric groups. These naturally have implications for the encouragement, or discouragement, of similar practices among small-scale contemporary societies. Beyond this, however, are examples in our own past of the consequences and effects of specific actions—not just short-term effects but long-term too. Forest clearance and over-exploitation of marginal land are just such cases and have already been discussed in some detail (p. 187). Relationships between complex societies and small-scale societies, the effects of trade across such boundaries, and the

implications for political and economic development are all important areas for study. After all, Britain's relationship with the Third World now is much the same as between the Roman world and Britain 2000 or so years ago. Mention may also be made of the ways in which goods are consumed. From our own past it is clear that periods of maximum innovation and technological development occurred when consumption and disposal of wealth peaked, for example at times when grave goods or ritual removed many objects from circulation and stimulated the production of replacements. Commensurately, when wealth (in the form of objects and equipment) is stored and accumulated, innovation is minimized.

Contributions to the present from prehistory will, of course, never provide straightforward solutions to current problems, but they can enrich the range of possible alternative courses of action, provide a more pragmatic basis for decision making and, in the longer term, allow a more balanced approach to understanding the working of societies and relations between and within them.

Prehistory tomorrow

It may at first sight seem perverse to finish a book on the ancient past with a look towards the future, but of course here lies the way forward for both the advancement of the discipline and the wider appreciation of prehistory as part of our heritage.

The single biggest problem facing prehistoric studies at present is the fact that the basic sources of information about the past are diminishing rapidly. Industrial development, high-intensity agriculture, land drainage, urban expansion and many other forms of change are collectively erasing the evidence remaining from prehistory at a faster rate than ever before. Despite widespread interest in the ancient past, financial considerations so often get in the way of preserving essentially priceless sites and monuments. It would be wrong to think that everything must be saved at all costs, but a conscious effort must be made to save the best of what we have for our own and future generations to enjoy.

Assuming that something remains to be studied, then academically the future looks bright. New discoveries, new excavations and new research will no doubt generate new insights into the past; details which are now obscure will in due course be clarified, and gaps in existing knowledge will, hopefully, be filled. Experimental and technical studies will no doubt extend our understanding of what is found.

As a financial asset, the prehistoric heritage is already proving its worth as a significant component in the expansion of the tourist and leisure industry. Income from such sources cannot easily be quantified because, in addition to direct revenue, local economies are stimulated in an unquantifiable way and visitor satisfaction and pleasure simply cannot be listed on a balance sheet. As a social contribution, the developing interest in the sociology of prehistory must not be underestimated. If studies of prehistory can stimulate a more positive attitude to material things, social relations, and the landscape in general then they will make a relevant contribution to the understanding of ourselves past, present, and future.

Notes and Select Bibliography

This bibliography makes no pretence to be exhaustive, and simply lists some of the major publications covering the subjects discussed in each chapter. Most of the works cited have their own extensive bibliographies which will lead interested readers deeper into the literature on specific periods or topics. Excavation reports have, in general, been excluded from the list unless they contain extensive discussion sections, or are referred to in a figure or table caption.

The following abbreviations have been used:

BAR	British Archaeological Reports
CBA	Council for British Archaeology
HMSO	Her Majesty's Stationery Office
Proc. Prehist. Soc.	Proceedings of the Prehistoric Society
RCHME	Royal Commission on the Historical Monuments of England

1 The Prehistoric Past *(pp. 13–27)*

Several general books on British prehistory provide accounts of specific aspects of the subject

On the effects of radiocarbon dating:

RENFREW, C. (ed.), 1974, *British Prehistory – A new outline*. Duckworth

On the environment:

SIMMONS, I. and TOOLEY, M. (eds.), 1981, *The environment in British Prehistory*. Duckworth

On settlement, economy and farming:

BRADLEY, R., 1978, *The prehistoric settlement of Britain*. Routledge and Kegan Paul

FOWLER, P. J., 1983, *The farming of prehistoric Britain*. Cambridge University Press

MERCER, R. (ed.), 1981, *Farming practice in British prehistory*. Edinburgh University Press

On society and politics:

BRADLEY, R., 1984, *The social foundations of prehistoric Britain*. Longman

For descriptive summaries of the archaeological evidence:

ASHBEE, P., 1978, *The ancient British*. Geo Books

MEGAW, J. V. S. and SIMPSON, D. D. A., 1979, *An introduction to British Prehistory*. Leicester University Press

On the development of interest in prehistoric archaeology:

ASHBEE, P., 1972, 'Field archaeology: Its origins and development' in FOWLER, P. J. (ed.) *Archaeology and the landscape*. John Baker, 38–74

DANIEL, G. E., 1962, *The idea of prehistory*. C. A. Watts

DANIEL, G. E., 1967, *The origins and growth of archaeology*. Penguin

DANIEL, G. E., 1975, *150 Years of archaeology*. Duckworth

MARSDEN, B. M., 1974, *The early barrow diggers*. Shire

MARSDEN, B. M., 1983, *Pioneers of prehistory*. G. W. and A. Hesketh

On changes in archaeological theory and practice since 1960:

ATKINSON, R. J. C., 1975, 'British prehistory and the radiocarbon revolution', *Antiquity* 49, 173–7

CLARK, G., 1966, 'The invasion hypothesis in British Prehistory', *Antiquity* 40, 172–89

DARVILL, T. C., PARKER PEARSON, M., SMITH, R. W. AND THOMAS, R. M. (eds.), 1978, *New approaches to our past: An archaeological forum*. Southampton University Archaeological Society

FOWLER, P. J., 1980, 'Traditions and objectives in British field archaeology', *Archaeological Journal* 137, 1–21

JONES, B., 1984, *Past imperfect. The story of rescue archaeology*. Heinemann Educational Books

RAHTZ, P. A. (ed.), 1974, *Rescue archaeology*. Penguin

On the recovery of archaeological evidence:

BARKER, P., 1977, *Techniques of archaeological excavation*. Batsford

COLES, J., 1972, *Field archaeology in Britain*. Methuen

COLES, J., 1984, *The archaeology of wetlands*. Edinburgh University Press

FASHAM, P., SCHADLA-HALL, R. T., SHENNAN, S. J. and BATES, P. J., 1980, *Fieldwalking for archaeologists*. Hampshire Field Club and Archaeological Society

GREEN, K., 1983, *Archaeology: An introduction*. Batsford

MACREADY, S. and THOMPSON, F. H. (eds.), 1985, *Archaeological field survey in Britain and abroad* (= Society of Antiquaries Occasional Paper (ns.) 6). Society of Antiquaries of London

MAXWELL, G. S. (ed.), 1983, *The impact of aerial reconnaissance on archaeology* (= CBA Research Report No. 49). CBA

WILSON, D., 1982, *Air photo interpretation for archaeologists*. Batsford

On data handling and analysis:

DORAN, J. E. and HODSON, F. R., 1975, *Mathematics and computers in archaeology*. Edinburgh University Press

HODDER, I. and ORTON. C., 1976, *Spatial analysis in archaeology* (= New Studies in Archaeology No. 1). Cambridge University Press

HODDER, I. (ed.), 1978, *Simulation studies in archaeology*. Cambridge University Press

ORTON, C., 1980, *Mathematics in Archaeology*. Collins

RICHARDS, J. D. and RYAN, N. S., 1985, *Data processing in archaeology*. Cambridge University Press

SHENNAN, S., 1985, *Experiments in the collection and analysis of archaeological survey data: The East Hampshire Survey*. Department of Archaeology and Prehistory, University of Sheffield

On technical studies:

BROTHWELL, D. R., 1972, *Digging up bones*. British Museum (Natural History)

BROTHWELL, D. and HIGGS, E. (eds.), 1969, *Science in archaeology* (2nd edition). Thames and Hudson

CORNWALL, I., 1974, *Bones for the archaeologist* (Revised edition). Dent

DIMBLEBY, G. W., 1985, *The palynology of archaeological sites*. Academic Press

HODGES, H., 1964, *Artifacts – An introduction to early materials and technology*. John Baker

LIMBREY, S., 1975, *Soil science in archaeology*. Academic Press

PHILLIPS, P. (ed.), 1985, *The archaeologist and the laboratory* (= CBA Research Report No. 58). CBA

SEMENOV, S. A., 1964, *Prehistoric technology*. trs. M. W. Thompson. Mooraker Press

TITE, M. S., 1972, *Methods of physical examination in archaeology*. Seminar Press

On the development of archaeological theory and current theoretical approaches:

BINFORD, L. R., 1972, *An archaeological perspective*. Seminar Press

BINFORD, L. R., 1983, *In pursuit of the past: decoding the archaeological record*. Thames and Hudson

BRADLEY, R. and HODDER, I., 1979, 'British prehistory: an integrated view', *Man* 14, 93–104

CLARKE, D. L., 1978, *Analytical Archaeology* (2nd edition). Methuen

HODDER, I. (ed.), 1982, *Symbolic and structural archaeology*. Cambridge University Press

MILLER, D. and TILLEY, C. (eds.), 1984, *Ideology, power and prehistory*. Cambridge University Press

RENFREW, C. (ed.), 1973, *The explanation of culture change: Models in prehistory*. Duckworth

RENFREW, C., 1973, *Social archaeology*. Southampton University (Inaugural lecture)

RENFREW, C., 1984, *Approaches to social archaeology*. Edinburgh University Press

RENFREW, C., ROWLANDS, M. J. and SEGRAVES, B. A. (eds.), 1982, *Theory and explanation in archaeology*. Academic Press

SPRIGGS, M. (ed.), 1984, *Marxist perspectives in archaeology*. Cambridge University Press

On ethnography and anthropology:

FRIED, M., 1967, *The evolution of political society*. Random House

HODDER, I., 1982, *The present past*. Batsford

ORME, B. J., 1981, *Anthropology for archaeologists: an introduction*. Duckworth

SERVICE, E. R., 1962, *Primitive social organisation*. Random House

SAHLINS, M., 1974, *Stone Age economics*. Tavistock Publications

On experimental archaeology:

COLES, J., 1973, *Archaeology by experiment*. Hutchinson

COLES, J., 1979, *Experimental archaeology*. Academic Press

REYNOLDS, P. J., 1979, *Iron-Age farm: The Butser experiment*. British Museum Publications Ltd

On radiocarbon dating:

GILLESPIE, R., 1984, *Radiocarbon user's handbook*
(= Oxford University Committee for Archaeology
Monograph No. 3). Oxford University Committee
for Archaeology

GOWLETT, J. A. J. and HEDGES, R. E. M., (eds.), 1986,
Archaeological results from accelerator dating.
(= Oxford University Committee for Archaeology
Monograph No. 11. Oxford University Committee
for Archaeology

RENFREW, C., 1973, *Before civilisation – The radiocarbon
revolution and prehistoric Europe.* Jonathan Cape

WATERBOLK, H. T., 1971, 'Working with radiocarbon
dates', *Proc. Prehist.* Soc. 37, 15–33

WATKINS, T. F. (ed.), 1975, *Radiocarbon, calibration and
prehistory.* Edinburgh University Press

*On environmental archaeology and reconstruction of the
prehistoric environment:*

COLES, B. and COLES, J., 1986, *Sweet Track to
Glastonbury – The Somerset Levels in prehistory.*
Thames and Hudson

EVANS, J. G., 1975, *The environment of early man in the
British Isles.* Paul Elek

EVANS, J. G., 1978, *An introduction to environmental
archaeology.* Paul Elek

EVANS, J. G., LIMBREY, S. and CLEERE, H. (eds.), *The
effect of Man on the landscape: the highland zone*
(= CBA Research Report No. 11). CBA

GODWIN, H., 1975, *History of the British flora* (2nd
edition). Cambridge University Press

HARDING, A. (ed.), 1982, *Climatic change in later
prehistory.* Edinburgh University Press

LIMBREY, S. and EVANS J. G., 1978, *The effect of Man on
the landscape: the lowland zone* (= CBA Research
Report No. 21). CBA

SHACKLEY, M., 1985, *Using environmental archaeology.*
Batsford

On the use of models and theories in prehistory:

BINFORD, L. R. (ed.), 1977, *For theory building in
archaeology.* Academic Press

CLARKE, D. L. (ed.), 1972, *Models in Archaeology.*
Methuen

Works cited in figure captions not referred to above:

BECKETT, S. C. and HIBBERT, F. A., 1979, 'Vegetational
change and the influence of prehistoric man in the
Somerset Levels', *New Phytologist* 83, 577–600

EVANS, J. G., 1971, 'Habitat change on the calcareous
soils of Britain: the impact of Neolithic Man' in
SIMPSON, D. D. A. (ed.), *Economy and settlement in
neolithic and early bronze age Britain and Europe.*
Leicester University Press. 27–73

PEARSON, G. W., PILCHER, J. R. and BAILLIE, M. G. L.,
1983, 'High precision measurement of Irish oaks to
show the natural ^{14}C variations from 200 BC to 4000
BC', *Radiocarbon* 25 (no. 2) 187–96

RENFREW, C., 1972, *The emergence of civilization.*
Methuen

2 Bands on the Run *(pp. 28–47)*

This chapter covers the periods traditionally referred to
as the palaeolithic and mesolithic. General works on these
periods include:

CLARK, G., 1967, *The stone age hunters.* Thames and
Hudson

MORRISON, A. M., 1980, *Early Man in Britain and
Ireland.* Croom Helm

PALMER, S., 1977, *The mesolithic cultures of Britain.*
Dolphin Press

ROE, D. A., 1981, *The lower and middle palaeolithic
periods in Britain.* Routledge and Kegan Paul

WYMER, J. J., 1982, *The palaeolithic age.* Croom Helm

On the Pleistocene Ice Age:

SPARKS, B. W. and WEST, R. G., 1972, *The ice age in
Britain.* Methuen

WEST, R. G., 1968, *Pleistocene geology and biology, with
special reference to the British Isles.* Longman

On the emergence and development of early man:

COLES, J. M. and HIGGS, E. S., 1969, *The archaeology of
early Man.* Faber and Faber

COLLINS, D., 1976, *The human revolution.* Phaidon Press

LEAKEY, R. E., 1981, *The making of Mankind.* Dutton

PFEIFFER, J. E., 1970, *The emergence of Man.* Nelson

On the Clactonian and Acheulian in Britain:

OAKLEY, K. P. and LEAKEY, M., 1937, 'Report on
excavations at Jaywick Sands, Essex (1934), with
some observations on the Clactonian industry, and
on the fauna and geological significance of the
Clacton Channel', *Proc. Prehist. Soc.* 3, 217–60

ROE, D. A., 1968, 'British lower and middle palaeolithic
hand-axe groups', *Proc. Prehist. Soc.* 34, 1–82

ROE, D. A., 1968, *Gazetteer of British lower and middle
palaeolithic sites* (= CBA Research Report No. 8).
CBA

WYMER, J. J., 1968, *Lower palaeolithic archaeology in
Britain as represented by the Thames Valley.* John
Baker

WYMER, J. J., 1974, 'Clactonian and Acheulian
industries in Britain: their chronological
significance', *Proceedings of the Geological
Association* 85 (3), 391–421

Notes and Select Bibliography

On the Swanscombe and Pontnewydd hominid remains:

COOK, J., STRINGER, C. B., CURRANT, A. P., SCHWARCZ, H. P. and WINTLE, A. G., 1982, 'A review of the chronology of the European middle pleistocene hominid record', *Yearbook of Physical Anthropology* (1982), 19–65

GREEN, S., 1984, *Pontnewydd Cave – A lower palaeolithic hominid site in Wales*. National Museum of Wales

OVEY, C. D. (ed.), 1964, *The Swanscombe skull*. Royal Anthropological Society of London

On the Mousterian in Britain:

MELLARS, P. A., 1974, 'The palaeolithic and mesolithic' in RENFREW, C. (ed.), *British prehistory – A new outline*. Duckworth, 41–99

On the hunter-gatherer society generally:

BAILEY, G., 1983 (ed.), *Hunter-gatherer economy in prehistory*. Cambridge University Press

LEE, R. B and DE VORE, I. (eds.), 1968, *Man the hunter*. Aldine

SERVICE, E. L., 1966, *The hunters*. Prentice Hall

On the Devensian period, including the discontinuity and resettlement:

CAMPBELL, J. B., 1977, *The upper palaeolithic of Britain: a study of Man and nature in the late ice age* (2 vols.). Clarendon Press

HALLAM, J. S., EDWARDS, B. J. N., BARNES, B. and STUART, A. J., 1973, 'A late glacial elk with associated barbed points from High Furlong, Lancashire', *Proc. Prehist. Soc.* 39. 100–28

JACOBI, R. M., 1980, 'The upper palaeolithic in Britain with special reference to Wales' in TAYLOR, J. A. (ed.), *Culture and environment in prehistoric Wales* (= BAR 76). BAR. 15–19

OELE, E., SCHUTTENHELM, R. T. E. and WIGGERS, A. J. (eds.), 1979, *The Quaternary history of the North Sea*. Uppsala

TAYLOR, J. A., 1980, 'Environmental changes in Wales during the Holocene' in TAYLOR, J. A. (ed.), *Culture and environment in prehistoric Wales* (= BAR 76). BAR. 101–206

RACKHAM, O., 1976, *Trees and woodland in the British landscape*. Dent

WALKER, D. and WEST, R. G. (eds.), 1970, *Studies in the vegetational history of the British Isles: essays in honour of Harry Godwin*. Cambridge University Press

On eighth- to sixth-millennium BC hunter-gatherer groups:

CLARK, J. G. D., 1954, *Excavations at Star Carr*. Cambridge University Press

CLARK, J. G. D., 1972, *Star Carr a case study in Bioarchaeology* (= Addison-Wesley Modular Publications, Module 10). Addison-Wesley

CLARKE, D. L., 1976, 'Mesolithic Europe: the economic basis' in SIEVEKING, G. DE. G, LONGWORTH, I. H. and WILSON, K. E. (eds.), *Problems in economic and social archaeology*. Duckworth. 449–81

COLES, J. M., 1971, 'The early settlement of Scotland: excavations at Morton, Fife', *Proc. Prehist. Soc.* 37 (2), 284–366

JACOBI, R. M., 1973, 'Aspects of the "mesolithic age" in Great Britain' in KOZLOWSKI, S. K. (ed.), *The mesolithic in Europe*. (Warsaw). 237–65

JACOBI, R. M., 1976, 'Britain inside and outside mesolithic Europe', *Proc. Prehist. Soc.* 42, 67–84

JACOBI, R. M., 1978, 'The settlement of northern Britain in the 8th millennium BC' in MELLARS, P. (ed.), *The early post-glacial settlement of northern Europe*. Duckworth. 295–332

JACOBI, R. M., 1979, 'Early Flandrian hunters in the south-west', *Proceedings of the Devon Archaeological Society* 37, 48–93

MELLARS, P. A. (ed.), 1978, *The early postglacial settlement of northern Europe*. Duckworth

SIMMONS, I. G., 1983, 'Mesolithic Man and environment in upland Britain: an historiographic approach' in BRIGGS, D. J. and WATER, R. S. (eds.), *Studies in quaternary geomorphology*. Geo Books. 215–22

On fifth- to fourth-millennium BC hunter-gatherer groups:

CARE, V., 1979, 'The production and distribution of mesolithic axes in southern England', *Proc. Prehist. Soc.* 45, 93–102

CARE, V., 1982, 'The collection and distribution of lithic raw materials during the mesolithic and neolithic periods in southern England', *Oxford Journal of Archaeology* 1, 269–85

CHURCHILL, D. M., 1965, 'The kitchen midden site at Westward Ho!, Devon, England: ecology, age and relation to changes in land and sea level', *Proc. Prehist. Soc.* 31, 74–84

FROOM, F. R., 1976, *Wawcott III: a stratified mesolithic succession* (= BAR 27). BAR

GENDAL, P. A., 1984, *Mesolithic social territories in north-western Europe* (= BAR S218). BAR

JACOBI, R. M., 1978, 'Population and landscape in mesolithic lowland Britain' in LIMBREY, S. and EVANS, J. G. (eds.), *The effect of Man on the landscape: the lowland zone* (= CBA Research Report No. 21). CBA. 75–85

JACOBI, R. M., 1984, 'The mesolithic of northern East Anglia and contemporary territories' in BARRINGER, C. (ed.), *Aspects of East Anglian prehistory*. Geo Books. 43–76

MELLARS, P. A., 1976, 'Fire ecology, animal populations and Man: a study of some ecological relationships in prehistory', *Proc. Prehist. Soc.* 42, 15–45

MELLARS, P. A., 1976, 'Settlement patterns and industrial variability in the British mesolithic' in SIEVEKING, G. DE. G., LONGWORTH, I. H., and WILSON, K. (eds.), *Problems in economic and social archaeology*. Duckworth. 375–99

WYMER, J. J., 1977, *Gazetteer of mesolithic sites in England and Wales* (= CBA Research Report No. 20). CBA

Works cited in figure captions not referred to above:

EVANS, J. G. and SMITH, I. F., 1983, 'Excavations at Cherhill, north Wiltshire, 1967', *Proc. Prehist. Soc.* 49, 43–118

PALMER, S., 1970, 'The stone age industries of the Isle of Portland, Dorset, and the utilisation of Portland Chert as artefact material in southern England', *Proc. Prehist. Soc.* 36, 82–115

WYMER, J., 1985, *The palaeolithic sites of East Anglia*. Geo Books

3   Harvest for the Year *(pp. 48–74)*

This chapter broadly covers the period traditionally referred to as the early and middle neolithic. The following provide general overviews of the period and its wider setting:

BRADLEY, R. and GARDINER, J. (eds.), 1984, *Neolithic studies* (= BAR 133). BAR

PIGGOTT, S., 1954, *The Neolithic cultures of the British Isles*. Cambridge University Press

SMITH, I. F., 1974, 'The Neolithic' in RENFREW, C. (ed.), *British Prehistory: A new outline*. Duckworth. 100–36

WHITTLE, A. W. R., 1977, *The earlier neolithic of southern England and its continental background* (= BAR S35). BAR

WHITTLE, A. W. R., 1985, *Neolithic Europe*. Cambridge University Press

On the change from hunter-gatherer to farming-based economies and the possible Continental origins:

BENDER, B., 1978, 'Gatherer-hunter to farmer: a social perspective', *World Archaeology* 10, 204–22

CASE, H. J., 1969, 'Neolithic explanations', *Antiquity* 43, 176–86

DE LAET, S. J. (ed.), 1976, *Acculturation and Continuity in Atlantic Europe mainly during the neolithic period and the bronze age* (= Dissertationes Archaeologicae Gandenses XVI). De Tempel

On early farming sites and the environmental background:

BIRKS, H. J. B., DEACON, J. and PEGLER, S., 1975, 'Pollen maps for the British Isles 5000 years ago', *Proceedings of the Royal Society of London* (B), 189, 87–105

WAINWRIGHT, G. J., 1972, 'The excavation of a neolithic settlement on Broome Heath, Ditchingham, Norfolk, England', *Proc. Prehist. Soc.* 38, 1–97

PENNINGTON, W., 1975, 'The effect of neolithic Man on the environment in north-west England: the use of absolute pollen diagrams' in EVANS, J. G., LIMBREY, S. and CLEERE, H. (eds.), *The effect of Man on the landscape: the highland zone* (= CBA Research Report No. 11). CBA. 74–85

On early farming and subsistence:

DENNELL, R. W., 1976, 'Prehistoric crop cultivation in southern England', *Antiquaries Journal* 56, 11–23

FOWLER, P. J., 1971, 'Early prehistoric agriculture in western Europe: some archaeological evidence' in SIMPSON, D. D. A. (ed.), *Economy and settlement in neolithic and early bronze age Britain and Europe*. Leicester University Press. 153–84

LEGGE, A. J., 1981, 'Aspects of cattle husbandry' in MERCER, R. (ed.), *Farming practice in British prehistory*. Edinburgh University Press. 169–81

ROWLEY-CONWY, P., 1981, 'Slash and burn in the temperate European neolithic' in MERCER, R. (ed.), *Farming practice in British prehistory*. Edinburgh University Press. 85–96

On crafts and technology:

CLOUGH, T. H. MCK. and CUMMINS, W. A. (eds.), 1979, *Stone axe studies* (= CBA Research Report No. 23). CBA

GREEN, H. S., 1980, *The flint arrowheads of the British Isles* (= BAR 75). BAR (2 vols.)

HOWARD, H., 1981, 'Ceramic production at Windmill Hill' in HOWARD, H. and MORRIS, E. (eds.), *Production and distribution: a cermaic viewpoint* (= BAR S120). BAR

PITTS, M. and JACOBI, R. M., 1979, 'Some aspects of change in flaked stone industries of the mesolithic and neolithic in southern Britain', *Journal of Archaeological Science* 6, 163–7

RACKHAM, O., 1977, 'Neolithic woodland management in the Somerset Levels: Garvin's, Walton Heath and Rowland's Tracks', *Somerset Levels Papers* 3, 65–72

Notes and Select Bibliography

On farmsteads and unenclosed settlements:

CLARK, J. G. D., HIGGS, E. S. and LONGWORTH, I. H., 1961, 'Excavations at the neolithic site at Hurst Fen, Mildenhall, Suffolk, 1954, 1957 and 1958', *Proc. Prehist. Soc.* 26, 202–45

PRYOR, F. M., 1974, *Excavation at Fengate, Peterborough, England: the first report* (= Royal Ontario Museum Archaeology Monograph No. 3). Royal Ontario Museum

WILLIAMS, A., 1952, 'Clegyr Boia, St David's (Pemb.): Excavation in 1943', *Archaeologia Cambrensis* 102, 20–47

On enclosures:

BAMFORD, H., 1985, *Briar Hill: Excavation 1974–1978*. Northampton Development Corporation

BARKER, G. and WEBLEY, D., 1978, 'Causewayed camps and early neolithic economies in central southern England', *Proc. Prehist. Soc.* 44. 161–86

BEDWIN, O., 1981, 'Excavations at the Neolithic enclosure on Bury Hill, Houghton, West Sussex 1979', *Proc. Prehist. Soc.* 47, 69–86

HEDGES, J. and BUCKLEY, D., 1978, 'Excavations at a neolithic causewayed enclosure, Orsett, Essex, 1975', *Proc. Prehist. Soc.* 44, 219–308

MERCER, R. J., 1980, *Hambledon Hill: A Neolithic landscape*. Edinburgh University Press

MERCER, R. J., 1981, 'Excavations at Carn Brea, Illogan, Cornwall, 1970–73', *Cornish Archaeology* 20, 1–204

SMITH, I. F., 1965, *Windmill Hill and Avebury – Excavations by Alexander Keiller 1925–1939*. Clarendon Press

WHITTLE, A. W. R., 1977, 'Earlier neolithic enclosures in north-west Europe', *Proc. Prehist. Soc.* 43, 329–48

On early burial monuments:

ATKINSON, R. J. C., 1965, 'Wayland's Smithy', *Antiquity* 39, 126–33

DARVILL, T. C., 1984, 'Neolithic Gloucestershire' in SAVILLE, A. (ed.), *Archaeology in Gloucestershire – From the earliest hunters to the industrial age*. Cheltenham Museum and Art Gallery & Bristol and Gloucestershire Archaeological Society. 80–112

PIGGOTT, S., 1972, 'Excavation of the Dalladies long barrow, Fettercairn, Kincardineshire', *Proceedings of the Society of Antiquaries of Scotland* 104, 23–47

POWELL, T. G. E., 1973, 'The excavation of the megalithic chambered cairn at Dyffryn Ardudwy, Merioneth, Wales', *Archaeologia* 104, 1–49

VYNER, B. E., 1984, 'The excavation of a neolithic cairn at Street House, Loftus, Cleveland', *Proc. Prehist. Soc.* 50, 151–95

On long barrows and chambered tombs:

ASHBEE, P., 1970, *The earthen long barrow in Britain*. Dent. (2nd edition, 1984, Geo Books)

BRITNELL, W. J. and SAVORY, H. N., 1984, *Gwernvale and Penywyrlod: two neolithic long cairns in the Black Mountains of Brecknock* (= Cambrian Archaeological Monograph No. 2). Cambrian Archaeological Association

CORCORAN, J. X. W. P., 1972, 'Multi-period construction and the origins of the chambered long cairn in western Britain and Ireland' in LYNCH, F. M. and BURGESS, C. (eds.), *Prehistoric Man in Wales and the West*. Adams and Dart. 31–64

CRAWFORD, O. G. S., 1925, *The long barrows of the Cotswolds*. John Bellows

DANIEL, G. E., 1950, *The prehistoric chamber tombs of England and Wales*. Cambridge University Press

DARVILL, T. C., 1982, *The megalithic tombs of the Cotswold-Severn region*. Vorda

FRASER, D., 1983, *Land and society in neolithic Orkney* (= BAR 117). BAR. (2 Vols.)

HEDGES, J. W., 1983, *Isbister – A chambered tomb in Orkney* (= BAR 115). BAR

HENSHALL, A. S., 1963 and 1972, *The chambered tombs of Scotland*. Edinburgh University Press. (2 Vols.)

MANBY, T. G., 1970, 'Long barrows of northern England: structural and dating evidence', *Scottish Archaeological Forum* (1970), 1–28

PIGGOTT, S., 1962, *The West Kennet long barrow – Excavations 1955–6* (= Ministry of Works Archaeological Reports No. 4). HMSO

POWELL, T. G. E., CORCORAN, J. X. W. P., LYNCH, F. and SCOTT, J. G., 1969, *Megalithic enquiries in the west of Britain*. Liverpool University Press

RCHME, 1979, *Long barrows in Hampshire and the Isle of Wight*. HMSO

STARTIN, B. and BRADLEY, R., (1981), 'Some notes on work organisation and society in prehistoric Wessex' in RUGGLES, C. N. L. and WHITTLE, A. W. R. (eds.), *Astronomy and society in Britain during the period 4000 – 1500 BC* (= BAR 88). BAR. 289–96

On early third-millennium BC round barrows

COLES, J. M. and SIMPSON, D. D. A., 1965, 'The excavation of a neolithic round barrow at Pitnacree, Perthshire, Scotland', *Proc. Prehist. Soc.* 31, 34–57

KINNES, I., 1979, *Round barrows and ring-ditches in the British Neolithic* (= British Museum Occasional Paper No. 7). British Museum

On burials in barrows and other contexts:

CHESTERMAN, J., 1977, 'Burial rites in a Cotswold long barrow', *Man* 12, 22–32

PRYOR, F., 1976, 'A neolithic multiple burial from Fengate, Peterborough', *Antiquity* 50, 232–3

SAVILLE, A., 1984, 'Preliminary report on the excavation of a Cotswold-Severn tomb at Hazleton, Gloucestershire', *Antiquaries Journal* 64, 10–24

SHANKS, M. and TILLEY, C., 1982, 'Ideology, symbolic power and ritual communication: a reinterpretation of neolithic mortuary practices' in HODDER, I. (ed.), *Symbolic and structural archaeology*. Cambridge University Press. 129–54

On population and society:

ATKINSON, R. J. C., 1968, 'Old mortality: some aspects of burial and population in neolithic Britain' in COLES, J. and SIMPSON, D. D. A. (eds.), *Studies in ancient Europe*. Leicester University Press. 83–94

BROTHWELL, D., 1971, 'Palaeodemography and earlier British population', *World Archaeology* 4, 75–87

BROTHWELL, D., 1973, 'The human biology of the neolithic population of Britain' in SCHWIDETZKY, I. (ed.), *Die Anfange des neolithikums vom orient bis nordeuropa – Teil VIIIa Anthropologie. 1 Teil.* Bohlau Verlag. 280–99

FLEMING, A., 1973, 'Tombs for the living', *Man* 8, 177–93

HODDER. I., 1984, 'Burials, houses, women and men in the European neolithic' in MILLER, D. and TILLEY, C. (eds.), *Ideology, power and prehistory*. Cambridge University Press. 51–68

KINNES, I., 1975, 'Monumental function in British neolithic burial practices', *World Archaeology* 7, 16–29

RENFREW, C., 1973, 'Monuments, mobilisation and social organisation in neolithic Wessex' in RENFREW, C. (ed.), *The explanation of culture change: models in prehistory*. Duckworth. 539–58

RENFREW, C., 1976, 'Megaliths, territories and populations' in DELAET, S. J. (ed.), *Acculturation and continuity in Atlantic Europe mainly during the neolithic period and the bronze age* (= Dissertationes Archaeologicae Gandenses XVI). De Tempel. 198–220

RENFREW, C., 1983, 'The social archaeology of megalithic monuments', *Scientific American* November 1983, 128–36

On trackways, exchange and interaction:

CAMPBELL-SMITH, W., 1965, 'The distribution of jade axes in Europe with a supplement to the catalogue of those from the British Isles', *Proc. Prehist. Soc.* 31, 25–33

CLARK, J. D. G., 1965, 'Traffic in stone axe and adze blades', *Economic History Review* 18, 1–28

CLOUGH, T. H. MCK. and CUMMINS, W. A. (eds.), 1979, *Stone axe studies* (= CBA Research Report No. 23). CBA

COLES, J. M. (ed.), 1975–1986, *Somerset Levels Papers* 1–12 (continuing)

COLES, J. M. and ORME, B. J., 1980, *The prehistory of the Somerset Levels*. Somerset Levels Project

CUMMINS, W. A., 1974, 'Neolithic stone axe trade in Britain', *Antiquity* 48, 201–5

CUMMINS, W. A., 1979, 'Neolithic stone axes – distribution and trade in England and Wales' in CLOUGH, T. H. MCK and CUMMINS, W. A. (eds.), *Stone axe studies* (= CBA Research Report No. 23). CBA. 5–12

HODDER, I. and LANE, P., 1982, 'A contextual examination of neolithic axe distributions in Britain' in ERICSON, J. E. and EARLE, T. K. (eds.), *Contexts for prehistoric exchange*. Academic Press. 213–35

PEACOCK, D. P. S., 1969, 'Neolithic pottery production in Cornwall', *Antiquity* 43, 145–9

On people, land-use and war:

DIXON, P. W., 1979, 'A neolithic and iron age site on a hilltop in southern England', *Scientific American* May 1979, 142–50

MERCER, R. J., 1985, 'A neolithic fortress and funeral center', *Scientific American* March 1985, 76–83

4 Sunrises and Other New Beginnings
(pp. 75–107)

This chapter covers the period traditionally defined as the late neolithic, beaker period and the early Bronze Age. General accounts of the period include:

BURGESS, C., 1980, *The age of Stonehenge*. Dent

PIGGOTT, S., 1954, *The neolithic cultures of the British Isles*. Cambridge University Press

WHITTLE, A. W. R., 1981, 'Late neolithic society in Britain, a realignment' in RUGGLES, C. and WHITTLE, A. W. R. (eds.), *Astronomy and society during the period 4000–150 BC* (= BAR 88). BAR. 297–342

On changes in the second half of the third millennium:

BRADLEY, R., 1972, 'Prehistorians and pastoralists in neolithic and bronze age England', *World Archaeology* 4, 192–203

BRADLEY, R., 1978, 'Colonisation and land use in the late neolithic and early bronze age' in LIMBREY, S. and EVANS, J. G. (eds.) *The effects of Man on the landscape: the lowland zone* (= CBA Research Report No. 21). CBA. 95–102

SMITH, R. W., 1984, 'The ecology of neolithic farming systems as exemplified by the Avebury region of Wiltshire', *Proc. Prehist. Soc.* 50, 99–120

WHITTLE, A. W. R., 'Resources and population in the British neolithic', *Antiquity* 52, 34–42

On burials in the second half of the third millennium BC

BRADLEY, R., CHAMBERS, R. A. and HALPIN, C. E., 1984, *Barrow Hills, Radley, 1983–4: An interim report.* Oxfordshire Archaeological Unit

KINNES, I., 1979, *Round barrows and ring ditches in the British Neolithic* (= British Museum Occasional Paper No. 7). British Museum

PETERSON, F., 1972, 'Traditions of multiple burial in later neolithic and early bronze age England', *Archaeological Journal* 129, 22–55

On cursus monuments:

HEDGES, J. and BUCKLEY, D., 1981, *Springfield cursus and the cursus problem* (= Essex County Council Occasional Paper No. 1). Essex County Council

PRYOR, F. M. M. and FRENCH, C. A. I., 1985, *The Fenland Project, Number 1: Archaeology and environment in the lower Welland valley* (= East Anglian Archaeology Report No. 27). Cambridgeshire Archaeology Committee. (2 Vols.)

On bank barrows:

BRADLEY, R., 1983, 'The bank barrows and related monuments of Dorset in the light of recent fieldwork', *Proceedings of the Dorset Natural History and Archaeological Society* 105, 15–20

On henges:

BURL, A., 1969, 'Henges: internal features and regional groups', *Archaeological Journal* 126, 1–28

HOULDER, C. H., 1968, 'The henge monuments at Llandegai', *Antiquity* 42, 216–21

JONES, S. J., GRIMES, W. F., FAWCETT, E. and TETLEY, H., 1938, 'The excavation of Gorsey Bigbury', *Proceedings of the University of Bristol Spelaeological Society* 5, 3–56

MERCER, R. J., 1981, 'The excavation of a late neolithic henge-type enclosure at Balfarg, Markinch, Fife, Scotland', *Proceedings of the Society of Antiquaries of Scotland* 111, 63–171

RITCHIE, J. N. G., 1976, 'The Stones of Stennes, Orkney', *Proceedings of the Society of Antiquaries of Scotland* 107, 1–60

THOMAS, N., 1955, 'The Thornborough circles near Ripon, North Riding', *Yorkshire Archaeological Journal* 38.3 (pt. 152), 425–45

WAINWRIGHT, G. J., 1969, 'A review of henge monuments in the light of recent research', *Proc. Prehist. Soc.* 35, 112–33

On late third-millennium BC tombs:

BRADLEY, R. and CHAPMAN, R. W., 1984, 'Passage graves in the European neolithic – a theory of converging evolution' in BERENHULT, G., *The archaeology of Carrowmore* (= Theses and Papers in North European Archaeology 14). Institute of Archaeology at the University of Stockholm. 348–56

FRASER, D., 1983, *Land and society in neolithic Orkney* (= BAR 117). BAR. (2 Vols.)

POWELL, T. G. E. and DANIEL, G. E., 1956, *Barclodiad Y Gawres.* Liverpool University Press

HERITY, M., 1974, *Irish passage graves.* Irish University Press

On Clava cairns and recumbent stone circles:

BURL, A., 1976, *The stone circles of the British Isles.* Yale University Press

HENSHALL, A. S., 1963, *The chambered tombs of Scotland: Volume 1.* Edinburgh University Press

On round barrow burial monuments:

ASHBEE, P., 1960, *The bronze age round barrow in Britain.* Phoenix

FOX, C., 1959, *Life and death in the bronze age.* Routledge and Kegan Paul

LYNCH, F. M., 1972, 'Ring cairns and related monuments in Wales', *Scottish Archaeological Forum* 4, 61–80

RITCHIE, J. N. G. and MACLAREN, A., 1972, 'Ring-cairns and related monuments in Scotland', *Scottish Archaeological Forum* 4, 1–17

On grooved ware:

WAINWRIGHT, G. J. and LONGWORTH, I. H., 1971, 'The Rinyo-Clacton culture reconsidered' in WAINWRIGHT, G. J. and LONGWORTH, I. H., *Durrington Walls: Excavations 1966–1968* (= Reports of the Research Committee of the Society of Antiquaries of London No. XXIX). Society of Antiquaries. 235–306

On trade and contact within the late third millennium:

NEEDHAM, S., 1979, 'The extent of foreign influence on early bronze age axe development in southern Britain' in RYAN, M. (ed.), *The origins of metallurgy in Atlantic Europe: Proceedings of the fifth Atlantic Colloquium.* (Dublin). 265–93

SHEE TWOHIG, E., 1981, *The megalithic art of western Europe.* Clarendon Press

SHENNAN, S. J., 1982, 'Exchange and ranking: the role of amber in the earlier bronze age of Europe' in RENFREW, C. and SHENNAN, S. (eds.), *Ranking, resource and exchange.* Cambridge University Press. 33–45

On beakers and associated graves and settlements:

BAMFORD, H. M., 1982, *Beaker domestic sites in the Fen edge and East Anglia* (= East Anglian Archaeology Report No. 16). Norfolk Archaeology Unit

BURGESS, C. and SHENNAN, S. J., 1976, 'The beaker phenomenon: some suggestions' in BURGESS, C. B. and MIKET, R. (eds.), *Settlement and economy in the third and second millennia BC* (= BAR 33). BAR. 309–327

CASE, H. J., 1977, 'The beaker culture in Britain and Ireland' in MERCER, R. J. (ed.), *Beakers in Britain and Europe* (= BAR S26). BAR. 71–101

CLARKE, D. L., 1970, *Beaker pottery of Great Britain and Ireland.* Cambridge University Press. (2 Vols.)

CLARKE, D. L., 1976, 'The beaker network – social and economic models' in LANTING, J. N. and VAN DER WAALS, J. D. (eds.), *Glockenbechersymposion Oberried, 1974.* Fibula-Van Dishoek. 459–77

GIBSON, A. M., 1982, *Beaker domestic sites* (= BAR 107). BAR. (2 Vols.)

HARRISON, R. J., 1980, *The Beaker Folk.* Thames and Hudson

LANTING, J. N. and VAN DER WAALS, J. D., 1972, 'British beakers as seen from the Continent', *Helinium* 12, 20–46

ROBERTSON-MACKAY, M. E., 1980, 'A head and hoofs burial beneath a round barrow, with other neolithic and bronze age sites on Hemp Knoll near Avebury, Wiltshire', *Proc. Prehist. Soc.* 46, 123–76

SIMPSON, D. D. A., 1971, 'Beaker houses and settlements in Britain' in SIMPSON, D. D. A. (ed.), *Economy and settlement in neolithic and early bronze age Britain and Europe.* Leicester University Press. 131–52

On large monuments of the late third millennium BC:

ATKINSON, R. J. C., 1970, 'Silbury Hill 1969–70', *Antiquity* 44, 313–14

BURL, A., 1979, *Prehistoric Avebury.* Yale University Press

WAINWRIGHT, G. J., 1975, 'Religion and settlement in Wessex, 3000–1700 BC' in FOWLER, P. J. (ed.), *Recent work in rural archaeology.* Moonraker Press. 57–71

WAINWRIGHT, G. J., 1979, *Mount Pleasant Dorset: Excavations 1970–71* (= Reports of the Research Committee of the Society of Antiquaries of London No. XXXVII). Society of Antiquaries

WAINWRIGHT, G. J. and LONGWORTH, I. H., 1971, *Durrington Walls: Excavations 1966–1968* (= Reports of the Research Committee of the Society of Antiquaries of London No. XXIX). Society of Antiquaries

On stone circles and rows:

ATKINSON, R. J. C., 1956, *Stonehenge.* Hamish Hamilton

BURL, A., 1976, *The stone circles of the British Isles.* Yale University Press

BURL, A., 1979, *Prehistoric stone circles.* Shire

EMMETT, S., 1979, 'Stone rows: the traditional view reconsidered', *Proceedings of the Devon Archaeological Society* 37, 94–114

On the uses of stone circles and alignments:

ATKINSON, R. J. C., 1974, 'Ancient astronomy; unwritten evidence' in HODSON, F. R. (ed.), *The place of astronomy in the ancient world.* 123–31

BURL, A., 1983, *Prehistoric astronomy and ritual.* Shire

HEGGIE, D. C., 1981, *Megalithic science.* Thames and Hudson

RUGGLES, C. R. and WHITTLE, A. W. R., 1981, *Astronomy and society in Britain during the period 4000–1500 BC* (= BAR 88). BAR

THOM, A., 1967, *Megalithic sites in Britain.* Oxford University Press

THOM, A., 1971, *Megalithic lunar observatories.* Oxford University Press

On power and prestige:

BRAITHWAITE, M., 1984, 'Ritual and prestige in the prehistory of Wessex c.2200–1400 BC: a new dimension to the archaeological evidence' in MILLER, D. and TILLEY, C. (eds.), *Ideology, power and prehistory.* Cambridge University Press. 93–110

CLARKE, D. V., COWIE, T. G. and FOXON, A., 1985, *Symbols of power at the time of Stonehenge.* National Museum of Antiquaries of Scotland

PIERPOINT, S., 1980, *Social patterns in Yorkshire Prehistory* (= BAR 74). BAR

On early second-millennium BC pottery:

GIBSON, A. M., 1978, *Bronze age pottery in the north-east of England* (= BAR 56). BAR

COWIE, T. G., 1978, *Bronze age food vessel urns* (= BAR 55). BAR

LONGWORTH, I., 1984, *Collared urns of the Bronze Age in Great Britain and Ireland.* Cambridge University Press

SIMPSON, D. D. A., 1968, 'Food vessels: associations and chronology' in COLES, J. and SIMPSON, D. D. A. (ed.), *Studies in Ancient Europe.* Leicester University Press. 197–211

On early second-millennium BC rich burials:

GERLOFF, S., 1975, *The early bronze age daggers in Great Britain, with a reconsideration of the Wessex culture* (= Prahistorische Bronzefunde VI. 2). (Munchen)

PIGGOTT, S., 1938, 'The early bronze age in Wessex', *Proc. Prehist. Soc.* 4, 52–106

On the European setting and foreign contact in the early to mid second millennium BC:

COLES, J. M. and HARDING, A. F., 1979, *The bronze age in Europe*. Methuen

COLES, J. and TAYLOR, J., 1971, 'The Wessex culture: a minimal view', *Antiquity* 45, 6–14

RENFREW, C., 1968, 'Wessex without Mycenae', *Annual of the British School and Athens* 63, 277–85

On crafts, economic growth and the development of metallurgy:

BRITTON, D., 1963, 'Traditions of metalworking in the later neolithic and early bronze age of Britain: part I', *Proc. Prehist. Soc.* 29, 258–325

BURGESS, C., 1978, 'The background of early metalworking in Ireland and Britain' in RYAN, M. (ed.), *The origins of metallurgy in Atlantic Europe*. Stationery Office, Dublin. 243–86

COLES, J., 1969, 'Scottish early bronze age metalwork', *Proceedings of the Society of Antiquaries of Scotland* 101, 1–110

COLES, J. M., HEAL, S. V. E. and ORME, B. J., 1978, 'The use and character of wood in prehistoric Britain', *Proc. Prehist. Soc.* 44, 1–46

ROE, F., 1979, 'Typology of stone implements with shaftholes' in CLOUGH, T. H. MCK. and CUMMINS, W. A. (eds.), *Stone axe studies* (= CBA Research Report No. 23). CBA. 23–48

SAVORY, H. N., 1980, *Guide catalogue of the Bronze Age collections*. National Museum of Wales

TAYLOR, J. J., 1980, *Bronze age goldwork of the British Isles*. Cambridge University Press

On society and politics in the early second millennium BC:

HODDER, I., 1979, 'Social and economic stress and material culture patterning', *American Antiquity* 44, 446–54

FLEMING, A., 1971, 'Territorial patterns in bronze age Wessex', *Proc. Prehist. Soc.* 37, 138–66

RENFREW, C., 1974, 'Beyond a subsistence economy: the evolution of social organisation in prehistoric Europe' in MOORE, C. B. (ed.), *Reconstructing complex societies* (= Supplementary Bulletin of the American School of Oriental Studies No. 20). American School of Oriental Studies. 69–93

SHENNAN, S., 1982, 'Ideology, change and the European early bronze age', in HODDER, I. (ed.), *Symbolic and structural archaeology*. Cambridge University Press. 155–61

On settlement and subsistence:

CLARKE, D. V., 1976, *The neolithic village at Skara Brae, Orkney, 1972–3 excavations – an interim report*. HMSO (Edinburgh)

JONES, M., 1980, 'Carbonised cereals from grooved ware contexts', *Proc. Prehist. Soc.* 46, 61–4

PRYOR, F. M., 1978, *Excavation at Fengate, Peterborough, England: the second report* (= Royal Ontario Museum Archaeology Monograph No. 5). Royal Ontario Museum

MANBY, T. G., 1974, *Grooved ware sites in the north of England* (= BAR 9). BAR

On standing stones and landscape organisation:

GRESHAM, C. A. and IRVINE, H. C., 1963, 'Prehistoric routes across north Wales', *Antiquity* 37, 54–8

BOWEN, H.C. and FOWLER, P.J. (eds.), 1978, *Early land allotment in the British Isles* (= BAR 48). BAR

WILSON, J. C., 1983, 'The standing stones of Anglesey', *Bulletin of the Board of Celtic Studies* 30, 210–33

Works cited in figure captions not referred to above:

ANNABLE, F. K. and SIMPSON, D. D. A., 1964, *Guide catalogue of the neolithic and bronze age collections in Devizes Museum*. Wiltshire Archaeological and Natural History Society

BRADLEY, R., 1984, *The social foundations of prehistoric Britain*. Longman

5 After the Gold Rush *(pp. 108–32)*

This chapter covers the period traditionally referred to as the middle and late Bronze Age. The following works cover this period in general and its European background:

BARRETT, J.C. and BRADLEY, R. (eds.), 1980, *Settlement and society in the British later bronze age* (= BAR 83). BAR (2vols.)

BURGESS, C., 1980, *The age of Stonehenge*. Dent

COLES, J. M. and HARDING, A. F., 1979, *The bronze age in Europe*. Methuen

On land management, settlement and subsistence:

BARRETT, J., 1980, 'The evolution of later bronze age settlement in BARRETT, J.C. and BRADLEY, R. (eds.), *Settlement and society in the British later bronze age* (= BAR 83). BAR. 77–95

BOWEN, H. C. and FOWLER, P. J. (eds.), 1978, *Early land allotment in the British Isles* (= BAR 48). BAR

BRADLEY, R., 1978, 'Prehistoric field systems in Britain and north-west Europe – a review of some recent work', *World Archaeology* 9, 265–77

FLEMING, A., 1978, 'The prehistoric landscape of Dartmoor. Part 1: south Dartmoor', *Proc. Prehist. Soc.* 44, 97–123

FLEMING. A., 1979, 'The Dartmoor reaves: boundary patterns and behaviour patterns in the second millennium BC', *Proceedings of the Devon Archaeological Society* 37, 115–31

FLEMING. A., 1983, 'The prehistoric landscape of Dartmoor Part 2: north and east Dartmoor', *Proc. Prehist. Soc.* 49, 195–242

DREWETT, P., 1978, 'Field systems and land allotment in Sussex, 3rd millennium BC to 4th century AD' in BOWEN, H. C. and FOWLER, P. J. (eds.), *Early land allotment in the British Isles* (= BAR 48). BAR. 67–80

DREWETT, P., 1979, 'New evidence for the structure and function of middle bronze age round houses in Sussex', *Archaeological Journal* 136, 3–11

PRYOR, F., 1980, *Excavation at Fengate, Peterborough, England: the third report* (= Royal Ontario Museum Archaeology Monograph No. 6). Royal Ontario Museum

JOBEY, G., 1980, 'Green Knowe unenclosed platform settlement and Harehope cairn, Peeblesshire', *Proceedings of the Society of Antiquaries of Scotland* 110, 72–113

JOBEY, G., 1983, 'Excavation of an unenclosed settlement on Strandrop Rigg, Northumberland, and some problems related to similar settlements between Tyne and Forth', *Archaeologia Aeliana* 5th series, 11, 1–22

SMITH, K. COPPEN, G., WAINWRIGHT, G. J. and BECKETT, S., 1981, 'The Shaugh Moor project: third report – settlement and environmental investigation', *Proc. Prehist. Soc.* 47, 205–74

On burnt mounds:

HEDGES, J., 1975, 'Excavation of two Orcadian burnt mounds at Liddle and Beaquoy', *Proceedings of the Society of Antiquaries of Scotland* 106, 39–983

NIXON, M. J., 1980, 'Burnt mounds in the south Birmingham area', *West Midlands Archaeological Newsletter* 23, 1980, 9–13

On burial ritual:

BRADLEY, R., 1981, 'Various styles of urn: cemeteries and settlement in southern England *c.*1400–1000 BC' in CHAPMAN, R. W., KINNES, I. and RANDSBORG, K. (eds.), *The archaeology of death.* Cambridge University Press. 93–104

BRITNELL, W., 1982, 'The excavation of two round barrows at Trelystan, Powys', *Proc. Prehist. Soc.* 48, 133–202

BURGESS, C., 1976, 'Burials with metalwork of the later bronze in Wales and beyond' in BOON, G. and LEWIS, J. M. (eds.), *Welsh antiquity.* National Museum of Wales. 81–104

DACRE, M. and ELLISON, A., 1981, 'A bronze age urn cemetery at Kimpton, Hampshire', *Proc. Prehist. Soc.* 47, 147–204

FOX, C., 1959, *Life and death in the bronze age.* Routledge and Kegan Paul

LYNCH, F. M., 1971, 'Report on the re-excavation of two bronze age cairns in Anglesey: Bedd Branwen and Treiorwerth', *Archaeologia Cambrensis* 120, 11–83

PETERSON, F. F., 1981, *The excavation of a bronze age cemetery on Knighton Heath, Dorset* (= BAR 98). BAR

On ritual connected with rivers, lakes and wet places:

BRADLEY, R., 1979, 'The interpretation of later bronze age metalwork from British rivers', *International Journal of Nautical Archaeology* 8, 3–6

BRADLEY, R., 1982, 'The destruction of wealth in later prehistory', *Man* 17, 108–122

BURGESS, C., COOMBS, D. and DAVIES, G., 1972, 'The Broadward complex and barbed spearheads' in LYNCH, F. and BURGESS, C. (eds.), *Prehistoric Man in Wales and the West.* Adams and Dart. 211–84

EHRENBERG, M., 1980, 'The occurrence of bronze age metalwork in the Thames: an investigation', *Transactions of the London and Middlesex Archaeological Society* 31, 1–15

On foreign connections:

BUTLER, J. J., 1963, 'Bronze age connections across the North Sea', *Palaeohistoria* 9

MUCKLEROY, K., 1980, 'Two bronze age cargoes in British waters', *Antiquity* 54, 100–9

MUCKLEROY, K., 1981, 'Middle bronze age trade between Britain and Europe: a maritime perspective', *Proc. Prehist. Soc.* 47, 275–97

O'CONNER, B., 1980, *Cross-channel relations in the later bronze age* (= BAR S91). BAR. (2 Vols.)

On domestic crafts and technology:

BARRETT, J. C., 'The pottery of the later bronze age in lowland England', *Proc. Prehist. Soc.* 46, 297–319

BESWICK, P., 1975, 'Report on the shale industry at Swaine Sty', *Transactions of the Hunter Archaeological Society* 10, 207–11

COLES, J. M., HEAL, S. V. E., and ORME, B. J., 1978, 'The use and character of wood in prehistoric Britain and Ireland', *Proc. Prehist. Soc.* 44, 1–46

FORD, S., BRADLEY, R., HAWKES, J. and FISHER. P., 1984, 'Flint working in the metal age', *Oxford Journal of Archaeology* 3, 157–73

MCGRAIL, S., 1978, *The logboats of England and Wales* (= BAR 51). BAR. (2 Vols.)

On metalworking and hoards:

BURGESS, C., 1968, 'The later bronze age in the British Isles and north-western France', *Archaeological Journal* 125, 1–45

BURGESS, C. and COOMBS, D. (eds.), *Bronze age hoards – some finds old and new* (= BAR 67). BAR

CHAMPION, T., 1971, 'The end of the Irish bronze age', *North Munster Journal of Archaeology* 14, 17–24

CHAMPION, T., 1980, 'The early development of iron working', *Nature* 284, 513–14

COLES, J., 1960, 'Scottish late bronze age metalwork: typology, distribution and chronology', *Proceedings of the Society of Antiquaries of Scotland* 93, 16–134

COLES, J., 1964, 'Scottish middle bronze age metalwork', *Proceedings of the Society of Antiquaries of Scotland* 97, 82–156

NEEDHAM, S. and BURGESS, C., 1980, 'The later bronze age in the lower Thames valley: the metalwork evidence' in BARRETT, J. C. and BRADLEY, R. (eds.), *Settlement and society in the British later bronze age* (= BAR 83). BAR. 437–70

POWELL, T. G. E., 1976, 'The inception of the iron age in temperate Europe', *Proc. Prehist. Soc.* 42, 1–14

PLEINER, R., 1980, 'Early iron metallurgy in Europe' in WERTIME, T. A. and MUHLY, J. D. (eds.), *The coming of the age of iron.* Yale University Press

ROWLANDS, M. J., 1976, *The production and distribution of metalwork in the middle bronze age in southern Britain* (= BAR 32) BAR (2 vols.)

On exchange and trade:

ELLISON, A., 1981, 'Settlement and regional exchange: a case study' in BARRETT, J. C. and BRADLEY, R. J. (eds.), *Settlement and society in the British later bronze age* (= BAR 83). BAR. 127–40

BRADLEY, R., 1985, 'Exchange and social distance – the structure of bronze artefact distributions', *Man* 20, 692–704

BRADLEY, R. J. and ELLISON, A., 1975, *Rams Hill: A bronze age defended enclosure and its landscape* (= BAR 19). BAR

NORTHOVER, P., 1982, 'The exploration of long-distance movement of bronze in bronze age and early iron age Europe', *Bulletin of the London University Institute of Archaeology* 19, 45–72

PIGGOTT, S., 1977, 'A glance at Cornish tin' in MARKOTIC, V. (ed.), *Ancient Europe and the Mediterranean.* Aris and Phillips. 141–5

On horseriding and wagons:

PIGGOTT, S., 1983, *The earliest wheeled transport.* Thames and Hudson

POWELL, T. G. E., 1971, 'The introduction of horse-riding to temperate Europe: A contributory note', *Proc. Prehist. Soc.* 37, 1–14

On early first-millennium BC environmental change:

HARDING, A. F. (ed.), 1982, *Climatic change in later prehistory.* Edinburgh University Press

PIGGOTT, S., 1972, 'A note on climatic deterioration in the first millennium BC in Britain', *Scottish Archaeological Forum* 4, 109–13

On 'ranch boundaries' and landscape change in the early first millennium BC:

BOWEN, H. C., 1978, 'Celtic fields and ranch boundaries in Wessex' in LIMBREY, S. and EVANS, J. G. (eds.), *The effect of Man on the landscape: the lowland zone* (= CBA Research Report No. 21). CBA. 115–21

RILEY, D., 1980, *Early landscapes from the air.* Department of Archaeology and Prehistory, University of Sheffield

SPRATT, D. (ed.), 1982, *Prehistoric and Roman archaeology in north-east Yorkshire* (= BAR 104). BAR

On defended enclosures and early hillforts:

AVERY, M., 1976, 'Hillforts of the British Isles: a students introduction' in HARDING, D. W. (ed.), *Hillforts: later prehistoric earthworks in Britain and Ireland.* Academic Press. 1–58

CUNLIFFE, B., 1978, *Iron Age Communities in Britain* (2nd Edition). Routledge and Kegan Paul

HARDING, D. W. (ed.), 1976, *Hillforts: later prehistoric earthworks in Britain and Ireland.* Academic Press

On weapons of the late second to mid first millennium BC:

COLES, J., 1962, 'European bronze age shields', *Proc. Prehist. Soc.* 28, 156–90

COOMBS, D., 1975, 'Bronze age weapon hoards in Britain', *Archaeologia Atlantica* 1, 49–81

COWEN, J. D., 1951, 'The earliest swords in Britain and their origins on the continent', *Proc. Prehist. Soc.* 17, 195–213

COWEN, J. D., 1967, 'The Halstatt sword of bronze: on the continent and in Britain', *Proc. Prehist. Soc.* 33, 377–454

EHRENBERG, M. R., 1977, *Bronze age spearheads from Berkshire, Buckinghamshire and Oxfordshire* (= BAR 34). BAR

On salt production:

DE BRISAY, K. and EVANS, K. (eds.), *Salt – the study of an ancient industry.* Colchester Archaeological Group

JONES, M. U., 'Prehistoric salt equipment from a pit at Mucking, Essex', *Antiquaries Journal* 57, 315–19

On developments in the north:

BREWSTER, T. C. M., 1963, *The excavation of Staple Howe.* East Riding Archaeological Research Committee

BURGESS, C., 1984, 'The prehistoric settlement of Northumberland: a speculative survey' in MIKET, R. and BURGESS, C. (eds.), *Between and beyond the walls: essays on the prehistory and history of north Britain in honour of George Jobey.* John Donald. 126–75

CHAPMAN, J. C. and MYTUM, H. C. (eds.), 1983, *Settlement in northern Britain 1000 BC–1000 AD* (= BAR 118). BAR

HAMILTON, J. R. C., 1956, *Excavations at Jarlshof, Shetland* (= Ministry of Works Archaeological Reports No. 1). HMSO

On society and politics:

BRADLEY, R., 1980, 'Subsistence, exchange and technology: a social framework for the bronze age in southern England *c.*1400–700 BC' in BARRETT, J. C. and BRADLEY, R. (eds.), *Settlement and society in the British later bronze age* (= BAR 83). BAR. 57–75

COLES, J., 1977, 'Parade and display: experiments in bronze age Europe' in MARKOTIC, V. (ed.), *Ancient Europe and the Mediterranean.* Aris and Phillips. 51–58

ELLISON, A., 1980, 'Deverel-Rimbury urn cemeteries: the evidence for social organisation' in BARRETT, J. C. and BRADLEY, R. (eds.), *Settlement and society in the British later bronze age* (= BAR 83). BAR. 115–26

ELLISION, A., 1981, 'Towards a socio-economic model for the middle bronze age in southern England' in HODDER, I., ISAAC, G. and HAMMOND, N. (eds.), *Pattern of the past.* Cambridge University Press. 413–38

FLEMING. A., 1982, 'Social boundaries and land boundaries' in RENFREW, C. and SHENNAN, S. (eds.), *Ranking, resource and exchange.* Cambridge University Press. 52–5

HAWKES, C. F. C. and SMITH, M. A., 1957, 'On some buckets and cauldrons of the bronze and early iron ages', *Antiquaries Journal* 37, 131–98

ROWLANDS, M. J., 1980, 'Kinship, alliance and exchange in the European bronze age' in BARRETT, J. C. and BRADLEY, R. (eds.), *Settlement and society in the British later bronze age* (= BAR 83). BAR. 15–55

Works cited in figure captions not referred to above:

ANNABLE, F. K. and SIMPSON, D. D. A., 1964, *Guide catalogue of the neolithic and bronze age collections in Devizes Museum.* Wiltshire Archaeological and Natural History Society

SAVORY, H. N., 1976, *Guide catalogue of the early iron age collections.* National Museum of Wales

6 Below the Salt *(pp. 133–61)*

This chapter covers the period traditionally termed the early and middle Iron Age. The following publications provide general accounts of the period and its continental setting:

COLLIS, J., 1977, *The iron age in Britain – a review.* Department of Prehistory and Archaeology, University of Sheffield

COLLIS, J., 1984, *The European iron age.* Batsford

CHAMPION, T. C. and MEGAW, J. V. S. (eds.), 1985, *Settlement and society: Aspects of west European prehistory in the first millennium BC.* Leicester University Press

CUNLIFFE, B., 1978, *Iron age communities in Britain* (2nd Edition). Routledge and Kegan Paul

HARDING, D., 1974, *The iron age in lowland Britain.* Routledge and Kegan Paul

RIVET, A. L. F. (ed.), . 1967, *The iron age in Northern Britain.* Edinburgh University Press

On southern and western England:

CUNLIFFE, B., 1984, 'Iron age Wessex: continuity and change' in CUNLIFFE, B. and MILES, D. (eds.), *Aspects of the iron age in central southern Britain* (— University of Oxford Committee for Archaeology Monograph No. 2). University of Oxford Committee for Archaeology. 12–45

GREEN F. J., 1984, 'Iron age, Roman and Saxon crops: the archaeological evidence from Wessex' in JONES, M. and DIMBLEBY, G. (eds.), *The environment of Man: the iron age to the Anglo-Saxon period* (= BAR s87). BAR. 129–153

HARDING, D., 1972, *The Iron Age in the upper Thames Basin.* Oxford

MALTBY, M., 'Iron age, Romano-British and Anglo-Saxon animal husbandry – A review of the faunal evidence' in JONES, M. and DIMBLEBY, G. (eds.), *The environment of Man: the iron age to the Anglo-Saxon period* (= BAR s87). BAR. 155–203

PALMER, R., 1984, *Danebury – An iron age hillfort in Hampshire: an aerial photographic interpretation of its environs* (= RCHME Supplementary Series No. 6). RCHME

REYNOLDS, P. J., 1974, 'Experimental iron age storage pits', *Proc. Prehist. Soc.* 40, 118–31

REYNOLDS, P. J., 1985, *Iron age agriculture reviewed.* CBA Regional Group 12

RCHME, 1976, *Iron Age and Romano-British monuments in the Gloucestershire Cotswolds.* RCHME

On the development of hilltop enclosures and hillforts:

CUNLIFFE, B., 1983, *Danebury. Anatomy of an iron age hillfort.* Batsford

CUNLIFFE, B., 1984, *Danebury: an iron age hillfort in Hampshire* (=CBA Research Report No. 52). CBA. (2 Vols.)

DIXON P. and BORNE, P., 1977, *Crickley Hill and Gloucestershire prehistory*. Crickley Hill Trust

FORDE-JOHNSON, J., 1976, *Hillforts of the Iron Age in England and Wales*. Liverpool University Press

GUILBERT, G. (ed.), 1981, *Hillfort studies – Essays for A. H. A. Hogg*. Leicester University Press

HARDING, D. W., (ed.), 1976, *Hillforts – later prehistoric earthworks in Britain and Ireland*. Academic Press

HOGG, A. H. A., 1975, *Hillforts of Britain*. Hart-Davis, MacGibbon Ltd

JESSON, M. and HILL, D. (eds.),1971, *The iron age and its hill-forts* (= University of Southampton Monograph Series No. 1). University of Southampton

On farmsteads and hamlets in southern and western England:

BERSU, G., 1940, 'Excavations at Little Woodbury, Wiltshire', *Proc. Prehist. Soc.* 6, 30–111

SAVILLE, A., 1979, *Excavations at Guiting Power iron age site, Gloucestershire, 1974* (= Committee for Rescue Archaeology in Avon, Gloucestershire and Somerset Occasional Paper No. 7). Committee for Rescue Archaeology in Avon, Gloucestershire and Somerset

WAINWRIGHT, G. J., 1968, 'The excavation of a Durotrigian farmstead near Tollard Royal in Cranborne Chase, southern England', *Proc. Prehist. Soc.* 34, 102–47

WAINWRIGHT, G. J., 1979, *Gussage All Saints – An iron age settlement in Dorset* (= Department of the Environment Archaeological Reports No. 10). HMSO

WAINWRIGHT G. J., AND SWITSUR, V. R., 1976, 'Gussage All Saints – a chronology', *Antiquity* 50, 32–9

On structure in the landscape:

COLLIS, J., 'A theoretical study of hillforts' in GUILBERT, G. (ed.), 1981, *Hillfort studies – Essays for A. H. A. Hogg*. Leicester University Press. 66–77

CUNLIFFE, B., 1976, 'Hillforts and *oppida* in Britain' in SIEVEKING, G. DE. G., LONGWORTH, I. H. and WILSON, K. (eds.), *Problems in economic and social archaeology*. Duckworth. 343–58

CUNLIFFE, B., 1982, 'Settlement, hierarchy and social change in southern Britain in the iron age', *Analecta Praehistorica Leidensia* 15, 161–87

GENT, H., 1983, 'Centralised storage in later prehistoric Britain', *Proc. Prehist. Soc.* 49, 243–68

JONES, M., 1984, 'Regional patterns in crop production' in CUNLIFFE, B., and MILES, D. (eds.), *Aspects of the iron age in central southern Britain* (= University of Oxford Committee for Archaeology Monograph No. 2). University of Oxford Committe for Archaeology 120–25

On eastern and central England:

DRURY, P., 1978, *Excavations at Little Waltham 1970–1* (= CBA Research Report No. 26). CBA

HINGLEY, R. and MILES, D., 1984, 'Aspects of iron age settlement in the upper Thames valley' in CUNLIFFE, B. and MILES, D. (eds.), *Aspects of the iron age in central southern Britain* (= University of Oxford Committee for Archaeology Monograph No. 2). Oxford Committee for Archaeology 52–71

GRANT, A., 1984 'Animal husbandry in Wessex and the Thames valley' in CUNLIFFE, B. and MILES, D. (eds.), *Aspects of the iron age in central southern Britain* (= University of Oxford Committee for Archaeology Monograph No. 2). Oxford Committee for Archaeology. 102–19

HAWKE-SMITH, C. F., 1979, *Man-land relations in prehistoric Britain – The Dove-Derwent interflueve, Derbyshire* (= BAR 64). BAR

KNIGHT, D., 1984, *Late bronze age and iron age settlement in the Nene and Great Ouse basins* (= BAR 130). BAR. (2 Vols.)

LAMBRICK, G., 1978, 'Iron Age settlement in the upper Thames Valley' in CUNLIFFE, B. and ROWLEY, T. (eds.), *Lowland Iron Age communities in Europe* (= BAR S48). BAR. 103–20

PRYOR, F., 1984, *Excavation at Fengate, Peterborough, England: the fourth report* (= Royal Ontario Museum Archaeology Monograph No. 7). Royal Ontario Museum

SMITH, C., 1979, *Fisherwick: the reconstruction of an iron age landscape (* = BAR 61). BAR

On Atlantic Britain:

CLARKE, D. L., 'A provisional model of an iron age society and its settlement system' in CLARKE, D. L. (ed.), *Models in Archaeology*. Methuen. 801–69

COLES, B. and COLES, J., 1986, *Sweet Track to Glastonbury – The Somerset Levels in prehistory*. Thames and Hudson

COLES, J. and ORME, B. J., 1980, *The prehistory of the Somerset Levels*. Somerset Levels Project

HARDING, D. W., 1984, 'The function and classification of brochs and duns' in MIKET, R. and BURGESS, C. (eds.), *Between and beyond the walls: essays on the prehistory and history of north Britain in honour of George Jobey*. John Donald. 206–20

LAMB, R. G., 1980, *Iron age promontory forts in the northern Isles* (= BAR 79). BAR

SMITH, C. A., 1977, 'Late prehistoric and Romano-British enclosed homesteads in north-west Wales: An interpretation of their morphology', *Archaeologia Cambrensis* 126, 38–52

WAINWRIGHT, G. J., 1967, *Coygan Camp*. Cambrian Archaeological Association

WAINWRIGHT, G. J., 1971, 'The excavation of a fortified settlement at Walesland Rath, Pembrokeshire', *Britannia* 2, 48–108

On northern England:

BURGESS, C., 1984, 'The prehistoric settlement of Northumberland: a speculative survey' in MIKET, R. and BURGESS, C., (eds.), *Between and beyond the walls: essays on the prehistory and history of north Britain in honour of George Jobey*. John Donald. 126–75

CHAPMAN, J. C and MYTUM, H. C., (eds.), 1983, *Settlement in North Britain 1000 BC–AD 1000* (= BAR 118). BAR

GATES, T., 1983, 'Unenclosed settlements in Northumberland' in CHAPMAN, J. C. and MYTUM, H. C. (eds.), *Settlement in North Britain 1000 BC–AD 1000* (= BAR 118). BAR. 103–48

JOBEY, G., 1977, 'Iron Age and later farmsteads on Belling Law, Northumberland', *Archaeologia Aeliana* (5th series) 5, 1–38

JOBEY, G., 1978, 'Iron Age and Romano-British settlement on Kennel Hall Knowe, N. Tynedale, Northumberland', *Archaeologia Aeliana* (5th series), 6, 1–28

JOBEY, G., 1983, 'A note on some northern palisaded settlements' in O'CONNOR, A. and CLARKE, D. V. (eds.), *From the stone age to the 'forty-five*. John Donald 197–205

RITCHIE, A., 1970, 'Palisaded sites in northern Britain: their context and affinities', *Scottish Archaeological Forum* 2, 48–67

On eastern Scotland:

FEACHEM, R. W., 1966, 'The hillforts of Northern Britain' in RIVET, A. L. F. (ed.), *The iron age in northern Britain*. Edinburgh University Press. 59–88

FEACHEM, R. W., 1973, 'Ancient agriculture in the highland zone of Britain', *Proc. Prehist. Soc.* 39, 332–53

HARDING, D. W. (ed.), *Later prehistoric settlement in south-east Scotland* (= University of Edinburgh, Department of Archaeology Occasional Paper No. 8). University of Edinburgh

MCINNES, L., 1984, 'Settlement and economy: East Lothian and the Tyne-Forth province' in MIKET, R. and BURGESS, C. (eds.), *Between and beyond the walls: essays on the prehistory and history of north Britain in honour of George Jobey*. John Donald. 176–98

On crafts, industry and exchange:

ALLEN, D., 1967, 'Iron currency bars in Britain', *Proc. Prehist. Soc.* 33, 307–35

DE BRISAY, K. and EVANS, K., 1975, *Salt – the study of an ancient industry*. Colchester Archaeological Group

MACGREGOR, M., 1976, *Early Celtic art in northern Britain*. Leicester University Press. (2 Vols.)

MORRIS, E. L., 1981, 'Ceramic exchange in western Britain: a preliminary view' in HOWARD, H. and MORRIS, E. L. (eds.), *Production and distribution: a ceramic viewpoint* (= BAR S120). BAR. 67–81

MEGAW, J. V. S., 1970, *Art of the European iron age: a study of the elusive image*. Adams and Dart

NORTHOVER, P., 1984, 'Iron age bronze metallurgy in central southern England' in CUNLIFFE, B. and MILES, D. (eds.), *Aspects of the iron age in central southern Britain* (= University of Oxford Committee for Archaeology Monograph No. 2). University of Oxford Committee for Archaeology, 126–45

PEACOCK, D. P. S., 1969, 'A contribution to the study of Glastonbury ware from south-western Britain', *Antiquaries Journal* 49, 41–61

SALTER, C. and EHRENREICH, R., 1984, 'Iron age metallurgy in central southern Britain' in CUNLIFFE, B. and MILES, D. (eds.), *Aspects of the iron age in central southern Britain* (= University of Oxford Committee for Archaeology Monograph No. 2). University of Oxford Committee for Archaeology, 146–61

WAINWRIGHT, G. J. and SPRATLING, M., 1973, 'The iron age settlement of Gussage All Saints', *Antiquity* 47, 109–30

On foreign trade and continental setting:

CHAMPION, T. C., 1975, 'Britain in the European Iron Age', *Archaeologia Atlantica* 1, 127–45

CUNLIFFE, B., 1978, *Hengistbury Head*. Paul Elek

HARBISON, P. and LAING, L., 1974, *Some iron age Mediterranean imports in England* (= BAR 5). BAR

SMITH, R. A., 1926, 'Two early British bronze bowls', *Antiquaries Journal* 6, 276–83

On burial and ritual:

DENT, J., 1985, 'Three cart burials from Wetwang, Yorkshire', *Antiquity* 59, 85–92

FITZPATRICK, A. P., 1984, 'The deposition of La Tène iron age metalwork in watery contexts in southern England' in CUNLIFFE, B. and MILES, D. (eds.), *Aspects of the iron age in central southern Britain* (= University of Oxford Committee for Archaeology Monograph No. 2). University of Oxford Committee for Archaeology, 178–90

ROSS, A., 1959, 'The human head in insular pagan Celtic religion', *Proceedings of the Society of Antiquaries of Scotland* 91, 10–43

ROSS, A., 1967, *Pagan Celtic Britain*. Routledge and Kegan Paul

STEAD, I., 1979, *The Arras culture*. Yorkshire Philosophical Society

WHIMSTER, R., 1977, 'Harlyn Bay reconsidered: the excavations of 1900–1905 in the light of recent discoveries', *Cornish Archaeology* 16, 61–88

WHIMSTER, R., 1977, 'Iron age burial in southern Britain', *Proc. Prehist. Soc.* 43, 317–27

WHIMSTER, R., 1981, *Burial practices in iron age Britain* (= BAR 90). BAR. (2 Vols.)

On society and politics:

CUNLIFFE, B., 1978, 'Settlement and population in the British iron age: some facts, figures and fantasies' in CUNLIFFE, B. and ROWLEY, T. (eds.), *Lowland iron age communities in Europe* (= BAR S48). BAR. 3–24

DENT, J., 1983, 'Weapons, wounds and war in the iron age', *Archaeological Journal* 140, 120–8

HINGLEY, R., 1984, 'Towards social analysis in archaeology: Celtic society in the iron age of the upper Thames valley' in CUNLIFFE, B. and MILES, D. (eds.), *Aspects of the iron age in central southern Britain* (= University of Oxford Committee for Archaeology Monograph No. 2). University of Oxford Committee for Archaeology, 72–88

POWELL, T. G. E., 1980, *The Celts* (2nd Edition). Thames and Hudson

7 Questions of Balance *(pp. 162–84)*

This chapter covers the period traditionally referred to as the late Iron Age, with a little overspill into the early Roman period. The following works include general treatments of this period:

CUNLIFFE, B., 1978, *Iron age communities in Britain* (2nd edition). Routledge and Kegan Paul

FILIP, J., 1977, *Celtic civilization and its heritage*. Collet's Academia

On the effects of the Romans in Gaul and written sources:

CHAMPION, T. C., 1984, 'Written sources and the study of the European iron age' in CHAMPION, T. C., and MEGAW, J. V. S. (eds.), *Settlement and society: aspects of west European prehistory in the 1st millennium BC*. Leicester University Press. 9–22

CUNLIFFE, B., 1981, 'Money and society in pre-Roman Britain' in CUNLIFFE, B. (ed.), *Coinage and society in Britain and Gaul: some current problems* (= CBA Research Report No. 38). CBA. 29–39

JACKSON, K. H., 1964, *The oldest Irish tradition – a window on the iron age*. Cambridge University Press

NASH, D., 1976, 'The growth of urban society in France' in CUNLIFFE, B. and ROWLEY, T. (eds.), *Oppida in barbarian Europe* (= BAR S11). BAR. 95–134

NASH, D., 1976, 'Reconstructing Poseidonios' Celtic ethnography: some considerations', *Britannia* 7, 111–26

TIERNEY, J. J., 1960, 'The Celtic ethnography of Posidonius', *Proceedings of the Royal Irish Academy* 60, 189–275

On international trade 100–55 BC:

CUNLIFFE, B., 1978, *Hengistbury Head*. Paul Elek

FITZPATRICK, A., 1985, 'The distribution of Dressel I amphorae in north-west Europe', *Oxford Journal of Archaeology* 4, 305–40

KENT, J. P. C., 1981, 'The origins of coinage in Britain' in CUNLIFFE, B. (ed.), *Coinage and society in Britain and Gaul: some current problems* (= CBA Research Report No. 38). CBA. 41–3

MACREADY, S. and THOMPSON, F. H. (eds.), 1984, *Cross channel trade between Gaul and Britain in the pre-Roman iron age* (= Society of Antiquaries of London Occasional Paper (ns.) IV). Society of Antiquaries

PEACOCK, D. P. S., 1971, 'Roman amphorae in pre-Roman Britain' in JESSON, M. and HILL, D. (eds.), *The iron age and its hillforts* (= University of Southampton Monograph No. 1). University of Southampton. 161–88

On the problem of the Belgae in Britain:

ALLEN, D. F., 1944, 'The Belgic dynasties of Britain and their coins', *Archaeologia* 90, 1–46

BIRCHELL, A., 1965, 'The Aylesford-Swarling culture: the problem of the Belgae reconsidered', *Proc. Prehist. Soc.* 31, 241–367

HACHMANN, R., 1976, 'The problem of the Belgae seen from the continent', *Bulletin of the London Institute of Archaeology* 13, 117–37

HAWKES, C. F. C., 1968, 'New thoughts on the Belgae', *Antiquity* 42, 6–16

HAWKES, C. F. C. and DUNNING, G. C., 1930, 'The Belgae of Gaul and Britain, *Archaeological Journal* 87, 150–541

On Caesar's expeditions to Britain:

FRERE, S. S., 1967, *Britannia – a history of Roman Britain*. Routledge and Kegan Paul

HAWKES, C. F. C., 1978, 'Britain and Julius Caesar', *Proceedings of the British Academy* 63, 125–92

HAWKES, C. F. C., 1980, 'Caesar's Britain: an oppidum for Cassivellaunus', *Antiquity* 54, 138–9

On the core zone in south-eastern England:

COLLIS, J. R., 1971, 'Functional and theoretical interpretations of British coinage', *World Archaeology* 3, 71–83

COLLIS, J. R., 1981, 'Coinage, *oppida* and the rise of Belgic power: a reply' in CUNLIFFE, B. (ed.), *Coinage and society in Britain and Gaul: some current problems* (= CBA Research Report No. 38). CBA. 53–5

CUNLIFFE, B., 1976, 'The origins of urbanisation in Britain' in CUNLIFFE, B. and ROWLEY, T. (eds.), *Oppida in barbarian Europe* (= BAR S11). BAR. 135–62

HASELGROVE, C., 1982, 'Wealth, prestige and power: the dynamics of late iron age political centralisation in south-east England' in RENFREW, C. and SHENNAN, S. (eds.), *Ranking, resource and exchange*. Cambridge University Press. 79–88

RODWELL, W., 1976, 'Coinage, *oppida* and the rise of Belgic power in south-eastern Britain' in CUNLIFFE, B. and ROWLEY, T. (eds.), *Oppida in barbarian Europe* (= BAR S11). BAR. 181–366

RODWELL, W., 1978, 'Buildings and settlements in south-east Britain in the late iron age' in CUNLIFFE, B. and ROWLEY, T. (eds.), *Lowland iron age communities in Europe* (= BAR S48). BAR. 25–42

On oppida *and settlements in the core zone:*

FULFORD, M., 1985, *Guide to the Silchester excavations – Forum basilica 1982–84*. Department of Archaeology, University of Reading

HAWKES, C. F. C. and HULL, M. R., 1947, *Camulodunum – first report on the excavations at Colchester 1930–1939* (= Reports of the Research Committee of the Society of Antiquaries of London No. XIV). Society of Antiquaries

PARTRIDGE, C., 1981, *Skeleton Green – A late iron and Romano-British site* (= Britannia Monograph Series No. 2). Society for the Promotion of Roman Studies

SAUNDERS. C. and HAVERCROFT, A. B., 1982, 'Excavations on the line of the Wheathampstead bypass', *Hertfordshire Archaeology* 8, 11–39

On first-century AD trade:

CUNLIFFE, B. W., 1982, 'Britain, the Veneti and beyond', *Oxford Journal of Archaeology* 1, 39–65

HASELGROVE, C., 1976, 'External trade as a stimulus to urbanisation' in CUNLIFFE, B. and ROWLEY, T. (eds.), *Oppida in barbarian Europe* (= BAR S11). BAR. 25–50

MACREADY, S. and THOMPSON, F. H. (eds.), 1984, *Cross channel trade between Gaul and Britain in the pre-Roman iron age* (= Society of Antiquaries of London Occasional Paper (ns.) 4). Society of Antiquaries

TIMBY, J. R., 1987, 'The distribution of *terra nigra* and *terra rubra* to Britain', *Rei Cretariae Romanae Favtorvm Acta* XXV/XXVI, 291–310

WILLIAMS, D. F., 1981, 'The Roman amphorae trade with late iron age Britain' in HOWARD, H. and MORRIS, E. L. (eds.), *Production and distribution: a ceramic viewpoint* (= BAR S120). BAR. 123–32

On burials, temples and ritual:

BUSHE-FOX, J. P., 1925, *Excavation of the late Celtic urnfield at Swarling, Kent* (= Reports of the Research Committee of the Society of Antiquaries of London No. V). Society of Antiquaries

COLLIS, J., 1973, 'Burials with weapons in iron age Britain', *Germania Anzeiger* 51, 121–33

COLLIS, J., 1977, 'Pre-Roman burial rites in north-west Europe' in REECE, R. (ed.), *Burial in the Roman world* (= CBA Research Report No. 22). CBA. 1–13

EVANS, A. J., 1890, 'On a late Celtic urnfield at Aylesford, Kent', *Archaeologia* 52, 315–388

PIGGOTT, S., 1968, *The Druids*. Thames and Hudson

RODWELL, W. (ed.), 1980, *Temples, churches and religion in Roman Britain* (= BAR 77). BAR. (2 Vols.)

STEAD, I. M., 1967, 'A La Tène III burial at Welwyn Garden City', *Archaeologia* 101, 1–62

WHIMSTER, R., 1981, *Burial practices in iron age Britain* (= BAR 90). BAR. (2 Vols.)

On the periphery zone of central and southern England:

CUNLIFFE, B., 1984, 'Gloucestershire and the iron age of southern Britain', *Transactions of the Bristol and Gloucestershire Archaeological Society* 102, 5–16

CLIFFORD, E. M., 1960, *Bagendon – A Belgic oppidum*. Heffer

HASELGROVE, C. C. and TURNBULL, P., 1984, *Stanwick: excavation and fieldwork – second interim report 1984* (= University of Durham, Department of Archaeology, Occasional Paper No. 5). University of Durham, Department of Archaeology

MAY, J., 1978, 'The growth of settlements in the later iron age in Lincolnshire' in CUNLIFFE, B. and ROWLEY, T. (eds.), *Oppida in barbarian Europe* (= BAR S11). BAR. 163–80

WHEELER, R. E. M., 1943, *Maiden Castle, Dorset* (= Reports of the Research Committee of the Society of Antiquaries of London No. XII). Society of Antiquaries

On the outer zone of western, northern and Atlantic Britain :

CHRISTIE, P. M. L., 1978, 'The excavation of an iron age souterrain and settlement at Carn Euny, Sancreed, Cornwall', *Proc. Prehist. Soc.* 44, 309–434

HOGG, A. H. A., 1966, 'Native settlement in Wales' in THOMAS, C. (ed.), *Rural settlement in Roman Britain* (= CBA Research Report No. 7). CBA. 1–14

JONES, B., 1975, 'The north-west interface' in FOWLER, P. J. (ed.), *Recent work in rural archaeology.* Moonraker Press. 93–106

MACKIE, E., 1975, 'The brochs of Scotland' in FOWLER, P. J. (ed.), *Recent work in rural Archaeology.* Moonraker Press. 72–92

STEAD, I. M., BOURKE, J. B. and BOTHWELL, D. (eds.), 1986, *Lindow Man–The body in the bog.* Guild Publishing

THOMAS, C. (ed.), 1972, *The iron age in the Irish Sea province* (= CBA Research Report No. 9). CBA

WILLIAMS, G., 1985, *Fighting and farming in iron age west Wales.* Dyfed Archaeological Trust

On political manoeuvrings :

ALLEN, D. F., 1944, 'The Belgic dynasties of Britain and their coins', *Archaeologia* 90, 1–46

ALLEN. D. F., 1970, 'The coins of the Iceni', *Britannia* 1, 1–33

SELLWOOD, L., 1984, 'Tribal boundaries viewed from the perspective of numismatic evidence' in CUNLIFFE, B. and MILES, D. (eds.), *Aspects of the iron age in central southern Britain* (= University of Oxford Committee for Archaeology Monograph No. 2). University of Oxford Committee for Archaeology. 191–204

On the coming of Rome :

DUDLEY, D. R. and WEBSTER, G., 1965, *The Roman conquest of Britain.* Batsford

FRERE, S. S., 1967, *Britannia – a history of Roman Britain.* Routledge and Kegan Paul

MANNING, W. H., 1976, 'The conquest of the west country' in BRANIGAN, K. and FOWLER, P. J. (eds.), *The Roman west country.* David and Charles. 15–41

RIVET, A. L. F., 1971, 'Hillforts in action' in JESSON, M. and HILL, D. (eds.), *The iron age and its hillforts* (= University of Southampton Monograph No. 1). University of Southampton. 189–202

TODD. M., 1984, 'Oppida and the Roman army. A review of recent evidence', *Oxford Journal of Archaeology* 4, 187–200

WACHER, J., 1979, *The coming of Rome.* Routledge and Kegan Paul

WARMINGTON, B. H., 1976, 'Nero, Boudicca and the frontier in the west' in BRANIGAN, K. and FOWLER, P. J. (eds.), *The Roman west country.* David and Charles. 42–51

WEBSTER, G., 1970, 'The military situation in Britain between AD 43 and 71', *Britannia* 1, 179–97

WEBSTER, G., 1981, *Rome against Caratacus.* Batsford

On changes after the Conquest :

BREEZE, D. and DOBSON, 1985, 'Roman military deployment in north England', *Britannia* 16, 1–20

DENT. J., 1983, 'The impact of Roman rule on native society in the territory of the Parisi', *Britannia* 14, 35–44

FOWLER, P. J., 1976, 'Farms and fields in the Roman west country' in BRANIGAN, K. and FOWLER, P. J. (eds.), *The Roman west country.* David and Charles. 162–82

HOLDER, P. A., 1982, *The Roman army in Britain.* Batsford

MILES, D. (ed.), 1982, *The Romano-British Countryside – studies in Rural settlement and economy* (= BAR 103). BAR. (2 Vols.)

TODD, M., 1971, *Roman Britain.* Harvester Press

TODD. M., 1984, 'Hembury (Devon): Roman troops in a hillfort', *Antiquity* 58, 171–4

Works cited in figure captions not referred to above :

MEGAW, J. V. S. and SIMPSON, D. D. A. (eds.), 1979, *An introduction to British prehistory.* Leicester University Press

8   All Things Must Pass *(pp. 185–93)*

Very little has been published on the subjects covered in this chapter, and there are no general works available

On social change and prehistoric society :

CHILDE, V. G., 1941, *Man makes himself.* Watts and Co

CHILDE, V. G., 1951, *Social evolution.* Watts and Co

FRIEDMAN, J. and ROWLANDS, M. J. (eds.), 1977, *The evolution of social systems.* Duckworth

RENFREW, C. (eds.), 1973, *The explanation of culture change.* Duckworth

On the prehistoric inheritance:

COLES, J. M. and ORME, B. J., 1977, 'Neolithic hurdles from Walton Heath, Somerset', *Somerset Levels Papers* 3, 6–29

DARVILL, T. C., 1986, *The archaeology of the uplands.* CBA and RCHME

DIMBLEBY, G. W., 1974, 'The legacy of prehistoric Man' in WARREN, A. and GOLDSMITH, B. (eds.), *Conservation in practice.* Wiley. 279–89

GELLING, M., 1978, *Signposts to the past.* Dent

On prehistory as a social science and as a contribution to society today:

BLOCH, M., 1977, 'The past and the present in the present', *Man* 12, 278–92

CHILDE, G. V., 1947, 'Archaeology as a social science', *Institute of Archaeology in London Annual Report.* 3, 49–60

CLARK, G., 1957, *Archaeology and society* (3rd edition). Methuen

HODDER, I., 1981, 'Towards a mature archaeology' in HODDER, I., ISAAC, G. and HAMMOND, N. (eds.), *Pattern of the past.* Cambridge University Press. 1–13

HODDER, I, 1982, *Symbols in action.* Cambridge University Press

HODDER, I., 1982, *The present past.* Batsford

RENFREW, C., 1982, *Towards an archaeology of mind.* Cambridge University Press. (Inaugural Lecture)

REYNOLDS, P., 1979, *Iron age farm: the Butser experiment.* British Museum Publications Ltd

On prehistory tomorrow:

CLEERE, H. (ed.), 1984, *Approaches to the archaeological heritage.* Cambridge University Press

FOWLER, P. J., 1977, *Approaches to archaeology.* A and C Black

THE PREHISTORIC SOCIETY, 1984, *Prehistory, priorities and society: the way forward.* Prehistoric Society

THOMAS, C., 1971, 'Ethics in archaeology, 1971', *Antiquity* 45, 268–74

Works cited in figure captions not referred to above:

FOWLER, P. J., 1978, 'Lowland landscapes: culture, time and personality' in LIMBREY, S. and EVANS, J. G. (eds.), *The effect of Man on the environment: the lowland Zone* (= CBA Research Report No. 21). CBA. 1–11

Index